OUR COLONIAL HERITAGE

DIPLOMATIC AND MILITARY

James Trapier Lowe

UNIVERSITY
PRESS OF
AMERICA

Lanham • New York • London

Copyright © 1987 by

University Press of America,® Inc.

4720 Boston Way
Lanham, MD 20706

3 Henrietta Street
London WC2E 8LU England

British Cataloging in Publication Information Available

Library of Congress Cataloging-in-Publication Data

Lowe, James Trapier.
  Our colonial heritage.

  Bibliography: p.
  Includes index.
  1. United States—Foreign relations—Colonial
period, ca. 1600-1775.   2. United States—Foreign
relations—1783-1815.   I. Title.
E188.L864   1987   327.73   87-10397
ISBN 0-8191-6391-0 (alk. paper)
ISBN 0-8191-6392-9 (pbk. : alk. paper)

All University Press of America books are produced on acid-free
paper which exceeds the minimum standards set by the National
Historical Publication and Records Commission.

dedicated to

WILLIAM   FRANKLIN   SANDS

TO:

MARY JANE, KAREN, KAYE,

SANDI, AND STEPHANIE

Full credit for the design and art work goes to Bob
Lamme; Mary Gill did all the typing.

v

C O N T E N T S

Book One

The Diplomatic Heritage

Introduction by James Brown Scott   1

Chapter I: The Agency System 17

Chapter II: Intercolonial Diplomacy 59

Chapter III: The More Perfect Union 93

Book Two

The Strategic Heritage

Chapter IV: The Indian Nations 159

Chapter V: Diplomacy and War 211

Index   313

PREFACE

For the purpose of clarity, the subject has been
divided into two parts: Book One is the Diplomatic
Heritage, and Book Two is the Strategic Heritage. This
does not mean that the one or the other is the better
method of approach. Each has its own advantages, and
the use of the two together helps to clarify the whole
with a minimum of redundance.

James Wilson, on the floor of the Pennsylvania State Convention, called to ratify the Constitution said on December 11, 1787:

"And now is accomplished what the great mind of

Henry IV of France had in contemplation-- a system of

government for large and respectable dominions, united

and bound together, in peace, under a superintending

head, by which all their differences may be accommo-

dated, without the destruction of the human race."

ABOUT THE AUTHOR

James Trapier Lowe, formerly a professor of the School of Foreign Service, Georgetown University, a professorial lecturer at the George Washington University, and an adjunct professor at the School of Advanced International Studies at the Miami University, he is also a Carnegie Fellow in International Law, and a recipient of Georgetown's Vicennial Medal. He has contributed to a number of scholarly journals, and recently published two books, <u>Geopolitics and War: Mackinder's Philosophy of Power</u> (1981), and <u>A Philosophy of Air Power</u> (1984).

Book One

THE DIPLOMATIC HERITAGE

INTRODUCTION

The present volume is a thesis and a demonstration. The thesis is that our diplomacy began in America with the first permanent English settlement; that it grew in strength, in frequency and in importance with the growth of the Colonies, only changing its name to extend its application to the world at large by the astounding declaration of the 4th day of July, 1776.

The demonstration arises from the examination of the relations of the Colonies with the Crown and with one another from the standpoint of diplomacy and diplomatic intercourse as then and now understood by the law of nations.

But the book is a challenge as well as a demonstration,--a challenge to the reader who does not go beyond the school books. As the thesis is fundamental, what was and is the conception of diplomacy upon which it is based?

The authors of our day who deal with foreign relations neither frame a definition of diplomacy nor include within the definition which they adopt the American Colonies and their relations. Indeed they have to all intents and purposes, omitted any consideration of the Colonies in their disquisitions. As regards to meaning of diplomacy, they are disposed to accept the definitions from two modern works on the subject whose authority is unquestioned, because they cannot be successfully controverted.

The first definition is none other than that given in *A Guide to Diplomatic Practice*, by the late Sir Ernest Satow, a diplomatist from the cradle, one might say, representing Great Britain to many a nation as well as the Second Hague Peace Conference,--the last of the successful world conferences -- and whose life was, in a word, diplomacy.

The first edition of this authoritative work appeared in 1917; the second, from which the quotation is made, in 1922. Each edition is in two volumes--exhaustive but not exhausting -- and the definition of diplomacy is identical in each: "Diplomacy is the application of intelligence"--which the Colonists possessed in full measure-- "and tact" -- which they also possessed, otherwise they would have ceased to be Colonists -- "to the conduct of official relations" -- their relations with the Crown were official, not personal -- "between the governments of independent states"--which the erstwhile Colonies are admitted to be--"extending sometimes also to their relations with vassal states"--which characterization the reader may apply to the Colonies, if he be so minded.[1]

Now for the definition which Sir Ernest himself quotes from the opening paragraph of De Garden's *Traite Complete de Diplomatie*, published in 1855, which may be thus Englished: "Diplomacy ... is the science of the respective relations and mutual interests of States, or the art of conciliating the interests of peoples; in a more definite sense, the science or art of negotiation.

"Diplomacy embraces the whole system of interests born of the relations established between nations; its general object is the security of those relations, their tranquility and their respective dignity.   The direct and immediate object of diplomacy is-- or should be--to maintain peace and harmony among the Powers."[2]

It is to be observed that the Comte de Garden's definition dwells upon the fact that states have mutual interests which are to be conciliated, not as the interests of the states as such but of their peoples, and that the conciliatory arrangement of these interests raises negotiation to the position of a science or art; perhaps it would be better to say both.

But this is not enough.   The Comte de Garden, who was a diplomatist by profession and therefore knew whereof he spoke, considered his science or his art as having two objects, the generally accepted one of promoting the security, the tranquility and the dignity of the relations between peoples.   There may, however, be security, dignity, even a measure of tranquility, without peace, yet peace was to de Garden a desirable if not essential element in the relations between nations. Therefore he lays down the principle that the specific, or the direct, or the immediate object of diplomacy is --we know from history, from century to century -- "to maintain peace and harmony among the Powers."   Now if the fundamental purpose of diplomacy is the maintenance of peace and harmony, it is evident that it necessarily applies to communities, whether they be states or vassals; for without peace and harmony they cannot exist.

It is evident, therefore, that the relations of the American Colonies came directly within the definition of diplomacy as conceived by the diplomatic profession, although the texts of our school books--and indeed of the larger treatises--seem to be unaware of this fact. It would not have hurt the authors of the various texts if they had been familiar with books of diplomacy, as well as with the troubles and trials and achievements of the American Plantations.

Now if diplomacy is the intercourse of states, sovereign or vassal, it must be based upon rules, and these rules, taken together, form what was called, in an earlier day, the law of nations,--a law which has been defined in various ways, but for our purpose there is no better definition, specifying at one and the same time its content, than that of President Cleveland in a classic State Paper. "The law of nations is founded," our distinguished President said, "upon reason and justice, and the rules of conduct governing individual relations between citizens or subjects of a civilized state are equally applicable as between enlightened nations."

Now the Colonists were possessed of both reason and justice in their mutual relations, and those rules of reason and justice were equally applicable between the Colonies, which, if not full sovereignties, were at least vassal states. Therefore, according to no less an authority than Mr. Cleveland, the Colonies had a law of nations and this law of nations they applied from time to time in their mutual relations, for the general purpose of conciliating their interests, in order to procure not only their security, tranquility and respective dignity but also for the fundamental purpose of diplomacy; to maintain peace and harmony among themselves.

There was not a single Colony of the thirteen English Colonies of North America, it may safely be said, which did not at various times enter into negotiations with its neighboring colonies. More picturesque were the relations of the Colonies with their Indian neighbors,--making with them those formal agreements, which in the law of nations are called treaties. In specific

3

cases not one, but a number of Colonies, met by their
delegates to negotiate treaties with the Indians, especially the Six Nations. The most striking instances of
these different forms of negotiations are set forth in
the present volume under appropriate headings and
chapters.

The agreements of conventions among the Colonies
were not limited to the smaller things which the unini-
tiated reader would expect from Colonies; they related
to international matters of war and of peace, neutrality, arbitration and especially the commercial relations among themselves entered into in order to bring
about free trade with neighboring and distant Colonies
and foreign States.

The present volume contains numerous concrete examples to demonstrate the thesis of the author, -- that
the Colonies, among themselves and the foreign nations,
embarked upon the stormy as well as the placid waters
of diplomacy and within the large and ever-widening
boundary of the law of nations,-- a law based upon the
rights and duties not only of the Colonists and of the
Indians but of the foreign countries with which they
had relations.

But these relations were as ordinary occurrences.
On more than one occasion, however, the relations of
the Colonies were of a transcendant nature, being pre-
cedents not merely for the Confederation of the Colonies when they had declared their independence and obtained it but also for the diplomatic union, that large
grouping of the English-speaking peoples which we have
grown accustomed to think of as the British Commonwealth of Nations.

The American settlers began early; indeed the Pilgrim Fathers entered into an association the night before they landed on Mrs. Hemans' "stern and rock-bound
coast." On that night one hundred and two in all, with
seventy men, --for men only counted in those days-- "in
the presence of God, and one of another," covenanted
and combined themselves "into a civill body politick,"
for their "better ordering and preservation," and "to
enacte, constitute, and frame such just and equall
lawes, ordinances, acts, constitutions, and offices,
from time to time, as shall be thought meete and convenient for the generall good of the Colonie, unto which
we promise all due submission and obedience."[3]

This was in 1620,--to be accurate, on the 11th day of November.

Some one hundred and sixty years thereafter "the people," to quote the exact language, "Inhabiting the territory formerly called the Province of Massachusetts Bay," did "hereby solemnly and mutually agree with each other, to form themselves into a free, sovereign, and independent body-politic, or State, by the name of THE COMMONWEALTH OF MASSACHUSETTS."[4] This was in 1780.

The neighboring people of Connecticut were able to maintain their charter during the entire Colonial period, and it had been found so adequate that in their Constitution of 1776--of but four articles-- they provided in the first article of but two sentences: "That the ancient Form of Civil Government, contained in the Charter from *Charles* the Second, King of *England*, and adopted by the People of this State, shall be and remain the Civil Constitution of this State, under the sole authority of the People thereof, independent of any King or Prince whatever. And this Republic is, and shall forever be and remain, a free, sovereign and independent State, by the Name of the STATE of CONNECTICUT."[5]

Here we have three examples: one of the formation of a political community or state, without any authority from the Crown or title to a foot of soil; the second of the transformation into a State of a Colony without a charter-- for Massachusetts had lost its charter; and the third, as is the case of Connecticut, of a Colony retaining its charter after it became a State.

The American State was not a creation; it developed from a Colony. There is here no break with the past but merely a change of name.

But this was not all. The Colonies formed themselves into a Confederation of Colonies just as the States, after the Declaration of Independence, formed themselves into a Confederation of States.

The first instance of confederation is that of the United Colonies of New England, consisting of the colonies of Massachusetts Bay, the Plymouth Colony, the Colony of Hartford and the Colony of New Haven. Rhode Island, the ungodly neighbor, was not admitted to this Confederation of the Lord's elect.

5

It is not the purpose of these words of introduction to go into details, but no fair-minded person can read the text of the Articles of Confederation of the United Colonies of New England without seeing that they were more than a precedent for the Articles of Confederation of the United States. Instead of the four neighboring Colonies in the earlier confederation, there were thirteen contiguous States in the later confederation, which shortly developed into a federation, expanding from generation to generation into these United States of America. The American past, here as everywhere, is deeply embedded in the present. Thus it is by the way of the Colonies that we eventually reach the most perfect union which we reverently call the Constitution of the United States.

As in the New England Confederation, Rhode Island and New Hampshire existed, yet were not admitted, so also Vermont existed at the time of the Confederation of States of 1781 but was not admitted until the more perfect union under the Constitution was formally made and duly ratified.

However, between the two Confederations there were attempts at general confederations which failed of realization.

Among the first was William Penn's plan of 1698, for "a Briefe and Plaine Scheam how the English Colonies in the North parts of America Viz: Boston Connecticut Road Island New York New Jerseys, Pensilvania, Maryland, Virginia and Carolina may be made usefull to the Crowne, and one anothers peace and safety with an universal concurrence." Of this project it can only be said in passing that the several Colonies were to meet once a year or oftener during war-- war is a characteristic of a vassal as well as of a sovereign state-- and at least once every two years in times of peace, "by their stated and appointed Deputies," whose purpose was "to debate and resolve of such measures as are most adviseable for their better understanding, and the public tranquility and safety."[6]

These are the very objects of diplomacy as stated by the Comte de Garden in his treatise on diplomacy.

There was to be a place of meeting,--not in Philadelphia, as might be expected, but in a more central position, the town of New York--and the representatives or deputies composing the Congress were to meet under the presidency of the "Kings High Commissioner during the Session after the manner of Scotland"--which was at the time a kingdom, with the King of England as King of Scotland, just as he was the King of every one of the American Colonies.

What ground is there for stating that the English monarch was King of each of the thirteen colonies? Evidence, indeed proof, is at hand. The relationship between King and Colonies was not lost upon admirers of Queen Elizabeth, and the evidence in question occurs in a place where we would not expect to find it, -- the dedication of Spenser's *Faerie Queene* (A delicate compliment to an unfairylike person):

To the Most High Mightie and Magnificent
EMPRESSE
renowned for Pietie Vertve and all
Gratiovs Givernment
E L I Z A B E T H
by the Grace of God qveene of England
Fravnce and Ireland and of Virginia
Defendevr of the Faith &c

Her Most Humble Zervaunt
EDMVD SPENSER
Doth in all Humilitie
Dedicate Present and Consecrate
These his Labovrs
To Live with the Eternitie of Her Fame.

Because of Spenser's dedication, if for no other reason, Virginia as a kingdom under the English Crown seems destined to live forever with "his Empresse renowned for Pietie and Vertve."

But the case of king and his colonial kingdoms does not end there. The Virginians were apparently proud of their connection with the Tudor "Faerie Queene"' for the seal of Virginia used for official purposes was the royal seal and remained so throughout the entire course of its colonial history until it became a free, sovereign and independent state by its declaration of June 12, 1776. Thereupon the colonial and royal seal, with its inscription, was replaced by a warning to tyrants, "*Sic Semper Tyrannis*."

In the early days, Sir William Berkeley, Royal Governor of Virginia--the word "royal" suggests the relation of kingship--issued a patent to certain lands in

Virginia under date of July 2, 1669, with the seal of the Colony displaying the Stuart arms and the words in the exergum, "*En dat Virginia Quintum (regnum)*," that is to say, "Behold Virginia gives the fifth (kingdom)." Thus we find that in 1669 there were five, instead of four, kingdoms as in the dedication of Spenser's *Faerie Queene* to the "Virgin Queen," because in the meantime a Stuart had become King of England; and therefore the seal speaks of five without naming them, the five being England, Scotland, France, Ireland and Virginia.

And so the seal stood until in Queen Anne's reign the union of Scotland with England reduced the number of kingdoms to four again, and the seal was appropriately changed to conform to the fact. The Crown, however, is understood instead of Kingdom, so the motto runs, "*En dat Virginia quartam (coronam)*."

What was express in the case of Virginia was implicit in the other American Colonies, so that it would be unjust to their royal majesties previous to July 4, 1776, to deprive them of their kingdoms on this side of the water.

But a later and better known "Scheam" of grouping the Colonies is Benjamin Franklin's "Plan for a Union of the Several Colonies," adopted at Albany in 1754, which, however, proved to be unacceptable to the Colonies as acknowledging too much power in the King, and unacceptable to the King because of a too great acknowledgment of power in the Colonies.

What were the Colonies? They were separate entities independent of one another but subject to the direction of a higher power, the King of England. What is the relation of the states of the American Union? They are independent of one another but dependent upon a higher authority of their own making, the Federal Union.

While these statements are simple to an elementary degree, nevertheless it is desirable to invoke the authority of an adjudged case or two.

The first is *Nathan* v. *Commonwealth of Virginia*.[7] decided in the September term, 1781, of the Court of Common Pleas of Philadelphia County, -- approximately three weeks before the capitulation of Yorktown put the seal upon the independence which the Colonial statesmen had proclaimed and France had made a reality. There being then no judicial department under the Confederation, the case was tried in the Court of Common Pleas of Philadelphia. The syllabus of the case is but a single line, to the effect that the property of a sister state is not liable to attachment in Pennsylvania. The holding, however, is of immense importance, inasmuch as the decision implied that each of the thirteen states was sovereign, free and independent of the other, as stated in the third of the Articles of Confederation.

What were the facts of the case? They are so interesting and so important that it seems best to quote them from the statement of the case itself: "A foreign attachment was issued against the Commonwealth of Virginia, at the suit of Simon Nathan; and a quantity of clothing, imported from France, belonging to that State, was attached in Philadelphia." Whereupon, "the delegates in Congress from Virginia, conceiving this" --to quote again -- "a violation of the laws of nations, applied to the Supreme Executive Council of Pennsylvania, by whom the sheriff was ordered to give up the goods."

So much for the facts.

The Attorney General, on behalf of the sheriff and by direction of the Supreme Executive Council had shown cause and prayed that the writ should be discharged. "He promised" --quoting the language of the report -- "that though the several states which form our federal republic, had, by the confederation, ceded many of the prerogatives of sovereignty to the United States, yet these voluntary engagements did not injure their independence of each other; but that each was a sovereign, 'with every power, jurisdiction and right, not expressly given up.'" He insisted, and properly, "that every kind of process issued against a sovereign, is a violation of the laws of nations."

In the course of his argument in support of the position which he had taken, "that all sovereigns are in a state of equality and independence"--unless otherwise with their own consent--he said "that sovereigns, with regard to each other, were always considered as individuals in a state of nature, where all enjoy the same prerogatives, where there could be no subordination to a supreme authority, nor any judge to define their rights or redress their wrongs"; that "all jurisdiction implies superiority over the party, and authority in the judge to execute his decrees; but there

9

could be no superiority." And the inference which he drew from the views advanced, and others in support of them--which are not needed for this purpose--was "that the court having no jurisdiction over Virginia, all its process against that State must be *coram non judice*, and consequently void."[8] For this he vouched the authority of Vattel.[9]

Having stated that there was no instance in our law books of a process against a sovereign, the Attorney-General considered suits against their representatives. The stock example, of course, was the immunity of diplomatic officers, existing by the law of nations, the violation of which was to be punished in England under the famous statute of 7 Queen Anne, Chapter 12, which statute did not introduce the immunity of diplomatic agents but was merely declaratory of the law of nations, with "nothing new in it," except the clause prescribing a summary mode of punishment"' and he concluded, under this heading, that this statute was a "part of the common law of the land before, and consequently extended to Pennsylvania."

As the writ of the sheriff was as null and void against a representative as against the sovereign, the sheriff attaching the goods in question was liable to punishment. To show the "inconveniences" which might follow if the converse were true, the Attorney-General referred to the calamity which might happen to the body politic, if the sheriff attached the goods addressed to a sovereign or its representative: "that any disaffected person, who happened to be a creditor of the United States, might injure our public defence, and retard or ruin the operations of a campaign; that he might issue an attachment against the cannon of General Washington, or seize the public money designed for the payment of the army,"[10]--a fanciful incident to us but a very real one with Washington's army then closing in upon Lord Cornwallis at Yorktown.

The second of the cases is *Penhallow* v. *Doane*, decided in 1795.[11] From the opinion of Mr. Justice Iredell some passages are lifted here and there --Mr. Justice Iredell's opinions carrying today as great--if not greater -- weight than when they were originally delivered. Indeed his dissenting opinion in the case of *Chisholm* v. *Georgia*[12] may be said to have the force of law, occasioning, as it did, the Eleventh Amendment to the Constitution, thus making his opinion the law of the land. Now in the case of *Penhallow* v. *Doane*, the learned Justice had occasion to speak of the Colonies before the Declaration of Independence and the thirteen States under the Articles of Confederation, saying: "Under the British government ... each province in America composed (as I conceive) a body politic, and the several provinces were no(t) otherwise connected with each other, than as being subject to the same sovereign. Each province had a distinct legislature, a distinct executive (subordinate to the king), a distinct judiciary; and in particular, the claim as to taxation, which began the contest, extended to a separate claim of each province to raise taxes within itself; no power then existed, or was claimed, for any joint authority on behalf of all the provinces to tax the whole. There were some disputes as to boundaries, whether certain lands were within the bounds of one province or another, but nobody denied that where the boundaries of any one province could be ascertained, all the permanent inhabitants within these boundaries were members of the body politic, and subject to all the laws of it.[13]

In the case of *Chisholm* v. *Georgia*, the Supreme Court held that a state could be sued by an individual citizen of another state. From this opinion Mr. Justice Iredell dissented, and dissent was confirmed --as previously stated--by the Eleventh Amendment to the Constitution. In the course of his opinion in that case, Mr. Justice Iredell said: "Every state in the Union, in every instance where its sovereignty has not been delegated to the United States, I consider to be as completely sovereign, as the United States are in respect to the powers surrendered. The United States are sovereign as to all the powers of government actually surrendered; each state in the Union is sovereign, as to all the powers reserved. It must necessarily be so, because the United States has no claim to any authority but such as the states have surrendered to them; of course, the part not surrendered must remain as it did before."[14]

The third case is that of the *State of Texas* v. *White*[15] in which Chief Justice Chase took occasion to define the nature of the state and the relations of the state to the United States, citing with approval Mr. Justice Iredell's opinion in the very case of *Penhallow* v. *Doane*. In a passage which has become classic, the Chief Justice said: "Under the Articles of Confederation each State retained its sovereignty, freedom, and independence, and every power, jurisdiction, and right not expressly delegated to the United States."[16]

And speaking of the states under the Constitution, Chief Justice Chase quoted from his opinion in the case of *County of Lane* v. *The State of Oregon*,[17] that "the people of each State compose a State, having its own government, and endowed with all the functions essential to separate and independent existence," and that "without the States in union, there could be no such political body as the United States." From this statement he drew the conclusion-- concurred in by the majority of the court--that "not only, therefore, can there be no loss of separate and independent autonomy to the States, through their union under the Constitution, but it may be not unreasonably said that the preservation of the States, and the maintenance of their governments, are as much within the design and care of the Constitution as the preservation of the Union and the maintenance of the National government." He concluded this portion of his opinion --the opinion of the majority of the court -- in terms which will last as long as the United States: "The Constitution, in all its provisions, looks to an indestructible Union, composed of indestructible States."[18]

It thus appears that each American Colony was independent of every other American Colony, but each independent upon higher authority, --the king, that after their Declaration of Independence each was a separate state, as independent of the others as of a foreign state.

Our Marshall, the greatest of our Chief Justices, gave fuller expression to this thought in his opinion in the leading case of *McCulloch* v. *State of Maryland*,[19] considered by many competent critics to be the greatest of his opinions. In the first place, he calls "the defendant (Maryland) a sovereign state." If this be so, then all of the American states are sovereign, and none the less sovereign because they have granted to the government of the United States the exercise of certain of their sovereign powers. He refers to the way in which the Constitution of the United States contains the grants of the powers made by the states to the United States, that way being a reference from the Continental Congress to conventions, to be elected in each one of the thirteen sovereign states, to ratify, if they were so disposed, the Constitution, which, by such action, became the Constitution for general purposes of the states so ratifying, just as the State Constitutions of their own making were their Constitutions for local purposes. The submission was not to the legislatures of the states, as they were the agents of the people, but to the people themselves in each of the States, as the source of power. Chief Justice Marshall says of the people of each of the States:

> They acted upon it in the only manner in which they can act safely, effectively and wisely, on such a subject, by assembling in convention. It is true, they assembled in their several states -- and where else should they have assembled?

To this question the Chief Justice, a loyal son of Virginia, and therefore a loyal son of these United States, answered in terms which will remain as long as we have the Government of the Fathers: "No political dreamer was ever wild enough to think of breaking down the lines which separate the states, and of compounding the American people into one common mass. Of consequence, when they act, they act in their states."[20]

Still later, it was maintained in the argument in the Supreme Court of the United States in the case of *Gibbons* v. *Ogden*[21] that "anterior" to the Constitution, the states "were sovereign, were completely independent, and were connected with each other only by a league." Upon this statement of the case Chief Justice Marshall contented himself with a sentence of three words: "This is true."

Marshall should have known, because he lived through that period when his native state of Virginia ratified the treaties of Amity and Commerce and of Alliance with France, concluded by the United States in Congress assembled. Indeed, Virginia exchanged ratifications with the French Minister in Philadelphia, the instruments of ratification themselves being today preserved in the Ministry of Foreign Affairs of the French Republic.

The Chief Justice, knowing what was the situation under the Articles of Confederation, stated that these allied sovereigns converted their league into a government"; they converted their congress of ambassadors, deputed to deliberate on their common concerns, and to recommend measures of general utility, into a legislature." The government and the legislature which John Marshall had in mind were none other than those of the United States of America.

13

The process was and is clear. The group of men and women known as the Pilgrims formed themselves into a body politic; the New England Colonies formed themselves into a Confederation; the American Colonies later declared themselves independent states and, following the New England example, created a Confederation, to end in the present union of states which we call the United States of America. It was a continuing process, and we cannot understand what we are today unless we know what we were in the living past.

How and why did this happen? James Russell Lowell has told us in one of his *Biglow Papers*, "Mason and Slidell: A Yankee Idyll"-- in which the Concord Bridge discourses with the Bunker Hill monument:

O strange New World, that yit wast never young,
Whose youth from thea by gripin' need was wrung,
Brown foundlin' o' the woods, whose baby-bed
Was prowled roun' by the Injun's cracklin' tread,
An' who grew'st strong thru shifts an' wants an'
     pains,
Nussed by stern men with empires in their brains.

And the latest of the empires which the English-speaking peoples carry in their "brains" is the British Commonwealth of Nations, which we cannot understand unless we are familiar with the origin, the nature and the development of the English-speaking colonies in the Western World. Indeed the British Commonwealth as well as the United States is the outcome of a continuous, conscious development.

This is the thesis of Mr. Lowe, and his demonstration of it is the volume to which these lines are in the nature of a prologue.

James Brown Scott (Secretary of the Carnegie Endowment for International Peace; President of the American Society of International Law: Member and past President of the Institut de Droit International)

FOOTNOTES--INTRODUCTION

[1]Rt. Hon. Sir Ernest Satow, *A Guide to Diplomatic Practice*, 1st ed. (London, 1917), p. 1.

[2]"La Diplomatie ... est la science des relations exterieures ou affaires estrangeres des Etat: dans un sens plus determine, c'est la science our l'art des negociations. Elle embrasse le systeme entier des rapports etablis entre les nations; elle a pour objet leur surete, leur tranquilite, leur dignite respectives, en son but direct, immediat, est le maintien de la paix et de la bonne harmonie."--Comte de Garden, vol. i, pp. 1-2.

[3]William Bradford, *History of Plymouth Plantation* (The Massachusetts Historical Society, Boston, 1912), vol. 1, p. 191.

[4]*The Federal and State Constitutions, Colonial Charters, and Other Organic Laws of the United States* (Washington, Government Printing Office, 1877), Pt. 1, p. 960.

[5]*Ibid.*, pp. 257-8.

[6]*Documents Relative to the Colonial History of the State of New York*, J. R. Broadhead (1851 ed.) vol. iv, p. 296-7.

[7]1 Dallas, 77, footnote (*a*).

[8]*Ibid.*, p. 78.

[9]Vol. 1, p. 2, 133.

[10]1 Dallas, 79.

[11]3 Dallas, 54.

[12]2 Dallas, 419.

[13]3Dallas, 89.

[14]2 Dallas, 435.

[15]7 Wall, 700.

[16] *Ibid.*, p. 725.

[17] Wall. 71, 76.

[18] Wall. 725.

[19] Wheat. 316.

[20] *Ibid.*, p. 403.

[21] Wheat. 1, 187.

CHAPTER I

THE AGENCY SYSTEM

One of the characteristics of the English language is the fact that words do not necessarily have the same meaning to all Americans. The word diplomacy is one such. Diplomacy may mean anything in our common useage from a synonym of that vagary of modern commercial life, sales psychology, to some merely flattering and rather false politeness of expression. To many of us diplomacy means only a sort of magnified horse-trading technique applied to international relations. Our intelligentsia, falling into the easy trap of semiliteracy, twist Sir Henry Wotton's famous pun and insist that a diplomat is an honest person sent abroad to lie for the good of his country. They lose the whole force of his play on words, for the point of that pun depends on the position within the sentence of the words "to lie" meaning a short sojourn while traveling instead of a permanent residence. Read in that way Sir Henry's definition of a diplomat as "an honest man sent to lie abroad for the good of his country" did not need to be twisted. It did, of course, contain a sly humorous dig at the doctrines of Niccolo Machiavelli, still famous for the most callously utilitarian treatise on the conduct of Princes ever written. Whether Niccolo meant what he said exactly as we understand him is another matter. Machiavelli was a cynic. He had good reason to be. It is not certain, however, whether he believed in the utterly unscrupulous conduct he seemed to advocate, and to which he conformed in his own diplomatic missions, or whether he was cynically satirizing the usual procedures of the diplomats of his period. In any case, Machiavelli has become the symbol and personification of diplomacy to many people.

Perhaps the lowest and least excusable of all popular definitions of diplomacy is the one that has been allowed to become exclusively American, that of diplomatic office as a "sinecure," and the profession of diplomacy as "feeding at the public trough." There is a depth of degradation in that conception of one of the most important functions of the executive power

17

which augurs ill for the successful conduct of international relations if it be widespread. That it is so, however, is rather sadly evident. There is no other country in the world where diplomacy is so degraded in the public mind. If one looks on diplomatic office as "a job" in the gift of government, it tends inevitably and of course to lower public understanding of the nature of an important profession. Considered as a political reward for vote getters a little too important for minor federal office and not quite big enough for senate, house of representatives, or cabinet, diplomatic office has been used too frequently by political party managers as a convenient shelf on which to lay such men.

Shallow as they are, these are reasons enough, unfortunately, for the disrepute of American diplomacy as a profession. Exactly the opposite should be the case. Instead of distorting and degrading the profession of diplomacy, we should look upon it as one of the most exacting, one of the most broadening careers to which a man may dedicate himself, one in which many Americans have taken an honorable and an important part in building the fabric of America. Far from being the "undemocratic" institution it is also called, diplomacy is a profession which a democracy above all other forms of political communities should appreciate at its true value and importance, for it is the channel through which democracy's own ideals are communicated to other peoples, and by which those ideals are fostered and protected when established in practice.

In spite of all these ignorant and illiterate perversions, diplomacy has a true and definite meaning. The classic textbook definition is the one advanced by Sir Ernest Satow in 1917, that diplomacy is "the application of intelligence and tact to the conduct of official relations between the governments of independent states, extending sometimes also to their relations with vassal states."[1] In his authoritative book on the subject Sir Ernest quoted the Count de Garden on the art and science of diplomacy, particularly its object. De Garden said that the essential element of the art and science of diplomacy was the spirit of conciliation or negotiation, more specifically that diplomacy "embraces the whole system of interests born of the relations established between nations; its general object is the security of those relations, their

18

tranquility and their respective dignity. The direct and immediate object of diplomacy is--or should be--to maintain peace and harmony among the Powers."[2]

If it is possible to add an additional definition to the wisdom of such diplomatic sages as Sir Ernest and Count de Garden, diplomacy may be considered as a bridge of which the two foundation structures, on either side of the precipitous ravine that habitually separates any two Peoples are: exact knowledge of one's own fundamental national character and aspirations and vital needs, and equally exact knowledge of those of the nation or people with whom one is dealing. The bridge, if built at all, should be designed to serve as a safe and permanent means of communication and interdependence in the best interests of both. And that is the essence of diplomacy. In that sense it expresses the fundamental aspirations of democracy in its world relations.

Diplomacy is not the only word that carries different meanings to different people in our complex society today. Empire is another such word. Today, empire is a word full of bad connotations, such as "evil empire." It is almost a dirty word, bringing to mind an image of predatory imperialism, an era in history wherein a few Great Powers in Western Europe brought the rest of the world to heel. Actually, the word empire meant something quite different in Anglo-American history. In 1533, when King Henry VIII boasted that this realm of England "is an empire" he meant that England was an independent country, an empire of its own, and intended to remain that way, no matter what the designs of others might be. Joel Hurstfield, in a delightful essay on the Elizabethan people and nation, said:

> to Henry VIII and to the English parliamentarians, empire meant independence. In declaring that England was an empire, Henry VIII was issuing a declaration of independence: England was a self-governing nation, free from any kind of exterior control by any authority. In this context he was thinking of the Pope. But his language and policy left no doubt that if the Emperor Charles V (who was also King of Spain) wished to pull some of the papal chestnuts out of

the fire, then this was an announcement
of defiance to him too. The declaration of empire of 1533 is as important
in English history as the Declaration
of Independence of 1776 is in the history of America or the Declaration of
Rights of Man of 1789 is in the history
of France.[3]

In the great debate over the ratification of our own
Constitution--in fact, in number 1 of the *Federalist*--
Alexander Hamilton argued that what was at stake was
nothing less than "the fate of an empire in many respects the most interesting in the world."[4]

Isolation is another word that has been dealt with
harshly by the forces of history. For long years the
British Empire was held together by a policy of
"splendid isolation" from the alliance systems of the
warring powers of Europe, and did not abandon the policy until her own survival was at stake. After our independence from the British Empire was won, we were
quick to adopt a policy of "splendid isolation" for
ourselves. The First President laid it down as "the
great rule" for us in foreign affairs to have as
little to do with the "broils and wars" of Europe as
was humanly possible. The idea of "no entangling alliances" was another manifestation of this fundamental
feeling on our part, as was President Monroe's ringing
declaration of December 2, 1823. It took a Franklin D.
Roosevelt to make "isolationism" a dirty word in the
United States. Woodrow Wilson tried, but failed, and
the failure probably cost him his life. To the Founding Fathers, isolationism was a glory word, a policy
objective of the highest order, and the greatest importance.

In other words, most Americans are unfamiliar
with the colonial past. To them, it is a closed book.
They do not know that there is any such thing as American diplomacy within the British Empire, or that
there is a colonial heritage, diplomatic and military.
They are satisfied that isolationism is a dirty word
when applied to foreign policy, and are not aware of
the fact that empire-building was the polar star of
our existence for the first 300 years of our history,
if one counts time from the days of Jamestown and Plymouth to the present. They also do not know that practically all the major problems we face today in the
field of foreign policy were problems that confronted

20

us in the first period of our existence. Nothing changes too much. During the colonial period each separate colony had to manage its own affairs much if not most of the time, and as a result we became steeped in the practice of government, including the management of foreign affairs. The problems we had to face included problems of war and peace, of trade and commerce, of disputed boundaries, of alliance, of sudden attack, of balance of power, of trade, of arbitration, on neutral rights of innocent passage, of navigation, of prisoners of war, of hostages, of duplicity on the part of uncertain allies, of slave uprisings, of Indian relations, of covert and overt traffic in arms, and nearly every other problem that confronts (or confounds) us today.

A people cannot cut itself off from its roots, and expect to survive in a competitive world. For us there is no solution unless we consent to treat the whole of our existence as part of our history. If we do that, we will see that when we have had reasonable foreign policy objectives we have managed creditably and with dignity. The obverse is also true. When our foreign policy objectives have been poorly defined or conceived on the basis of unreality the results have been disappointing or disastrous, depending on the circumstances. The key to successful diplomacy in a democracy is an informed public opinion. It is not possible to achieve this as long as the guiding first principles of American diplomacy are unknown or are treated as fable and mythology. The solution fo the problem is not in the transfer to the executive branch of the exclusive management of diplomacy. That is the dictatorial solution that we, as a democratic people, should stoutly resist. In our system, the public welfare is guarded, as it should be, by popular representation in Congress. The solution in our case cannot come out of the constant tensions between the two branches of government, with secretiveness on one side, and stubborn obstructionism on the other, but only if we agree to get back to first principles, to look at ourselves objectively in history, and to plot our course on the basis of clear and consistent policies, consciously adopted and steadfastly maintained. We cannot survive in today's world without a diplomacy that is based on solid foundations. Whimsy and emotionalism are no substitutes for experience, right reason, and clarity in the formulation of foreign policy.

21

The unwillingness of Americans to come to grips
with their past is evident not only in the conduct of
diplomacy, but even in the history books, not only
those of the textbook variety, but in some of the
larger treatises as well. For example, one of the most
distinguished of the colonial historians, Professor
Charles M. Andrews, in a classic book that ran through
eight printings said:

> little that took place in America in
> the seventeenth century can be con-
> strued as American, in any proper sense
> of the word. To scrutinize that cen-
> tury for the purpose of extracting
> therefrom something analogous to modern
> notions of liberty and progress is to
> disturb the whole historical process
> and to run the risk of admitting prepo-
> sitions that have already done much to
> mislead the popular mind as to what the
> earliest period of English life on Ame-
> rican soil really means.[5]

In sharp contrast, another outstanding colonial
historian, Max Savelle, stated the case for the con-
tinuity of history in an article (later a book) entitled "Colonial Origins of American Diplomatic Principles." Dr. Savelle rejected the idea that America
sprang like Athena fully armed from the brow of Zeus
in 1776, and said:

> that the ideas underlying the permanent
> bases of American diplomacy were al-
> ready old, even traditional, long be-
> fore the time of American independence;
> that those ideas are as old as European
> settlement in America, because they
> arose out of needs which were inherent
> in the geographic situation of the col-
> onies here; and that they developed
> simultansously in America and in Europe,
> out of the intercolonial relations of
> English, Spanish, Dutch and French
> colonies, on the one hand, and out of
> the adaptation of European diplomacy to
> the new international situation pre-
> sented by the appearance of colonial
> empires in the western hemisphere, on
> the other.[6]

American diplomacy began, as Max Savelle said it did, as soon as the first permanent English settlements were made in the New World. As our ancestors felt their way up from the beaches along the rivers to the mountains, they very quickly became aware of the existence of their ancient enemies, France and Spain; and in the forests beyond unexplored mountain ranges of the existence of Indians, not as mere isolated individuals, villages, or savage tribes, but of nations of Indians behind the tribes, and of confederations behind the nations. We could not live our self-governing lives in the face of that menace. We would not accept for ourselves any such imperial regimentation (as we saw it) as the Spaniards and the French. Our answer was a union of self-governing dominions, each one an entity in itself, whether it was Virginia, Massachusetts, New York, or Pennsylvania.

The 16th Century was an era of grandiose personal adventuring in America. Such sporadic attempts as were made by Elizabethan gallants to plant settlements in America were ill-ordered, poorly captained, and vanished into the mists that still hung over our legendary coast. The 17th Century took another course, more practical though still idealistic. The men who were boys when Elizabeth and her glamorous train were in their glory had come to understand that no permanent settlements could be established in America by dropping a group of someone's personal servants and tenants at some lonely spot on the far-away coast of Virginia with the injunction: increase and multiply—go, take the land before you—and when you are strong enough, go singe the beard of the King of Spain.

These men, more cunning than the great spendthrifts of the passing generation, recognized that initial capital and reserves were necessary to plant a colony and to maintain it. Therefore, they formed capital resources and reserves behind the groups with which they proposed to conquer and settle the New World. On their investments, they expected great returns in precious minerals and commerce. The settlers were to produce those returns for them, and in reward they were to be enabled to strike out for themselves, once they had taken a firm grasp on the edges of the new continent.

Queen Elizabeth set the pattern for the establishment of the British Empire in America when she made the decision that it would have to be done with

23

private, not public financing. Flattered as she was
that the New Found Land should be called Virginia "as
a memorial   that   it had been discovered during the
reign of a virgin queen,"[7] nevertheless the Queen refused to let the treasury bear the burden of exploiting the great discovery. If England was to win the
race for dominion in America, private enterprise would
have to foot the bill. This is in striking contrast
to the decision centuries later to put a man on the
moon. The race to be first in space was won by the
state, not by private enterprise. However, in Elizabeth's time the engine of progress was captained by an
enterprising private sector. The spirit of Elizabeth's
time was the same as that of 1776; when the signers of
the great Declaration affixed their signatures to the
great document they did so in the full knowledge that
they were risking "our Lives, our Fortunes and our
sacred Honor."[8]

It was not enough to devise protection and maintenance for settlers after they arrived in America.
They must first be induced to come. Charters must be
obtained to guarantee them certain desirable things in
their new homes from the only one who could grant them
--the King. He was the only source of right to the
soil in the conventions of the age of exploration and
discovery. Charters therefore were obtained from the
King by feudal lords Proprietary, by commercial stock
companies, and by groups of individuals sharing capital expenses. The accepted way to take title to the
soil was to plant the banner of the King under whom
the discoverer served, and to claim in his name all
adjacent territory. The charters thus obtained were
not mere grants of land to be settled for commercial
development and profit. They asserted soverdignty and
allegiance for all time, and in the carefully worded
feudal legal terminology of the time defined the relationship between King and subjects emigrating to found
colonies in new lands. These charters in most instances specifically guaranteed to the colonists all
the ancient liberties of Englishmen, even though many
of the liberties were under attack in England at the
same time they were being guaranteed to the colonists.

The colonial charters were granted under the dual
influence of the old feudal relation of the free Englishman to his overlord, which was voluntary (any free-
man could change his overlord at will) and definite
(land and protection in return for allegiance), and of

24

the liberal philosophies of men like Milton, John
Locke and Sir Thomas More. *Utopia*, it will be recalled,
was published at the time the New World was being made
known to the Old, and Raphael Hythloday, who tells the
story of Sir Thomas's imaginary island, is represented
as being a member of the expeditions of Amerigo
Vespucci.

The colonial charters not only guaranteed personal
liberties to the men who could be induced to settle in
the New World; they carefully defined the allegiance
expected of them, defined it in the clear legal terms
of usage at that time. Grants were made in free and
common socage, not in capite, nor for Knight's service.
A grant for Knight's service meant that the grantee
was obliged, in return for land and protection, to
supply military aid to the grantor, if needed, for a
definite number of days a year, at his own expense. A
grant in capite meant that the grantee must perform
some court service. A grant of land in soc, on the
other hand, established a separate jurisdiction cut
off from the ordinary authorities, without regular
military or court services. In all these instances,
however, the grants of land set up a direct relationship between the grantor, in this case the King, and
the grantees, whether they be chosen individuals,
Lords Proprietary, or commercial stock companies.

In this feudal charter relationship there was no
room for a third party to interpose himself between
the King and his colonies. Also within this relationship, absolute monarchy had no place. Long before the
American charters were drawn up, the great English
charter, Magna Carta, had set up a procedure whereby a
King who violated that relation could be brought to
justice. Americans followed that procedure exactly
when centuries later they refused to recognize the
sovereignty over them of the London Parliament (a
third party) and, in consequence, renounced their allegiance to a King whose "long train of abuses and usurpations, pursuing invariably the same Object evinces
a design to reduce them under absolute Despotism."[9]

In 1607, the first permanent English settlement in
the New World was made on the banks of the James River
in Virginia. The first charter of Virginia (1606)
contained the familiar provision guaranteeing to the
settlers the rights of free Englishmen, "to all Intents and Purposes, as if they had been abiding and

25

born, within this our Realm of England."[10]

The second charter of Virginia enlarged the mainland jurisdiction of the colony by providing that it should run "throughout from Sea to Sea, West and Northwest; and also all the Islands lying within one hundred Miles along the Coast of both Seas."[11] Thirteen years later, while the first colony was trying to survive within its imperial domain, a second permanent English colony was established. The Pilgrim Fathers began their sixty-five day voyage to the New World on September 16, 1620, and made the landfall not where they wanted to, in the neighborhood of the Hudson River, but far to the north at the tip of Cape Cod. Here they decided to stay because of the danger of encountering winter storms at sea. The only trouble was that Plymouth was outside the jurisdiction of the London Company which had issued them a patent, and since King James had refused to give them a charter, this left the Plymouth settlers without authority from the Crown or title to a foot of soil. Worse than that, it raised the question of law. Were the Plymouth settlers in a state of nature in this wild region? beyond any man-made law? To resolve the issue a meeting was held in the cabin of the *Mayflower* on November 21, and there a very famous document was drawn up and signed. This was the Mayflower Compact, of course, and in the opening sentence the settlers acknowledged that they were "Loyal Subjects of our dread Sovereign Lord King James," and then proceeded to establish their "civil Body Politick," pledging and promising "all due Submission and Obedience."[12]

The Pilgrim Fathers were doing something quite simple and at the same time profoundly moving in 1620. What they proposed was the establishment of a colony or body politic in the New World, entirely independent of the London and Plymouth companies in England, and to govern themselves as they saw fit, subject only to the legitimate power of the King. There in one phrase, "all due Submission and Obedience," is the root of much of the century and a half of controversy with the mother country that followed. The American vision was that of a New World, in the form of the British Empire, triumphant over all rivals, coupled with a great fear here, lest that vision be lost in the political evolution and the dynastic struggle of England. We were still Britons, but we were no longer English in the

26

narrow insular sense. We were Americans, though Britons in a broad, continental, and imperialistic sense. Benjamin Franklin was giving voice to no new thought when he spoke of a British Empire that was "constant'y increasing," and would shortly extend its "influence round the whole globe, and awe the world."[13]

Yes--Benjamin Franklin was thinking imperially, but not in isolation from the rest of his fellow Britons in America, nor as part of any new great flashing revelation. It was a traditional vision in America, and had been so ever since Virginia's second charter had granted the South Sea, the Pacific Ocean, as Virginia's western boundary. Franklin was thinking imperially, and he was also thinking of imperial organization, for in the same vein he says, "Where the frontier people owe and pay obedience, there they have a right to look for protection. No political proposition is better established than this."[14] But to whom did Americans acknowledge they owed and were willing to pay obedience? That, for the purpose of this account, is of paramount importance, and its understanding not only establishes the fact of American diplomacy within the British Empire, but carries us straight back to our earliest beginnings, in its consistent and continuous practice.

Franklin was selected to go to London in 1757 to present to the King the position of Pennsylvania in the controversies which had arisen between the Proprietor and the freemen with respect to the colony. This was 19 years before our separation from the empire. Franklin was sent to the King for the best of all reasons, for the same reason the Declaration of Independence is, after its preamble, a plain, direct, and personal indictment of the King for things that it was his duty to do but which he had not done, and for acts in which he had usurped powers that were not rightfully his. But whence did Britons (though Americans like Franklin) draw any such seemingly fantastic notions as the possibility of indicting the lawful sovereign, in person? From the charters that they were granted personally by Kings of England, particularly in the carefully worded feudal legal terminology of the Proprietary charters. The relation between King and freemen was direct and personal. The charters continued that relation to the King's successors. Obedience was due to the King and to him alone, but our obedience to the King and his rights over us were definite and limited.

27

The issue is nowhere better recorded than in Franklin's preliminary conversation with Lord Grenville in 1757. "You Americans," he said, "have wrong ideas of the nature of your constitution; you contend that the King's instructions to his governors are not laws, and think yourselves at liberty to regard or disregard them at your discretion. But those instructions are not like the pocket instructions given to a minister going abroad, for regulating his conduct in some trifling point of ceremony. They are first drawn up by judges learned in the laws; they are then considered, debated, and perhaps amended in Council, after which they are signed by the king. They are then, so far as they relate to you, the law of the land, for the king is the LEGISLATOR OF THE COLONIES."[15]

That was true, and we too, so understood it, but with one essential difference; in the ideas we brought from England absolute monarchy had no place. We acknowledged the King as "legislator" but not as absolute. We still held to Magna Carta, modified by the later struggle for constitutional monarchy. And there again we made a difference; we were prepared to admit the principle of "King and Parliament" as joint legislators--but not the King and the London Parliament. That was for England. For us, the proper form was the King and each of our own parliaments, assemblies, or whatever local name they bore. There, clearly, is the principle for which we fought continually and against which the London government fought us.

Franklin records his rejection of any such conception of absolute government. To him, as to all his breed, the fact was that the colonies were English colonies and nothing else, and that, as free Englishmen, we had certain rights and privileges even against the King. We possessed these rights all the more truly since both rights and privileges had been set down under royal guarantees in the early charters. This, to our way of thinking, was not a subject for Lord Grenville's opinion, nor even for that of the King himself.[16] If the issue is clear, it is possible to speak correctly of American diplomacy within the British Empire: "the science"--according to de Garden--"of the respective relations and mutual interests of States," the art of "conciliating the interests of Peoples," with the general object of the "security of these relations, their tranquility and their respective dignity."[17]

Franklin's appointment as Agent for the Pennsylvania colony in 1757 was a very important event, as it
turned out, but there was nothing singular or excep-
tional about it at the time. The Agency System got
its start in 1624 when John Pointis of Virginia was
appointed to represent his colony to the King, and by
the time of Franklin's appointment the Agency System
was a well established institution in the relationship
between the mother country and the colonies. During
the colonial period some 200 Agents were sent to the
imperial capital to represent their individual colonies to the King. As a particularly careful scholar
of the period, Professor E. P. Tanner of Columbia
University, said, "though the impulse for the agency
proceeded from America, it was aided, systematized and
enforced by the conscious policy of the British
government."[18]

Why were Agents necessary in the colonial system?
What practical purpose did they serve? Were the individual colonies largely ungovernable as they hardened
into little republics, and was this a reason a channel
had to be opened to conduct the official relations between the London government and the colonial governments? As the gap widened did it become more and more
apparent that without the application of intelligence
and tact on both sides the irrepressible break would
be irrepressible? Largely because this was so, it became necessary for the colonies to be represented in
London. It did not and does not matter whether the
arguments of the colonies were well founded in law or
not, negotiations were in order to present them at the
imperial capital, and to defend them when they ran up
against opposing views on the part of the mother
country.

Skills of the highest order were required on the
part of colonial Agents because the problems they had
to face were complex ones involving questions of war
and peace, of the preservation of charters, of boundary disputes between the colonies, and with their
rival claimants to empire in America, of Indian policy
and free trade in the world markets, to say nothing of
the claim as to taxation, which began the contest.
These were diplomatic problems of high importance to
both parties, and come within Sir Ernest Satow's definition of diplomacy, as "the application of Intelligence and tact to the conduct of official relations

between the governments of independent states, extending sometimes also to their relations with vassal states."[19]

Beginning in 1901 with E. P. Tanner's study of "Colonial Agencies in England," a growing number of such studies, including book-length treatises, have appeared in England and the United States. The authors have adhered to high levels of scholarship in making these studies, and they have looked at the system from different points of view. The subject is of obvious importance because it was carefully nurtured in the colonies and in the home government in England, not excluding the sovereigns themselves who on more than one occasion demanded that Agents be sent over with full powers to treat or negotiate with them on specific points that were troubling the relations between king and colony. Some of the Agents were powerful enough, or persuasive enough, to effect fundamental changes in imperial policy. It is a challenging subject, not only because of its intrinsic importance, but because of its many facets.

The point emphasized by Tanner in his pioneering study on the subject was the extent to which the system "epitomizes the political history of the colonies."[20] Dr. Ella Lonn paid particular attention to the colonial Agents of the southern colonies, and advanced the striking conclusion that the Agents "in forcing the repeal of the Stamp Act may have delayed the Revolution about a decade."[21] In 1968, Professor Michael G. Kammen published a scholarly work on the colonial Agents in the light of British politics, and the American Revolution. It was his view that the Agents should be looked at as "paid lobbyists"[22] and in this sense they were the precursors of the powerful special interest groups that sometimes control and dominate both houses of Congress. However, it is possible to look at the Agents and the Agency System from another point of view, the diplomatic point of view. Arthur Lee, one of the last colonial Agents, became the first of the colonial patriots to represent the country as a whole when he was appointed to be representative of the Continental Congress in London. His mission was "to inquire as to the disposition of foreigh powers"[23] in the event of a war between the colonies and the mother country. What the Congress had in mind was the attitude of France and Spain, England's traditional rivals and enemies. Professor Kammen recognized the significance of this transition when he said, "through one of those touches of irony that makes history endlessly fascinating, the expiring agency was nourishing its own progeny -- the foreign service of a new nation."[24]

It was more than that. The Agency System *was* a Foreign Service for the individual colonies all during the colonial period, and it was through this channel that each colony communicated directly with the mother country. On the other hand, the royal governors were the ordinary conduit of communication when the King communicated with the individual colonies. The theory was that since the King could not be in fourteen places at the same time, that is in London and in the capitals of the 13 American colonies, he should have governors to represent him in the 13 colonies, and the colonies in turn should have Agents to represent them to the King in the imperial capital. In other words, let an assembly in the New World address the King, Privy Council, or even Parliament, and the Agent would be the point of contact. By the same token, let the King address a colony, and the governor's job would be to serve as the official channel of communication with the colony. As the system developed, the prestige of the Agents increased, and there was a corresponding decline in the influence of the governors. However, taken together the Agents and the governors represented the official channel of communication between King and colonies. In their hands was placed the delicate problem of reconciling distinctly opposing points of view concerning imperial growth and organization.

Professor Kammen said, quite rightly, that the Agency System embraced more than one kind of Agent. In fact, he said "the genus 'agent' included various species,"[25] and among the varieties were the official and unofficial Agents, depending upon whether they represented some special, usually private, interest in the colonies, or whether they represented a public interest, either on the part of the colony as a whole, the governor, the council, or a colony assembly. In addition, there was the important difference between the Regular and Special Agents, the former being posted to the imperial capital for a specified period of time, and the latter for a particular mission. Of all these different types the only ones that were lobbyists in a modern sense were those representing private interests, usually commercial. All the others were diplomatic in nature in that they represented a government, or some important segment of it, at a foreign court. The difference between the Regular and Special Agents was the same as that which exists today between our regular Ambassadors and the Ambassadors Extraordinary on a special diplomatic mission. The true type of Agent in the colonial period was the one whose appointment stemmed from the colony as a whole rather than a particular branch of the government such as a colonial assembly or a governor's council. However, as long as they represented a government as opposed to a private interest they were Ambassadors in the modern sense of the term, no matter what the priorities in their instructions were, whether they were military, political, social, or economic. Even today we have diplomatic officers in our embassies abroad who are specialists such as military attaches, economic attaches, cultural attaches, and so forth.

The colonists were every bit as careful about the Instructions to their Agents as the King was about his Instructions to the royal governors. Not only were they just as careful but, from all accounts, they were more successful. The word *impower* was used constantly throughout the annals of the colonies in connection with Agents, and that use of the word is notable. The records are clear as to just what those powers were, how far the Agents were bound by their Instructions, to what extent any Agent could bind his colony, and so forth. The practice in all these matters conformed exactly to the established and recognized diplomatic usage of Europe at the time. It is identical with recognized diplomatic practice today. The Agent was always accredited to the King, and was bound by the Instructions from his colony, not by the King. The King himself recognized that limitation. Governor Hutchinson of Massachusetts records that on one occasion, being frustrated in a negotiation, "the King commanded that agents should be sent over, to appear before him in six months after receipt of this letter, fully instructed and impowered to answer."[26]

This is evidence, surely, that even the King recognized the fact that it was useless to negotiate unless the Agent had proper credentials, and the Agent's colony was the only authority that could give him the necessary credentials. When the Agent's colony did not permit him to satisfy on all points, that is to yield to the crown, the remedial action of the King was, to be sure, a threat to revoke the charter. The fact remains that within the charter the King was obliged to respect the limitations imposed upon the colonial negotiators. He could only get around the increasingly evident diplomatic character of the relation by an exercise of purely arbitrary authority cancelling the guaranteed status of the colony, and that is what Americans claimed with very good reason that he could not do.

Another notable thing in connection with the Agency System is the frequency of a phrase that deals with a fundamental idea in all the colonies, the phrase being "the interest of the colony." Thus in the Instructions given to the Agents from Massachusetts at a critical time it was said, "the court, this year, expecting great revolutions were at hand in England, sent over, as their agents, two of the ministers, Mr. Thomas Weld, and Mr. Hugh Peters, and one of the representatives, Mr. William Hibbins, in order to establish the interest of the colony."[27] This phrase, the interest of the colony, was a bed-rock principle of our early British-American relations. It was something apart from the internal revolutions of insular England, and had nothing to do with any kind of feeling of collective solidarity on the part of the colonies. It was an expression of the individuality of the colonies, and it was something that was firmly embedded in the minds of early Americans. To some extent, this idea was even accepted in London, as Charles II, for example, upon his formal restoration, ordered a new seal for the colony of Virginia which bore the inscription, "Behold! Virginia Gives The Fifth (Kingdom) --En Dat Virginia Quintum." Charles II had a special debt to Virginia because of the loyalty of the Old Dominion during the years of his exile. It was his way of paying the debt. On the whole, however, the idea of individual kingdoms or nations was stoutly rejected by the ruling monarchs in England.

Tanner's disquisition on the "Colonial Agencies in England" contains two sets of formal Instructions sent to colonial Agents in London, one from the Massachusetts colony dated 1694, and the other from Connecticut shortly after the outbreak of the Seven Years' War, which would put it some fifty years later. The Massachusetts Instructions were as follows:

> (1) It is necessary that applications be made unto their majesties, the ministers of state (and if need be to the Parliament) for the restoration of as

33

many of our ancient privileges as may
be obtained. The success of Maj. Winthrop on behalf of Connecticut is en-
couraging.

(2) We think it necessary that all
means be used to prevent the designs of
any persons to incommode the Province
by Charters or anything interfering
with our liberties or properties.

(3) We think it necessary and needful
to lay before their majesties the insupportable burden lying upon the province
in maintaining a garrison at Pemaquid,
and that their majesties be addressed
to take it into their royal care.

(4) It may be expedient to represent to
their majesties the necessity of reducing Canada and the extreme incapacity
and calamity whereto the Province is
brought by the miscarriage of our former expeditions and by our present war
with the Indians which makes us unable
to do anything in this matter.[28]

The Instructions to the Connecticut Agent over
fifty years later show how the duties of the colonial
Agents remained the same over the years, changing only
in particulars relevant to the parent colony, and how
much was expected of the Agents. In this case the
Agent was told:

(1) You are with all convenient speed
to embrace the first safe and good opportunity to embark for England and
there to transact on behalf of this
colony in all affairs and concerns
thereof...

(2) You are to represent the state of
this colony in every needful respect,
especially what share and burden it
hath sustained for the defense and security of his majesty's territories in
America...

(3) You are to take prudent care of the
affair of the Mohawk Indians to prevent

34

any further proceedings in the case.

(4) You are to take due care of our interest with relation to the four towns challenged by Massachusetts Bay and which lie to the south of the line between the two governments that no injury be done to us therein and that all disputes about it may be prevented.

(5) You are as occasion may require to represent the whole transaction relating to the Spanish ship, St. Joseph and St. Helen and her cargo, which we doubt not when truly known will set us in a favorable light on that head.

(6) You are to advise with and consult council learned in the law in any case wherein there is occasion; and in all things wherein you transact for the colony you are to take such advice and assistance in all measures and steps as you shall judge prudent and likely to promote our interest.[29]

It is clear from the Instructions to the two Agents that they were not lobbyists, attorneys, or mere commercial factors in their duties and functions. Their primary duty was to safeguard and protect the charters of their respective colonies, but in addition to this the two Agents were charged with the adjudication of boundary disputes, with the determination of Indian policy, with the building of forts, with problems of general foreign policy, including military operations against Canada, with maritime problems such as the one relating to the Spanish ship, and with any other problems that might arise in connection with the external affairs of the colony. In other words, the Agents were Agents Plenipotentiary in the scope of their official duties, responsibilities, and functions.

The final paragraph in the Instructions to the Connecticut Agent throws some light on how the Agency System worked. The Agent was specifically ordered "to transmit from time to time accounts of all your proceedings and everything done therein relative to our affairs by every convenient opportunity after your arrival at Great Britain and to observe such further instructions as shall hereafter be given you by this assembly."[30] In other words, each Agent in the field was supervised, controlled, and directed by a duly constituted authority in the home government. Today we call this authority the Department of State. In the colonial period it was a Committee of Correspondence in each colony. These were powerful committees, and in some cases they were even given the appointment and removal powers over the Agents. Only men of the first importance, as Dr. Lonn said, were allowed to serve on the "Committee of Correspondence, thus bearing witness to the importance of the office: the speaker was pretty regularly of the membership; the service was regarded as of sufficient importance to command the attention of some members for long years of service; some colonies wisely utilized the experience of members who had served on the committee as special agents, and, conversely, placed agents after their return on the committee."[31] So important were these committees that it became a toss-up as to whether it was more important to be on the committees or to be an Agent in the field. The same thing is true today in our State Department, and to a lesser extent in the Department of Defense. Active diplomats in the field and command generals in the theaters do not always have the highest opinions of the cookie-pushers in the State Department and the desk generals in the Pentagon. At first, the committees were controlled by the governors and their councils, but as the lower houses gained strength and influence, the balance began to change, and it was not long before the committees were under the control of the lower house.

What type of person was most likely to succeed as an Agent: It depended. Just as today, the qualities required for success as a Special Agent were quite different from those required for a Regular Agent. For the latter the qualities most desirable were those necessary in any large field, the most important being a good knowledge of all the important problems, and the ability to negotiate fairly in order to reconcile opposing points of view, in other words good judgment and common sense. In particular, the Agent had to be able to present himself at court, before the Privy Council, and if needs be before Parliament. He was expected to anticipate and ward off legislation prejudicial to his colony, and to take the necessary steps to get all the laws approved as they came from his colony. Among other things, he was expected to be able to present the colony's point of view on military

strategy, on Indian affairs, on boundary disputes, on
commerce and trade, and on anything else that affected
the interest of the colony, including the protection
of its charter. Dr. Lonn outlined the job qualifications when she said:

> ambassador of good will, liaison offi-
> cer, shrewd business man with a knowl-
> edge of all sorts of trade, Lawyer con-
> versant with British as well as colon-
> ial legislation, diplomat with the tact
> and finesse of the best French tradition
> -- all these and more the agent of
> one of the American colonies needed to
> be.[32]

The Agency system in colonial days was a magnet
that attracted the most able people in political life.
Appointments to office were coveted and much sought
after, even though the rewards were not great, and the
penalties for failure were often harsh. Governor
Hutchinson, looking back over a period of years, said
that "of all the agents which they have sent over unto
the court of England for now 40 years together, I know
not any one who did not, at his return, meet with some
very froward entertainment among his countrymen."[33]
Nevertheless, some of the most celebrated names of
colonial history, British as well as American, were
among those who served as colonial Agents, including
Edmund Burke, Edward Winslow, Increase Mather, Arthur
Lee, Joseph Dudley, and Benjamin Franklin. This is a
parade of greats. Positions as Agent were fought over
and sought after because, as Dr. Lonn said, the position of Agent was a very "dignified respectable post--
in a word, a gentleman's position."[34]

The salaries of the Agents varied greatly from
colony to colony, but the average was in the neighborhood of 250 pounds for the full-time services of the
Agent. By contrast, William Berkeley of Virginia was
paid a salary of 2,000 pounds a year as governor. The
highest salary paid a regular Agent was 800 pounds.
This was the salary Benjamin Franklin got for his
second term as a Pennsylvania Agent. For the first
term, Franklin's salary was 500 pounds, the same that
Edmund Burke got for his New York Agency. Georgia
paid Franklin 150 pounds for his part-time services,
and New Jersey 100 pounds. Massachusetts promised to
pay Franklin 300 pounds a year, but since Governor
Hutchinson vetoed the assembly's appropriations after

1770, Franklin did not get the money. However, if that were included Franklin's salary from the four governments he represented would have been 1,350 pounds a year. This was hardly big pay. On the whole, therefore, and consistent with practice today, the salaries were too low for principal Agents. As today, the determining factor in the salary a diplomat was paid was the wealth and interest of the sending government. One of the early Massachusetts Agents found his allowance so scant that the Corporation for Propagating the Gospel allowed him 100 pounds for his aid in that direction--but claimed it back from the government.[35]

The terms of office for the Agents varied greatly. In Massachusetts it lasted, as it has continued to do until this day in the United States, for as long as the political party that appointed the Agent held its majority. Otherwise, and particularly during the experimental period of the 17th Century, the usual term was one year. However, as the need for greater permanance became apparent, the term was extended to two years. There were exceptions to the two-year term, of course. One Agent served Rhode Island for 44 years, another served Virginia for 31 years, and still a third New Hampshire for 28 years. Nevertheless, the rule was a one-year term in the beginning, gradually giving way to a two-year period.[36] Even so, the Agents were always in the cross-fire of politics at home and abroad, and could have their appointments terminated at either end, by becoming persona non grata at the imperial capital, or by having the sending colony lose confidence in him.[37] The situation is not too different today with the comings and goings of the diplomats in all the major capitals of the world.

Perhaps another point should be made at this time about certain oddities of the Agency System from the point of view of today's Foreign Service. One of these is the fact that non-nationals occasionally served as Agents, and another is that it was not uncommon for a single Agent to represent several colonies at the same time. It was also not uncommon for several Agents from a single colony to reside in London at the same time, and to confuse the London authorities as to which one could speak for the colony. This was a bad practice because disputes between the Agents were common, particularly when one had his credentials from the assembly, and the other from the governor. This bad practice has been repeated frequently. Franklin lost a good opportunity to obtain the cession of Canada to the United States in the general treaty of peace because of John Jay's legalistic objection to the wording of the British plenipotentiary's powers. Strong divergence of opinion among joint and equal American delegates to international conferences has wrecked them in more recent times.

On the subject of non-nationals, how could a Pennsylvanian represent Georgia, for example, at the capital, or how could a London businessman or statesman have enough in common with an American colony to be its representative at the court of St. James? On the face of it, the difficulties would appear to be insurmountable, not only for the British-born Agents, but also for the Americans attempting to represent two or more colonies at the same time. In some cases the difficulties were insurmountable, and at the end of 1766 Massachusetts decided that her interests were not being served well, nor could they be, by having a non-national as an Agent, particularly having one who was representing other colonies at the same time. Accordingly, she dismissed the Agent, saying that the "general Interests of the Colonies cannot be so effectually Served by uniting the Agency of several of them in the Same person, as by each having its own Separate agent."[38] However, on the whole, the British-born Agents, and even those who represented several colonies at the same time, did their jobs well, conflict of interest or no conflict of interest. As Dr. Lonn pointed out:

> the loyalty of Franklin, Knox, Lee, and other Americans we may take for granted, but Barlow Trecothick, Richard Jackson, and, above all, Edmund Burke and Charles Garth were towers of strength to the American cause.[39]

The duties of the Agents varied from colony to colony, and from season to season. It was the Agent's principal duty to represent the interests of his colony to the King. However, the Agent's duties no more stopped with this primary official function than a diplomat's duties cease today when contact is made with a foreign minister of state, or when an important note is regularly presented to the proper authorities. The Agent must do everything humanly possible to present to the key people in the home government his colony's views, and to present them in their best

39

light. As Professor Tanner said, "his success and
reputation as an agent depended upon his ability to
win, by hook or crook, a concession of what was demanded."[40] He must harmonize and reconcile opposing
points of view, whether such negotiations lead him to
the King's court, to the Privy Council, to the halls
of Parliament, or to the private rendezvous of influential statesmen. Thus it became one of the functions
of colonial Agents to explain to ministers of the
crown and on occasion to Parliament the evolution of
new peoples on this continent, to interpret their aspirations, to safeguard and to harmonize their respective interests. In a word, they performed under the
common imperial roof some of the general duties of
diplomacy as defined by the authorities. The Agents
were not only instructed by their own American authorities to perform these duties, but were frequently
called on by the King himself to carry out such assign-
ments, even when London ideas were most diametrically
opposed to their own. The Agents were definitely
limited in the points they could concede. They were
negotiators, not mere apologists, nor courthouse
lawyers, and certainly not practitioners of the sleazy
trade of lobbying.

     Franklin's role as an Agent, like everything else
in his illustrious life, was outstanding. Because of
his broad intercolonial experience at home and his
many notable success abroad, he was in a category by
himself as an Agent. He entered upon these duties late
in life at the age of 51, and served two long tours of
duty in London, from 1757 until 1762, and again from
1764 to 1775. The second tour of duty was during the
Stamp Act crisis. This was a period in which tempers
flared on both sides of the Atlantic. In England, what
caused concern in the Stamp Act crisis, aside from the
economic issue, was the fact that the colonial protest
was not confined to a single colony or section, but
was almost continental in scope, extending from Massachusetts to Virginia, and including the middle colonies as well. In addition to this was the fact that
the constitutional issue involved, whether taxation
without representation was tyranny, contained within
it the seeds of rebellion, and was a direct challenge
to both the authority of Parliament and the sovereignty of the King.

     But this was not all. There was also the prac-
tical fact of the economic issue in English politics.

A crushing load of debt had been piled up in the recent war, and the English taxpayers, particularly the landowners, were already paying 20 percent of their income in taxes. By contrast, the tax load in Massachusetts, one of the highest taxed of the colonies, was only one shilling per head as against 26 shillings per head in Britain. Why should not some additional revenue be raised in America? Had not the last war started in America? Had not it been fought in America? Was not it a war primarily to defend, protect, and secure the American colonies? In fact, carried to its logical extreme, could it not be said that in the Seven Years' War the mother country had been only pulling colonial chestnuts out of the fire? Why, then, would Britain be required to pay all the costs of the war? Were English taxpayers not entitled to any relief from this burdensome taxation? Could not even a small amount of it be shifted to the American beneficiaries of the war? These arguments, plus the American challenge to King and Parliament, meant that Grenville could brook no delay in the passage of the Stamp Act.

Even so, the British Prime Minister moved with only very deliberate speed in drafting the Stamp Act, and took every precaution humanly possible to make sure that the measure would not cause offense in the colonies. A year before the bill was even introduced in Parliament Grenville announced his intentions, and respectfully requested the colonists to offer an alternative plan if they so desired. He also consulted the colonial Agents in London, and gave them every opportunity to be heard on the matter, saying that stamp duties would be forgotten if they would raise the money some other way. Even after the Act was passed, but before it went into effect, Grenville summoned the colonial Agents together, including Franklin, and exhorted their cooperation. He explained that all the revenue raised from the stamps would remain in America, and would not even be collected by English officials, since it was his intention to appoint only Americans in this capacity. He then invited the Agents to nominate discreet and respectable persons in each colony for these new positions.

Franklin took the bait. He nominated his friend John Hughes of Pennsylvania as one of the new crown officials. His reasoning was that the bill was going to be law anyway, and that it would be best for it to be administered by decent, honest and loyal Americans.

However, this did not mean that he supported the bill. He opposed it on the ground that taxation without representation was unconstitutional, and argued that the best way to raise the money was "the usual constitutional way" by requisitions. Grenville's objection to this was a very practical one, that the colonists would never agree on a formula for the requisitions, and of course he was right. The Agents themselves tried their hand at it with no success. Opposition to the bill was obviously a lost cause, and the measure, introduced on February 13 as part of the Grenville budget message, became the law of the land on March 22. Only three members of the House of Commons spoke against the bill, and when the vote was taken it passed 205 to 49. The House of Lords passed it without division. The die was now cast.

The American reaction to the Stamp Act came as a stunning surprise to nearly everyone in England, including Franklin. Like the other Agents, Franklin believed the colonial protests against the Stamp Act would moderate with the passage of time, and the people would gradually accept it as another of the necessary evils, at least to the extent they could not nullify it by evasion and non-cooperation. He was wrong. A spark was ignited in the Virignia legislature on May 29, 1765, when a young firebrand named Patrick Henry introduced seven resolutions in a fiery speech bordering on treason. Gradually the flame spread to other colonies where it was fueled by the street people until it threatened to engulf the continent as a whole. This is not to say that America was on the verge of open revolt in 1765. Far from it. It is only to say that the Henry resolutions were quickly sent to disaffected groups in other colonies, and began appearing in local newspapers, periodicals, handbills, and other writings. In Boston, James Otis moved in the Massachusetts legislature that the other colonies be requested to send delegates to a congress in New York City in October. The motion was carried, but the whole movement soon slipped entirely out of the hands of the moderates to become the property of the radical elements. As soon as this happened, riots began to break out in Boston, Newport, New York City, Wilmington, Brunswick, and other places. In New York, force was used against the mob, but the crowds only grew larger, and the melee did not end until the governor, Cadwallader Colden, surrendered all the stamps to the leadership of the mob. The steeet people in

42

Massachusetts scored a similar victory. The house of
the stamp distributor, Andrew Oliver, was stormed, and
when Governor Hutchinson sought to intervene the mob
ransacked his residence as well.   The street people
proudly called themselves Sons of Liberty. By the time
the Stamp Act was to go into effect, November 1, the
enforcement machinery had broken down completely. All
the stamp distributors had been forced to resign or
flee from their homes. If someone wanted to buy stamps
they were nowhere to be found.

     Concurrently with the lawless behavior of the mobs
on the streets a more moderate effort was under way to
right the wrongs of the Stamp Act by constitutional
means.   On June 8, 1765, James Otis moved that the
Massachusetts legislature should issue a call for a
meeting of all the colonies in New York City the following October. This motion was carried and when the
congress convened on October 7, 28 delegates from nine
colonies put in their appearance. The absentees were
New Hampshire, Virginia, North Carolina, and Georgia,
four colonies whose governors had managed to prevent
the assemblies from sending delegates. Though by this
time the street people had gained control of the movement, and the initiative had clearly slipped from the
grasp of the moderates, the delegates to the Stamp Act
Congress were not willing to sell out to the radicals,
and insisted, though without unanimity, on issuing a
perfectly proper and highly dignified Declaration of
Rights and Grievances setting forth their objections
to the Stamp Act, and at the same time reaffirming
their loyalty to "his Majesty's person," as well as
"all due subordination to that august body the Parli-
ment of Great Britain."

     While the congress was respectfully petitioning a
redress of the colonial grievances, and the street
people were disrespectfully assaulting the bastions of
law and order, economic forces were at work on both
sides of the Atlantic.   These probably had more to do
with the resolution of the crisis than all the constitutional arguments on both sides.   The law-abiding
elements in America who were under the gun of the
Stamp Act provisions were not content with political
resolutions of one kind or another, and they were not
happy to be identified with the lawless street mobs.
On the other hand, they were riled up about the Stamp

Act indignities, and longed for a way to express themselves effectively. The result was a sort of grass-
roots movement for the imposition of economic sanctions. The idea was to boycott all exports from England, and to make-do with local products or do without.
Thus sage was substituted for imported tea, and homespun dresses and suits became a fashion. City merchants lined themselves up behind the ladies by pledging not to buy any British goods, and new manufactur-
ing plants began to spring up in America. On the whole,
the measures were successful, and the first to feel
the pinch were the London merchants and working-class
people. The London government began to be swamped with
petitions demanding that the government put an end to
the policy of taxing the American Colonists. The
workers in Bristol, Liverpool, and Manchester even
threatened to march on Westminster to back their demands.

At this juncture the friends of America in England,
with the solid support of the Agents, hit upon a bold
plan to force the hand of the government in England.
This was to put Franklin on the stand before the bar
of the House of Commons, and let him take on all
comers in the debate over government policy. The
Agent Franklin was chosen for the simple reason that
he was a world-figure in his own right, and for the
additional reason that he knew more about the subject
than anyone else on either side of the water. There
were also additional considerations. Franklin was an
experienced man in all the arts of negotiation, was
shrewd, and could be relied upon to take the measure
of even the ministers of state, if necessary. The date
was February 13, 1766, and the Examination, as it was
called, was one of the great moments of history. The
hard-liners in the administration pulled no punches in
posing their loaded and leading questions, and Franklin's replies stated the case for the colonies in such
a way that it could be understood by the King himself,
to say nothing of the many well-wishers for the colonies among the ministers and in the higher councils of
the government. In many ways this Examination of
Franklin threw a great deal of much needed light on
the main points dividing the mother country and her
American colonies, and after making allowances for
Franklin's fighting fire with fire in some of his re-
joinders, it is clear that the Examination also shed
some much needed light on a few of the important whys
and wherefores of the American Revolution. The following questions and answers have been lifted from the

44

record.[41] Author-added headings.

Temper of America

Q. What is your name and place of abode?

A. Franklin of Pennsylvania.

Q. What was the temper of America towards Great
Britain before the year 1763?

A. The best in the world. They submitted willingly to the government of the Crown, and paid, in all
their courts, obedience to acts of Parliament. Numerous as the people are in the several provinces, they
cost you nothing in forts, cidadels, garrisons, or
armies to keep them in subjection. They were governed
by this country at the expence only of a little pen,
ink, and paper. They were led by a thread. They had
not only a respect but an affection for Great Britain:
for its laws, its customs and manners, and even a fond-
ness for its fashions, that greatly increased the commerce. Natives of Britain were always treated with
particular regard; to be an Old England man was, of
itself, a character of some respect and gave a kind of
rank among us.

Q. And what is their temper now?

A. Oh, very much altered.

Q. In what light did the people of America use
to consider the Parliament of Great Britain?

A. They considered the Parliament as the great
bulwark and security of their liberties and privileges,
and always spoke of it with the utmost respect and
veneration. Arbitrary ministers, they thought, might
possibly at times attempt to oppress them, but they
relied on it that Parliament on application would always give redress.

Q. And have they not the same respect for
Parliament?

A. No, it is greatly lessened.

Q. To what causes is that owing?

45

A. To a concurrence of causes: the restraints lately laid on their trade by which the bringing of foreign gold and silver into the colonies was prevented; the prohibition of making paper money among themselves, and then demanding a new and heavy tax by stamps; taking away, at the same time, trials by juries and refusing to receive and hear their humble petitions.

Stamp Act

Q. Have you not heard of the resolutions of this House, and of the House of Lords, asserting the right of Parliament relating to America, including a power to tax the people there?

A. Yes, I have heard of such resolutions.

Q. What will be the opinion of the Americans on those resolutions?

A. They will think them unconstitutional and unjust.

Q. Was it an opinion in America before 1763 that the Parliament had no right to lay taxes and duties there?

A. I never heard any objection to the right of laying duties to regulate commerce; but a right to lay internal taxes was never supposed to be in Parliament, as we are not represented there.

Q. On what do you found your opinion that the people in America made any such distinction?

A. I know that whenever the subject has occurred in conversation where I have been present, it has appeared to be the opinion of everyone that we could not be taxed by a Parliament where we were not represented. But the payment of duties laid by an act of Parliament, as regulations of commerce, were never disputed.

Q. You say the colonies have always submitted to external taxes and object to the right of Parliament only in laying internal taxes. Now can you show that there is any kind of difference between the two taxes to the colony on which they may be laid?

A. I think the difference is very great. An external tax is a duty laid on commodities imported; that duty is added to the first cost and other charges on the commidity and, when it is offered for sale, makes a part of the price. If the people do not like it at that price, they refuse it; they are not obliged to pay it. But an internal tax is forced from the people without their consent, if not laid by their own representatives. The Stamp Act says we shall have no commerce, made no exchange of property with each other, neither purchase nor grant nor recover debts; we shall neither marry nor make our wills; unless we pay such and such sums; and thus it is intended to extort our money from us or ruin us by the consequences of refusing to pay it.

Q. Supposing the Stamp Act was continued, and enforced, do you imagine that ill-humor will induce the Americans to give as much for worse manufactures of their own, and use them, preferably to better of ours?

A. Yes, I think so. People will pay as freely to gratify one passion as another, their resentment as their pride.

Q. What used to be the pride of the Americans?

A. To indulge in the fashions and manufactures of Great Britain.

Q. What is now their pride?

A. To wear their old clothes over again till they can make new ones.

Q. If the act is not repealed, what do you think will be the consequences?

A. The total loss of the respect and affection the people of America bear to this country, and of all the commerce that depends on that respect and affection.

Q. Can anything less than a military force carry the Stamp Act into execution?

A. I do not see how a military force can be applied to that purpose.

Q. Why may it not?

A. Suppose a military force sent into America, they will find nobody in arms; what then are they to do? They cannot force a man to take stamps who chooses to do without them? They will not find a rebellion; they may indeed make one.

Q. Then no regulation with a tax would be submitted to?

A. There opinion is that when aids to the Crown are wanted they are to be asked of the several assemblies, according to the old established usage; who will, as they always have done, grant them freely. And that their money ought not to be given away, without their consent, by persons at a distance, unacquainted with their circumstances and abilities. The granting aids to the Crown is the only means they have of recommending themselves to their sovereign; and they think it extremely hard and unjust that a body of men in which they have no representatives should make a merit to itself of giving and granting what is not its own but theirs; and deprive them of a right they esteem of the utmost value and importance, as it is the security of all their other rights.

Q. But if the legislature should think fit to ascertain its right to lay taxes, by an act laying a small tax, contrary to their opinions, would they submit to the tax?

A. The proceedings of the people in America have been considered too much together. The proceedings of the assemblies have been very different from those of the mobs, and should be distinguished, as having no connection with each other. The assemblies have only peaceably resolved what they take to be their rights; they have taken no measures for opposition by force; they have not built a fort, raised a man, or provided a grain of ammunition, in order to such opposition. The ringleaders of riots, they think ought to be punished; they would punish them themselves, if they could. Every sober, sensible man, would wish to see rioters punished, as otherwise, peaceable people have no security of person, or estate.

But as to an internal tax, how small soever, laid by the legislature here on the people there, while they have no representatives in this legislature, I think it will never be submitted to. They will oppose it to the last. They do not consider it as at all necessary for you to raise money on them by your taxes; because they are, and always have been, ready to raise money by taxes among themselves, and to grant large sums, equal to their abilities, upon requisition from the Crown.

Bad Press

America has been greatly misrepresented and abused here, in papers, and pamphlets, and speeches, as ungrateful, and unreasonable, and unjust, in having put this nation to immense expence for their defence, and refusing to bear any part of that expence. The colonies raised, paid, and clothed near 25,000 men during the last war; a number equal to those sent from Britain, and far beyond their proportion; they went deeply into debt in doing this, and all their taxes and estates are mortgaged for many years to come, for discharging that debt.

Government here was at that time very sensible of this. The colonies were recommended to Parliament. Every year the king sent down to the house a written message to this purpose: that his Majesty being highly sensible of the zeal and vigour with which his faithful subjects in North-America had exerted themselves, in defence of his Majesty's just rights and possessions, recommend it to the house to take the same into consideration, and enable him to give them a proper compensation.

You will find those messages on your own journals every year of the war to the very last; and you did accordingly give 200,000 Pounds annually to the Crown, to be distributed in such compensation to the Colonies.

This is the strongest of all proofs, that the colonies, far from being unwilling to bear a share of the burden, did exceed their proportion; for if they had done less, or had only equalled their proportion, there would have been no room or reason for compensation. Indeed, the sums, reimbursed them, were by no means adequate to the expence they incurred beyond their proportion; but they never murmured at that; they esteemed their Sovereign's approbation of their zeal and fidelity, and the approbation of this house, far beyond any other kind of compensation; therefore there was no occasion for this act, to force money from a willing people; they had not refused giving money for the purpose of the act; no requisition had been made; they were always willing and ready to do what could reasonably be expected from them, and in this light they wish to be considered.

Defense of America

Q. But suppose Great-Britain should be engaged in a war in Europe, would North-America contribute to the support of it?

A. I do think they would as far as their circumstances would permit. They consider themselves as a part of the British Empire, as having one common interest with it; they may be looked on here as foreigners, but they do not consider themselves as such. They are zealous for the honor and prosperity of this nation; and, while they are well used, will always be ready to support it, as far as their little power goes.

In 1739 they were called upon to assist in the expedition against Carthagena, and they sent 3,000 men to join your army. It is true, Carthagena is in America, but as remote from the Northern Colonies, as if it had been in Europe. They make no distinction of wars, as to their duty of assisting in them. I know that the last war is commonly spoke of here, as entered into for the defence, or for the sake, of the people in America. I think it is quite misunderstood. It began about the limits between Canada and Nova-Scotia; about territories to which the Crown indeed laid claim but were not claimed by any British Colony; none of the lands had been granted to any colonist; we had therefore no particular concern or interest in that dispute.

As to the Ohio, the contest there began about your right of trading in the Indian country; a right you had by the treaty of Utrecht, which the French infringed; they seized the traders and their goods, which were your manufactures; they took a fort which a company of your merchants, and their factors, and correspondents, had erected there to secure that trade. Braddock was sent with an army to retake that fort, (which was looked on here as another encrouchment of the king's territory) and to protect your trade. It was not until after his defeat, that the Colonies were attacked. They were before in perfect peace with both French and Indians; the troops were not, therefore, sent for their defence.

The trade with the Indians, though carried on in America, is not an American interest. The people of America are chiefly farmers and planters; scarce any thing that they raise or produce is an article of commerce with the Indians.

The Indian trade is a British interest; it is carried on with British manufactures, for the profit of British merchants and manufactures; therefore the war, as it commenced for the defence of territories of the Crown the property of no American, and for the defence of a trade purely British, was really a British war, and yet the people of America made no scruple of contributing their utmost towards carrying it on, and bringing it to a happy conclusion.

Q. Do you think, then, that the taking possession of the King's territorial rights, and strengthening the frontiers is not an American interest?

A. Not particularly, but conjointly a British and an American interest.

Q. You will not deny, that the preceding war, the war with Spain, was entered into for the sake of America; was it not occasioned by captures made in the American seas?

A. Yes; captures of ships carrying on the British trade there with British manufactures.

Q. Was not the late war with the Indians, since the peace with France, a war for America only?

A. It was more particularly for America than the former; but was rather a consequence or remains of the former war, the Indians not having been thoroughly pacified; and the Americans bore by much the greater share of the expence. It was put an end to by the army under General Bouquet; there was not above 300 regulars in that army, and above 1,000 Pennsylvanians.

Q. Is it not necessary to send troops to America, to defend the Americans against the Indiana?

51

A. No, by no means; it never was necessary. They
defended themselves when they were but a handful, and
the Indians much more numerous.   They continually
gained ground, and have driven the Indians over the
mountains, without any troops sent to their assistance
from this country. And can it be thought necessary now
to send troops for their defence from these diminished
Indian tribes, when the Colonies are become so populous and so strong? There is not the least occasion for
it; they are very able to defend themselves.

The Examination of Franklin before the bar of the
House of Commons was a singular event.   It came to an
end on February 13, and within a month, on March 4, by
a lopsided vote of more than two to one, with the
King's support, the Commons voted to rescind the Stamp
Act. Franklin was the toast of the town, not only in
America, but in many parts of England as well. It was
a victory not only for the protean Franklin, but for
the Agency System and colonial diplomacy as well. The
irrepressible conflict was repressed for a good 10
years.

The Agency System was strained into something
that was never intended by the Stamp Act crisis in
1765, and after it was over the Agents and the system
as a whole quickly reverted to its original form and
intent.   It was all very well for the Agents to flit
about London as ambassadors-at-large, but that was a
far cry from what was originally intended. None of the
Agents, including the great and many-sided Franklin,
had any authority to act outside the formal Instructions each had from his parent colony. Franklin never
pretended to have any authority to represent the
colonies as a whole, and as soon as the crisis was
over reverted to his role as Agent for Pennsylvania.
The fact that he picked up three part-time Agencies
(Georgia, New Jersey, and Massachusetts) in the post-
crisis period did nothing to give him any authority to
speak for the colonies as a whole. However, during the
crisis period the Agents displayed a remarkable spirit
of cooperation among themselves, and had regular
monthly meetings to agree on a unified front.   This
period came to an end about 1770, and beyond that date
not only did the regular meetings cease to take place,
but there was no further evidence of the capacity and
willingness of the Agents to cooperate among themselves. The non-cooperative attitude of the Agents in
London did not mean that the spirit of cooperation

52

among the colonies was dead. Far from it. It was only
dead within the Agency System. The spirit itself
awakened by the Stamp Act Congress in 1765 got a new
lease on life in 1772 when Sam Adams began organizing
his revolutionary committees of correspondence. These
should not be confused with the committees of correspondence in each colony that supervised and directed
(sometimes even appointed and removed) the colonial
Agents. The basic objective of the latter was to promote the self-interest of each individual colony, and
the basic objective of the former was to submerge par-
ticularism in favor of the revolutionary spirit. South
Carolina was the only colony that used its old Agency
Committee as the nucleus for its new radically-
oriented Committee of Correspondence.

The Agency System was both a training and a prov-
ing ground for the diplomats of the revolutionary and
post-revolutionary period. Their greatest triumph was
in the 1760s when they succeeded in delaying the revolution for almost a decade.[43]   The pity is that this
was as far as they could go.   It was the limits of
diplomacy.   Also, the success that crowned their
efforts in the 1760s could not be repeated in the
1770s.   The resort to arms is always the exit line for
the diplomacy of peace, and 1776 was not an exception
to this rule.   However, the outbreak of war does not
mean sudden unemployment for the diplomats. Quite the
reverse. As Karl von Clausewitz observed in the 1830s,
war is a continuation of politics, and diplomacy is
the language of international politics.[42]   The diplomacy of the Revolutionary War leaned very heavily on
the Agency System in that many of its products, including Franklin and Arthur Lee, were among the most effective representatives of the young Republic. The life-
giving alliance with France, in its covert and overt
forms, was negotiated by them, and Franklin above
everyone else was responsible for the very favorable
terms of the treaty of peace at the end of the war.

After the shooting was over, and independence was
finally recognized, the question of Agents came to the
fore again. This happened when King George III was
queried about an exchange of ministers. He was not
wild with enthusiasm at the prospect, and instead proposed an alternative. "As to the question whether I
wish to have a minister accredited from America," he
said, "I certainly can never say that it will be agree-
able to me, and I should think it wiser for both

parties if only Agents were appointed."[44]   The Agency
System was thus merged very smoothly into the diplomacy of the Republic.

[1]Rt. Hon. Sir Ernest Satow, *A Guide to Diplomatic Practice* (London: Longmans, Green and Co., 2nd and revised ed., 1922), 1.

[2]*Ibid*, pp. 1-2.

[3]Joel Hurstfield, *The Elizabethan Nation* (New York: Harper & Row, 1967), 9.

[4]Alexander Hamilton, *The Federalist*, No. 1 (New York: E. P. Dutton & Co., 1934), 1.

[5]Charles M. Andrews, *Our Earliest Colonial Settlements* (Ithaca: Cornell University Press, 1973), v.

[6]Max Savelle, "Colonial Origins of American Diplomatic Principles," *The Pacific Historical Review* (Sept. 1934), vol. III, no. 3, p. 334.

[7]John Marshall, *A History of the Colonies* (Philadelphia: Abraham Small, 1824), 17.

[8]The Declaration of Independence. *The Federal and State Constitutions, Colonial Charters, and Other Organic Laws*, ed. Francis Newton Thorpe (Washington: G.P.O., 1909), I, 6.

[9]*Ibid.*, I, 4.

[10]*Ibid.*, VII, 3788.

[11]*Ibid.*, VII, 3795.

[12]*Ibid.*, III, 1841

[13]Benjamin Franklin, *The Writings of*, ed. by Albert Henry Smyth (New York: The Macmillan Company, IV, 4.

[14]*Ibid.*, 50.

[15]*Ibid.*, 434-35.

[16]*Ibid.*, I, 435.

[17]Rt. Hon. Sir Ernest Satow, *op. cit.*, 1-2.

[18]E. P. Tanner, "Colonial Agencies in England" (New York: *Political Science Quarterly*, March 1901), 30-31.

[19]Rt. Hon. Sir Ernest Satow, *op. cit.*, 1.

[20]E. P. Tanner, *op. cit.*, 42.

[21]Ella Lonn, *The Colonial Agents of the Southern Colonies* (Chapel Hill, The Universith of North Carolina Press, 1945), 381.

[22]Michael G. Kammen, *A Rope of Sand: The Colonial Agents, British Politics, and the American Revolution* (Ithaca: Cornell University Press, 1968), 4.

[23]Paul A. Varg, *Foreign Policies of the Founding Fathers* (Michigan: Michigan State University Press, 1963), 15.

[24]Michael G. Kammen, *op. cit.*, 318.

[25]*Ibid.*, 3.

[26]Thomas Hutchinson, *The History of the Colony and Province of Massachusetts-Bay* (Cambridge: Harvard University Press, 1936), I, 264-65.

[27]*Ibid.*, I, 86.

[28]E. P. Tanner, *op. cit.*, 43.

[29]*Ibid.*, 37-38.

[30]*Ibid.*, 38.

[31]Ella Lonn, *op. cit.*, 259.

[32]*Ibid.*, 211.

[33]Thomas Hutchinson, *op. cit.*, I, 190.

[34]Ella Lonn, *op. cit.*, 373.

[35]Thomas Hutchinson, *op. cit.*, II, 99.

[36]Ella Lonn, *op cit.*, 146-49.

[37]Michael Kammen, *op. cit.*, 180-82.

[38]*Ibid.*, 127.

[39]Ella Lonn, *op. cit.*, 389

40

[41]Benjamin Franklin, *op. cit.*, iv, 412-48.

[42]Ella Lonn, *op. cit.*, 381.

[43]Karl von Clausewitz, *On War* (New York: The Modern Library, 1943 tr. O. J. Matthijs Jolles) Bk. VIII, 596.

[44]Michael G. Kammen, *op. cit.*, 319.

CHAPTER II

INTERCOLONIAL DIPLOMACY

American diplomacy within the British Empire began with the establishment and growth of the Agency System. This provided an orderly and efficient channel through which the governments in the New World could, by the peaceful processes of diplomacy, work out their differences with the mother country over a wide variety of public issues. The determination of these issues was critical for the individual colonies, and for the mother country as well. This may be one of the reasons London has remained our premier diplomatic post even to this day. It is a tradition that goes back to 1624, when the first Virginia Agent was posted to the Court of St. James.

The second field of American diplomacy within the British Empire was every bit as important as the first, and involved, as did the first, all the thirteen mainland colonies. This second field was intercolonial in the sense that it covered the official relations between the colonies and among them as they tried to find solutions to the many problems that arose in connection with their external relations. Their bilateral and multilateral negotiations were diplomatic in every sense of the word, and the men trained in that field were the American leaders in the revolutionary period as well as afterward, when the young Republic had to find its own way among the other sovereign nations.

Conflict in England was endemic at the time the colonies were planted. In the wars of succession, of royal absolutism against constitutional monarchy, of republicanism against royal absolutism, each side furnished material for emigration to America, not only from its misfits and malcontents, but also from the ranks of its bitter recalcitrants, who though beaten in England, were still unwilling to compromise their principles. This is the reason it is simply wrong to treat American history as if it were the story of misfits and malcontents thrown together in a huge melting pot. That might be called an Ellis Island interpretation of our history. The plain fact of the matter is that the original colonies were set apart from one another in order to preserve the New World from being engulfed by the flames that were threatening the mother country with a bloody civil war.

The physical separation of the colonies in America was one of the things that contributed to the tendency of the individual colonies to harden into little republics, and to develop a spirit of nationalism. Each colony was suspicious of the next, when it knew anything very much of its existence, and while each maintained direct relations with England, their preferred policy toward each other was one of studied aloofness. The colonial diplomats and leading men in each colony, for example, were much more at home in London than they were or could have been in any colony but their own. The minus side of that was that as soon as the colonies had spread out far enough to meet their next neighbors in the intervening forests, or when a King, forgetful of previous charters, granted to some new group a habitation that overlapped some previous charter, friction and sometimes open conflict resulted. Wars with or between Indian tribes smouldered everywhere, frequently bursting into full flame. There were also commercial wars between the colonies over the valuable fur trade with the Indians. In addition, there were armed conflicts between the colonies over fishing and navigation rights on the great intercolonial rivers.

No sooner was the colony of Georgia a reality than open warfare with Spain broke out.[1] At the same time, the usual intercolonial grievances arose, and a limited war with Carolina ensued. The Savannah River was claimed by both Carolina and Georgia, as the Potomac was claimed by Virginia and Maryland, and for the same reason. To both claimants in each case the river was the artery of the fur trade with the Indians, and that was a vital interest that had to be protected. Since fur was a major commercial commodity, a bed-rock commercial interest, it was a source of rivalry and potentially of war, on which no compromise was possible. In this case, Georgia seized the vessels belonging to Carolina, and seized them because the vessels were laden with rum, which in Georgia was a prohibited commodity. These vessels and this rum were for

60

use in trading with the Indians, and that trade belonged to Georgia. The Carolinians answered the complaints of Georgia by arming their vessels, and refusing to give up their trade with the Indians. This affair was just as international to the parties concerned as any similar question would be today concernint the navigation of international rivers, violations of territorial sovereignty, or even the sanctity of national honor.

War or the threat of war was inherent in every colonial controversy that touched on a vital interest. Most of the public disputes fell into this category, and the only way solutions could be found was through the give and take of colonial diplomacy or the final recourse of colonial arms. Appeals to the mother country were resorted to in some instances, but the process was a long and expensive one, and the results often fell short of expectations. The powerful colonies of that day were just as inclined to side-step or ignore unfavorable awards as the more powerful states today. Then as now the basic problems that divided the colonies were the same as those that confront the independent states of the world today; nationalism, imperialism, economic rivalry, balance of power, and national honor or prestige. Pride was just as much a matter of colonial concern as it is among the fiercely independent national states today. In the earlier period Massachusetts refused to enter into a defensive alliance with some of her sister colonies in New England because she felt it was beneath her dignity.

It was in this aloofness of the colonies, in their mutual suspicions, in their inherited jealousies, and in their individual aspirations to separate existence that is to be found the natural source of intercolonial correspondence, conferences, conventions, agreements, treaties, diplomacy and war. Out of these conditions proceeded the first attempts at federal union. All agreed (with some exceptions) that each should remain independent, and yet recognize some measure of interdependence. The key problem was how to adjust all these conflicting forces, and how to overcome these insuperable obstacles in order to form some sort of accommodated cooperative existance.

It is for this reason that the first tentative steps in the working out of the federal solution are worthy of study today. The first such step in this direction was the union of the three river towns in

what became the state of Connecticut in 1639. The
style of the unifying instrument was the Fundamental
Orders of Connecticut. James Bryce called this "the
oldest truly political constitution in America," and
Breckinridge Long said of it:

> The Fundamental Orders combined three
> towns into a federal government. Our
> constitution combined thirteen states
> into a federal government. The three
> towns had an existence prior to the ad-
> option of their federal government. So
> had the thirteen states. In both cases
> it was necessary to consider not only
> the individual inhabitants but to
> cater to the desires of the different
> independent political units. The in-
> habitants of one town were jealous
> that another town might assume control
> of the government and use it for its
> own advancement and to the detriment
> of the other towns; or that the feder-
> al government might do the same thing.
> The inhabitants of some of the thir-
> teen states were jealous that other
> states, or the federal government,
> would assume control of the system to
> the detriment of those individual
> states. In 1639, and in 1787, the
> problem was solved in the same way.[2]

Four years after the adoption of the Fundamental
Orders a second link in the chain of tentative solutions was forged. Again the solution was purely local,
and even confined to a chosen few in a sectional locality. The negotiations leading up to the settlement
of 1643 lasted for six years, and during this time
there was never any question about the diplomatic nature of the transaction. Both conference and congress
in diplomacy mean meetings of plenipotentiaries for
the discussion of international affairs. The long
series of inter-colonial meetings of full-powered delegates to agree on a great union of the New England
colonies were international conferences in every sense
of the word.

The negotiations antecedent to the New England
Confederation began in 1637, at the time the Pequot
War was drawing to its bloody end, and were concluded

on May 13, 1643, when the high contracting parties, Massachusetts, Plymouth, Connecticut, and New Haven, agreed to "the whole treaty,"[3] to quote the language of the document itself. Up to this time there had been a whole series of on-again-off-again negotiations leading first one way and then another. Connecticut took the lead in proposing the wider union called a Consotiation, and the following year Massachusetts seized the initiative. However, Connecticut hung back objecting to the provision that in cases of dispute a majority vote could decide the issue. Connecticut wanted the old Polish rule of unanimity. It was safer for a small colony. On the other hand, Connecticut could not let the negotiations lapse entirely. She felt menaced by the threat from New Netherland, and again took the initiative. In 1640 because of the threat of another Indian war the colonies of Rhode Island, Connecticut, and New Haven, joined to make another appeal to Massachusetts. This did not get anywhere, however, because of the presence of Rhode Island, a colony Massachusetts refused to recognize. It was not until the outbreak of the civil war in England, plus the threat of another Indian uprising, that the commissioners met in Boston, and agreed on the establishment of the New England Confederation.

Even so, however, there was a hitch. The full powers of the Plymouth delegates were deemed not to be adequate for the business at hand, the formation of a "perpetual Confederation,"[4] and it was therefore decided not to admit Plymouth into the union until her delegates had been given the necessary powers. By the time of the second meeting of the Confederates in Boston the following September the Plymouth delegates had the required full powers, and on September 7 the colony was formally admitted to this assembly of the Lord's elect. It was such an assembly because Rhode Island, Maine, and New Hampshire existed at the time, but were consciously excluded from membership.

The Articles of Confederation of the United Colonies of New England is a remarkable document in many ways. In the first place, the contracting parties were colonies, not independent states, and they were all subordinate to the Crown, if not also to the Parliament, but in their document they were acting like fully independent states, not amenable to any other power on earth. The articles of their Consotiation contain no reference to King or Parliament, and acknowledge no superior or external authority. Instead, they assumed unto themselves all the powers of sovereign states, including the treaty-making power, and the power to make war and peace. These are the ultimate powers of sovereighty because through them the state can surrender or lose its very existence.

Two words in Article 6 are especially significant. They are "aids" and "intermeddling." Aids to the crown or overlord, whether in goods, services, or men, were admissible because they were a voluntary act, the decision of a free man, not imposts or taxes. The members of the Confederation could be charged to support the efforts of the whole, but raising men and providing supplies had to be voluntary on the part of each member. The Confederation had no power to raise money by taxation, nor could it draft men in any of the colonies. This also explains the use of the word "intermeddling." When Americans finally recognized the need of union in some form, it was not the substance on which they disagreed, but the proposed form. The substance was the preservation and right evolution of their liberties and social system. Whether that could be done better in the form of an imperial unit or in that of a league of sovereign states was a matter of vital concern to early Americans. Clearly, there was nothing in this treaty-union that even implied a loss of independence on the part of the high contracting parties. The only oneness they admitted was in nation and religion. Otherwise,' the Articles strongly reaffirmed the treasured independence of each separate colony, not only from one another, but from the mother country as well.

Article 6 was a great victory for the weaker colonies of New England, Plymouth, Connecticut and New Haven. This was brought out in the provision relating to voting rights in the general body. At the time there were about 24,000 people in the New England area as a whole and 15,000 belonged to Massachusetts, leaving only about 3,000 each in the other three colonies. Massachusetts also controlled about two-thirds of the resources of the area. Yet the voting procedure within the Confederation was heavily weighted in favor of the smaller states. The provision was that "two Commissioners shall be chosen by and out of each of the four Jurisdictions."[5] Thus the smallest and weakest colony, New Haven, was given an equal voice with the largest and strongest, Massachusetts, in the managing and concluding of all affairs. A majority of six of the eight commissioners was required for all decisions of the general body, and if this could not be attained the matter had to be referred to the four General Courts. To rub it in, in the case of an enforcement action Massachusetts was required to send the bulk of the armed forces, namely a hundred men as against forty-five for each of the other governments. The only saving grace for Massachusetts was that "the whole advantage of the war (if it please God so to bless their endeavors) whether it be in lands, goods, or persons, shall be proportionately divided among the said Confederates."[6]

There is no question about it, while outwardly the New England Confederation was formed in the interests of the general welfare, the weaker colonies concerned regarded the arrangement quite definitely as a means of binding the powerful and aggressive Massachusetts Bay colony. The Massachusetts men for their part were not unmindful of the old axiom of European diplomacy that no matter what the science of mathematics has to say about it, the part may ultimately absorb the whole if the part be clever and strong enough. Machiavelli was thoroughly conversant with that sort of mental reservation on both sides of an agreement. He had seen it in operation in dynastic diplomacy as well as in the intrigues of the Italian oligarchies and republics in which he lived.

As to the powers of the Confederation, they were strictly limited to the conduct of the external relations of the contracting parties, and did not extend to the internal affairs of any of them, which were explicitly "preserved entirely to themselves" by the 6th Article. The powers of the Confederation over external affairs included all "affairs of our war, or peace, leagues, aids, charges, and numbers of men for war, division of spoils and whatsoever is gotten by conquest, receiving of more Confederates for Plantations into combination with any of the Confederates, and all things of like nature, which are the proper concomitants or consequents of such a Confederation for amity, offence, and defence."

There are two other provisions in the basic charter of the New England Confederation that are worthy of notice in passing. One relates to extradition and the other to membership in the union. In Article 8 it is provided "that if any servant run away from his master

65

into any other of these confederated Jurisdictions, that in such case, upon the certificate of one magistrate in the Jurisdiction out of which the said servant fled, or upon other due proof; the said servant shall be delivered, either to his master, or any other that pursues and brings such certificate or proof."[7] The provision was not only an extradition agreement, but conclusive evidence that not all were free men in these New England colonies. Extradition of any escaped prisoner whatsoever is also agreed upon, and extradition, it must be remembered, is connected with ownership and sovereignty.

The membership stipulation in the Articles was a strict one. It created a closed corporation, and provided that "no other Jurisdiction shall hereafter be taken in as a distinct head or member of the Confederation, nor shall any other Plantation or Jurisdiction in present being, and not already in combination or under the Jurisdiction of any of these Confederates, be received by any of them; nor shall any two of the Confederates join in one Jurisdiction without consent of the rest."[8] This closed the door on Rhode Island, New Hampshire, and Maine, and nailed it shut. Massachusetts considered New Hampshire and Maine to be merely fiefs of the Bay Colony, and when Rhode Island applied for membership in 1648 she was told that she could do so only on condition that she become incorporated into Massachusetts. As for the present membership of the league, Massachusetts was more than a match for any one of them, and wanted to keep it that way.

The New England Confederation, founded in 1643, lasted until 1684, when James II, by revoking the charter of Massachusetts, killed the union for all practical purposes. Before that time the union had been considerably weakened by the summary extinction of one of its members. This happened in 1662 when Charles II granted Connecticut a new charter extending its boundaries to include New Haven. By this arbitrary action the league of four was reduced to one of three. Whereas the Commissioners kept on holding their meetings the end was clearly in sight by 1662. However the 40-year history of the New England Confederation has an importance that goes beyond the dry facts of its successes and failures. The year 1648 was usually accepted as the date for the emergence of the modern idea of the territorial state with its absolutist concept of sovereignty. Thus it can be said that the remedy for the evil made its appearance in history at roughly the same time the evil itself became manifest. James Brown Scott, one of the outstanding legal scholars of the 20th Century, commented on the likeness between the 17th Century Articles of Confederation and the 20th Century League of Nations by saying:

> The dominant purpose of the League of Nations was peace. The means were threefold: the guarantee of territorial integrity and political independence of the members; peaceful settlement of international disputes; economic and military sanctions. The dominant purpose of the New England Confederation was likewise peace. The means were threefold: the safeguarding of territorial integrity and policical independence of the members; peaceful settlement of disputes likely to lead to a rupture between the members and their neighbors; economic and military sanctions. The similarity of the New England Confederation to the League of Nations, has it not been overlooked in our devotion to local matters? We are, however, justified in considering the Confederation as a diplomatic triumph and the unexpected prototype of the most international of international agreements.[9]

The validity of the comparison between the League of Nations in 1920 and the Articles of Confederation in 1643 is too obvious to merit additional comment. Indeed, it can and should be extended to the newest and most comprehensive of international agreements under the charter of the United Nations. There again the principles and objective were the same, the preservation of peace among the contracting parties, the prevention of war with others, and the territorial integrity of states. In both cases economic and military sanctions were contemplated and provided for in order to achieve the stated principles and objectives. Finally, the Charter and the Articles each provided machinery for the peaceful settlement of disputes likely to lead to a rupture of international relations. Very simply, the Articles of 1643 pledged the signatories to the task of "preserving the peace among themselves" and of "preventing as much as may be all occasion of war or differences with others."[10]

A few years after the New England Confederation was formed a case was laid before it that involved a controversy of long standing between Massachusetts and Connecticut. The question was whether Connecticut could impose a tax on goods imported or exported on the Connecticut River. The purpose of the tax was to raise revenue to maintain Fort Saybrook at the mouth of the river. Springfield was upstream from Saybrook, and the inhabitants refused to pay the tax. The Massachusetts attorneys argued that the Springfield inhabitants should not have to pay the tax because:

> Connecticut had no authority to lay a tax upon the inhabitants of another colony; that the fort was of no use to them; that a demand of this tax had hindered the union for several years; that the Massachusetts first took possession of the river and planted there, and had been at great expence, never expecting this tax; that the Massachusetts people had as good right to lay the same tax for all goods imported from Connecticut, to maintain the fort at Boston.[11]

In rebuttal, the Connecticut commissioners urged "the practice of many places in Europe; that the fort was a security to the whole river, and that the reason of this case was the same, as if Connecticut should be at any expence to make the river more navigable, Springfield surely would not in that case refuse to pay any part of the charge."[12]

Massachusetts agreed that Springfield ought to pay a proportionate share of any expense involved in making the river more navigable, but denied that this had anything to do with the case. The argument was that the fort was not a security against any vessel of force on the river, and that therefore the tax was nothing more than a pretext for gouging the citizens of another colony, contrary to all the laws of right reason and common sense. However, the decision of the court was against Massachusetts. This was a courageous decision because it was handed down by the commissioners from Plymouth and New Haven who could ill afford to risk the displeasure of the powerful Bay Colony. The Commissioners left themselves a loophole, however, saying that if the Massachusetts were of a mind to she was entitled to a new hearing at the 1648 meeting of the Confederates, particularly if she had any new evidence to submit or new arguments to make.

Massachusetts did not ignore the invitation to re-argue the case in 1648, and by the time this took place there were important new developments in the case. The central one was the fact that the fort in question had very mysteriously caught fire and burned to the ground, nobody knew by what cause or means. All that was known is the fact that Massachusetts took full advantage of the friendly fire to support her case against Connecticut. The Massachusetts startled the court by producing a general order from the legislature stipulating that henceforth:

> all goods, belonging or any way apper-
> taining to any inhabitants of the juris-
> diction of Plimouth, Connecticut or
> New-Haven, that shall be imported with-
> in the castle, or exported from any
> part of the bay, shall pay such custom
> as hereafter is expressed, viz. all
> skins of beaver, otter, moose, &c. two
> pence per skin, and all goods packed in
> hogsheads or otherwise ten shillings a
> ton, corn and meal two pence a bushel,
> biscuit six pence per hundred, on pain
> of forfeiture, &c.[13]

This was a public display of force on the part of the powerful Massachusetts Bay colony. It was directed not only against Connecticut, which had prevailed over Massachusetts in the legal battle, but also against New Haven and Plymouth, whose Commissioners had dared to rule against Massachusetts. The arguments the Bay Colony used would have made Machiavelli smile. They were to the effect that if there had been any justification for the Connecticut tax because of Fort Say-brook there was certainly none now since the fort was no longer in existence. On the other hand, it was pointed out that "this jurisdiction hath expended many thousand pounds in erecting and maintaining several forts, which others as well as ourselves have received the benefit of, and hath at present one principal fort or castle, of good force against any enemy of consider-able strength and well garrisoned and otherwise fur-nished with sufficient ammunition, besides several other forts and batteries whereby vessels and goods of all sorts are secured."[14]

The first reaction of the aggrieved targets of the Massachusetts broadside, Connecticut, Plymouth, and New Haven, was to walk out on Massachusetts by withdrawing from the Confederation. If other things had been equal this is what they would have done. But such was not the case. Other things were not equal. The weak needed the strong, and in this case Connecticut, Plymouth, and New Haven needed the alliance of Massachusetts. Without the protection of the powerful Bay Colony the smaller and weaker sisters faced a dim future in the face of the threats to their existence from their Indian neighbors plus the menacing presence of the French and the Dutch. They therefore did what turned out to be the only thing they could do under the circumstances, which was to discontinue their agitations against the powerful Massachusetts Bay, and to reconcile themselves to the realities of life in the larger world of power. However, as a sort of swan song to their dreams of equality in the Confederation the Commissioners of Plymouth and New Haven sorrowfully decided to recommend that the General Court of Massachusetts seriously reconsider "whether such proceedings agree with the law of love and the tenor and import of the Articles of Confederation; but in the mean time desire to be spared in all further agitation concerning Springfield."[15] The Massachusetts law was repealed in 1650.

The conduct of Massachusetts in the matter of the Connecticut tax was considered outrageous even at the time. Chief Justice Thomas Hutchinson, later the last American-born royal governor of the Bay Colony, said that "had the Massachusetts laid a duty on goods from Connecticut only, they might have had at least a colour, perhaps more than a colour, to justify them; but to extend their resentment to the other two colonies for giving judgment against them, no excuse can be framed for it. It was a mere exertion of power, and a proof of their great superiority, which enabled them, in effect, to depart from the union of combination whensoever they found it for their interest; and if done by a single magistrate would have been pronounced tyrannical and oppressive." Hutchinson concluded on a general philosophical note by adding the comment, "but in all ages and countries, by bodies or communities of men such deeds have been done, as most of the individuals of which such communities consisted, acting separately, would have been ashamed of. (It looks as if men imagined the guilt of each person to be diminished in proportion to the number concerned in an unjust act.)[16]

70

John Marshall, the greatest of our Chief Justices, in his general history of the American colonies, expressed the same concern about the conduct of Massachusetts in the matter of the Connecticut tax. "Thus," he said, "does a member of a confederacy, feeling its own strength, and the weakness of those with whom it is associated, deride the legitimate decisions of the federal body, when opposed to its own interest or passions, and obey the general will, only when that will is dictated by itself."[17]

This was not an isolated case in the annals of the New England Confederation. Massachusetts was a law unto itself, and, as Marshall said, never let the decisions of the federal body stand in its way when they were opposed to its interest or desires. The law that prevailed in the New England Confederation was that of the superior force, and this meant the dominance of the strongest member, Massachusetts. The only exception to this rule, if indeed it can be called that, occurred during the first Anglo-Dutch War of 1652-54. This was when Cromwell forced the Bay Colony to reverse itself on a position it had taken in opposition to all the other members of the New England Confederation.

Massachusetts had not been keen about the Dutch War in the first place because of its lucrative trade with the Dutch in New Netherland. Therefore, it decided to sit the war out, and not to become involved unless there was some reason for it in the New World. This coincided with the policy of Peter Stuyvesant who also desired peace in the New World, not so much because of trade, but for the reason that the slender forces at his disposal were no match for the much more numerous forces of the English. On the other hand, Connecticut and New Haven were eager for an English thrust at New Netherland to take the pressure off their backs. Because of geographical propinquity both were logical targets for Dutch ambition to the vital center of the English position on the Atlantic Coast.

Plymouth threw in her lot with Connecticut and New Haven, and brought the subject to a vote in a special meeting of the New England Confederation. There was a rumor making the rounds that Stuyvesant was secretly inciting the Indians to a general uprising against the English. Massachusetts did not put much stock in the rumor, and when the war resolution was put to a vote only one of the two delegates from the

71

Bay Colony supported it. However, since only six votes were necessary to carry the measure it passed with one vote to spare. This was too much for Massachusetts. The General Court of that colony simply resolved, "that no determination of the commissioners though they should all agree, should bind the general court."[18]

This was an old and familiar story, having Massachusetts exercise an unlawful but absolute veto over the constitutional decisions of the Confederation. But this time Connecticut and New Haven decided not to take it lying down, and joined forces by making an appeal to Cromwell to bring Massachusetts into line. The Lord Protector did as was requested, and sent a small force to the New World to reduce the Dutch colony. Cromwell also specifically ordered Massachusetts Bay to support the undertaking.

Massachusetts hesitated no longer. The General Court was called into emergency session, and pledged "their utmost to attend to his Highness's pleasure."[19] A force of 500 volunteers was raised and put on the ready for use against New Netherland. The only thing that saved Peter Stuyvesant on this occasion was the fact that the Anglo-Dutch War came to an end before the Lord Protector's force could be used.

The law of the superior force, in this case the heavy hand of Cromwell, is what prevailed in this case. The New England Confederation was only "a rope of sand,"[20] as Governor Hutchinson said it was, when it came to forcing the hand of the powerful Bay Colony. The only reason the Confederation lasted as long as it did, from 1643 to 1684, was because of the inability of the weaker members to stand alone. The lesson of the New England Confederation, in the final analysis, was the lesson of power.

Massachusetts itself was on the wrong end of the power equation in 1684 when the Court of Chancery in England declared her cherished charter to be null and void. The trouble began in 1676 when the English government dispatched a trouble shooter to the Bay Colony to make a first-hand report on the state of affairs there. His reception was a cool one, and his report was a devastating one, containing a long list of unauthorized powers that were being exercised by the unorthodox oligarchy in the Puritan colony. The result was the revocation of the Massachusetts charter, and the establishment of a royal government. This was only the first step in the implementation of a plan to reorganize the structure of the colonial system in North America.

The model was that of France. The centralized French colonial administration was in sharp contrast to the English system of discord and disunity, and the Stuart Kings were of a mind to correct this flaw. From the Stuart point of view, the only reason for the existance of colonies in the first place was to strengthen the mother country to improving her economic wellbeing and her military prowess. These two objectives could not be achieved until the mother country brought the colonies firmly under the control of a single strong hand. This was the purpose of the reorganization of the colonies. It was called the Dominion of New England, and the cornerstone of the effort was the revocation of the Massachusetts charter. Nothing could be done in the way of consolidating the New England colonies until the parent colony of the area had its wings clipped. This would also have the advantage of killing the already dying New England Confederation.

The first problem to face the planners of the Dominion after Massachusetts had been brought into line was the territorial scope of the New Dominion. The territorial boundaries of the existing colonies was completely disregarded, and the planners proceeded with their work of combining them into larger units. Plymouth, New Hampshire, and Maine could be merged into Massachusetts, and proceedings were instituted to include Rhode Island and Connecticut. However, the ultimate plan was to make New York, not Massachusetts, the center of the Dominion and the seat of its government. By the same token, the plan was to make Virginia the nucleus around which the southern colonies could be gathered.[21] Thus, through his royal governors and from a single center, London, all the affairs of the colonies would be controlled and directed under one all-embracing executive power. As far as the colonies were concerned, the absolute monarchy that the Stuarts dreamed about would be absolute, after the fashion of the French empire. It was the attempt of a king to make a theory of government, absolutism, stick in the colonies that Englishmen were refusing to accept for themselves in England.

On December 20, 1686, Sir Edmund Andros arrived in Boston as the governor-general of "Our Territory and Dominion of New England in America." By August of 1687 his jurisdiction had been extended to include the East and West Jersey as well as New York. The system of regimented control did violence to all the natural instincts of free Englishmen, and violated every constitutional right to which they were entitled. Nothing short of an army of occupation could have made the people of New England submit for long to a tyranny of this kind. However, Andros did not have an army of occupation to enforce his iron rule, and when the unpopular James II was forced to vacate his throne in England in favor of the Protestant succession, William and Mary, all hell broke loose in New England.

Not that the ground had not been carefully prepared for the ouster of Andros. It had. As early as 1688 the Old Guard in Massachusetts (sort of a government-in-exile) sent one of their most distinguished citizens to England as a Special Agent to undermine Andros, and to present the case for the restoration of the charter. The name of the Agent was Increase Mather. He did not have the usual credentials normally given Agents because the Andros government was in power, and Mather even had to resort to a disguise to get out of the country. However, he had a wide acquaintance in London, having lived abroad for a prolonged period early in life, and did not need the credentials of a formal diplomat to move around in the highest circles again. The king himself saw Mather on two occasions shortly after his arrival. At the royal request Mather prepared two statements of grievances and petitions for relief. He also published a series of pamphlets to make the case against Andros public. However, the Revolution was pressing too close on the king's affairs for him to take any decisive action, and Mather wisely let his suit lapse until he could reopen it with England's new sovereigns, William and Mary. He was granted an audience with King William on January 9, 1689, more than a month before his formal coronation. This was a God-send because a circular letter was already in preparation for the new King to sign confirming the governors in all the colonies, including New England. Mather succeeded in getting the letter to New England rescinded. It was a blessing that he was there, and could do this, because by this time the uprising in Boston was a *fait accompli*, Andros was in jail, and the old government was back in power. No diplomat ever served the best interests of his country more effectively than Increase Mather did at the time of the

74

Glorious Revolution in England.

The Andros plan was the third substantial link in the chain designed to unite the English speaking peoples in North America. It failed because the type of union it sought was administrative rather than diplomatic in character, because it was forged in London rather than in America, and because it could not be reconciled with the colonial preference for a union of equal states. Otherwise, the plan of union might have been successful. It was not union that the colonists objected to, but the idea of unit crystallization. This was something that could not be reconciled with the growing spirit of nationalism in each separate colony. The union that the colonists favored was one that would protect the individuality of each colony-state, and at the same time make it possible for them to speak with one voice in foreign affairs, military and economic, that is in connection with their external trade, as well as in their military confrontations, not only with the hostile Indian nations along their frontiers, but also with the rival European claimants to empire in America, the French, Spanish, Dutch and Swedes.

For 76 years after the Dominion of New England was laid to rest as a plan to unite the colonies, both sides kept up the effort to bridge the gap between their respective points of view. There were men of good will on both sides of the Atlantic, and it was not for lack of work that they failed. In 1695 King William himself devised a simple plan to unify the colonies by creating a general fund to be used by the King in the wars against the French and Indians. The Board of Trade, a development out of the Privy Council, provided the English authorities with any number of plans for colonial unions that were designed to facilitate the exploitation of the colonies by the mother country. William Penn's famous "Briefe and Plaine Scheam," produced in 1698, was outside the usual run of plans in the sense that he took into consideration the colonial point of view that he knew so well. The stated objectives of his plan were to make the colonies "more usefull to the Crowne, and one another's peace and safety." Penn also had in mind a Congress of the colonies that would meet once a year, or more often if need be, to hear and dispose of disputes "between Province and Province," as well as "to prevent or cure injuries in point of commerce."[22] The two new ideas that Penn threw into the pot were the settlement of inter-colonial disputes, and the regulation of trade not with the colonies but among them.

At the turn of the century Americans began to get into the act with proposals of their own for a union of the colonies. In 1701 two plans were produced. One was put forward under the anonym of "A Virginian," and the other by Robert Livingston of New York. The former took issue with Penn on the subject of representation, saying that instead of a perfect equality in the number of delegates each colony could send to the central body, the size of the delegations should be determined by the size, population, and strength of the sending colonies.[23] This was a very important difference. Livingston's plan was also quite different from Penn's in the fact that he would establish three confederations in North America instead of one, one in New England, a second in Middle America, and the third in the South, with the leading states being Massachusetts, New York or Pennsylvania, and Virginia.

By this time a distinct pattern had begun to emerge. Most of the plans came from the mother country. They were aimed at one target, reducing under the direct control of the Crown all the governments in North America to make better use of their military resources in time of war, and to exploit their economies more effectively in time of peace. The American plans of union up to this time were designed to guard their interests as self-governing colonies, and to take the wind out of the British sails by agreeing to some sort of union that would satisfy the mother country from the point of view of a better administration of the colonies, economic and military. For these reasons all the serious plans, British as well as American, made some provision for a British Captain-General or President-General as the chief executive officer, and a colonial Assembly or General Council to partake of the legislative function. At the same time the American plans raised two very divisive issues, sectionalism, more than one union (Livingston), and proportional representation instead of state equality (A Virginian).

Leaving aside the complexities of the problem, and Franklin probably understood them better than any other single individual on either side of the water, Franklin nevertheless was of the opinion that the problem could be solved, and said in 1750, "If you

76

were to pick out half a Dozen Men of good understanding and Address, and furnish them with a reasonable
Scheme and proper Instructions, and send them in the
Nature of Ambassadors to the other Colonies, where
they might apply particularly to all the leading Men,
and by proper Management get them to engage in promot-
int the Scheme; where, by being present, they would
have the Opportunity by pressing the Affair both in
publick and private, obviating Difficulties as they
arise, answering Objections as soon as they are made,
before they spread and gather Strength in the Minds of
the People, &c., I imagine such an Union might thereby
be made and established: For reasonable sensible Men,
can always made a reasonable Scheme appear such to
other reasonable Men, if they take pains, and have
Time and Opportunity for it; unless from some Circumstances their Honesty and good intentions are sus-
pected."[24]

As to the substance of the union, Franklin believed in 1750 that it should be limited in scope to
the terms of a general defensive alliance, and strict
regulation of the frontier. The colonies should be
represented in the general Assembly, he believed, on
the basis of the number of hundred pounds each paid into the common Treasury, the money to be raised by a
liquor tax levied in each colony. Finally, on the con-
troversial subject of the geographic location of the
general government, Franklin shrewdly proposed that
the meetings be held "at the Capitals of the several
Colonies, (that) they might thereby become better ac-
quainted with the Circumstances, Interests, Strength,
or Weakness, &cs., of all, and thence be able to judge
better of Measures propos'd from time to time; At
least it might be more satisfactory to the Colonies,
if this were propos'd as a Part of the Scheme; for a
Preference might create Jealousy and Dislike."[25]

As to the objections voiced then and later to the
general idea of a colonial union, that it was impracti-
cal, and could never be brought about, the Pennsylvanian had a quick and biting answer. He said, "It would
be a very strange Thing if Six Nations of ignorant
Savages should be capable of forming a Scheme for such
an Union, and be able to execute it in such a Manner,
as that it has sustained Ages, and appears indissoluble; and yet a like Union should be impracticable for
ten or a Dozen English Colonies, to which it is more
necessary, and must be more advantageous; and who cannot be supposed to want an equal Understanding of

77

their Interests."[26]

Under direct orders from the London government in 1753 a call went out to seven colonial governors to convene in a congress or conference to consider and repair their relations with the Iroquois League of Indians, and to agree on a united plan of defense against England's enemies in North America. The result was the Albany Congress of 1754. Of it, Max Savelle correctly said, "to be sure, the congress that met at Albany in 1754 and formulated the so-called 'Albany Plan of Union' was inspired by the Earl of Halifax, President of the Board of Trade, and was held in accord with instructions to the colonial governors from the Crown. The interest of the crown seems to have been chiefly in a union for defense and in restoring and maintaining good relations with the Indians, and the idea of a genuine colonial political union seems to have been originated by leaders in the colonies themselves."[27]

The colonial leaders who pushed the Albany Plan, notably Franklin, were in for the disappointment of their lives. The plan failed of acceptance in both London and America. In America, it was rejected in most of the colonies without the courtest of debate. Such was the case in Franklin's own Pennsylvania. In London, the King rejected the Albany Plan in favor of one prepared by the Lords of Trade. The London preference was for a purely military union to ensure the presence of a sufficiency of colonial troops and money to carry out His Majesty's designs in North America. Franklin summed it up by saying, "the assemblies did not adopt it, as they all thought there was too much *prerogative* in it, and in England it was judged to have too much of the *democratic*."[28] However, even late in life Franklin was convinced that "the different and contrary reasons of dislike to my plan makes me suspect that it was really the true medium; and I am still of opinion it should have been happy for both sides of the water if it had been accepted. The colonies, so united, would have been sufficiently strong to have defended themselves; there would have been no need of troops from England; of course, the subsequent pretence for taxing America, and the bloody contest it occasioned, would have been avoided. But such mistakes are not new; history is full of the errors of states and princes."[29]

After the Albany Plan of Union in 1754, the next important link in the chain of events that led to the more perfect union in 1787, was the Stamp Act Congress of 1765. At the call of Massachusetts, this Congress met in New York City from October 7 to 25, and delegates from nine colonies sent their representatives, the absentees being New Hampshire whose delegates failed to attend, and Virginia, North Carolina, and Georgia, who were prevented from sending delegates by their governors. The gathering was unique in several important respects. It was the first time a meeting of this kind was held in America on the initiative of the colonies. It was continental in scope, and not confined to a selected few in a regional locality. And the voice of the Congress was the voice of America, since the absentees quickly made it clear that they would agree to whatever was done by the Congress.

In the two and a half weeks of discussion in the Congress 12 resolutions were passed, and numerous petitions, memorials, and addresses were adopted, including an important Declaration of Rights and Grievances. The significance of all this debate and discussion was the fact that a consensus finally emerged that the fundamental issue between the mother country and her colonies was constitutional. The question was whether the mother country could tax the colonies without their consent? This was the same question that the barons had raised at Runnymede in 1215, and the colonial view was that Magna Carta still lived, that a tax imposed on them by a Parliament in which they were not represented was null and void.

In addition to clarifying the constitutional issue in the controversy between the mother country and her colonies, the Stamp Act Congress helped to solidify public opinion in the colonies against the Act, which resulted in a patriotic movement to boycott British goods in favor of homespun products, no matter how shoddy they were by comparison. Public protest also manifested itself when the street people calling themselves Sons of Liberty began making war on the stamp collectors confiscating their stamps and burning their homes. The result was a cave-in on the part of the British government, and the repeal of the Stamp Tax. However, this was not done gracefully, and it was flatly denied that the repeal signified that the colonists had won the legal battle, for on the day the King signed the repealing act Parliament passed the Declaratory Act reaffirming the right of Parliament to make laws for the colonies in all cases whatsoever.

The Stamp Act Congress adjourned sine die on October 25, 1765. This closed the door on any future meetings of the same body. Thus this first meeting of the colonies on their own initiative was a one-shot affair directed against a single issue, the Stamp Act, and in this respect as in many others it was quite unlike its successor, the formal Congress that convened on September 5, 1774, to take cognizance of the state of affairs that existed at that time. This Congress was called at the behest of the Virginia House of Burgesses, and while the issue between the mother country and the colonies was still the same, the sovereignty of the London Parliament over the colonies, what was at stake in 1774 was whether one colony, Massachusetts, could be crushed into obedience by a series of disciplinary measures. The Coercive Acts were designed to close the port of Boston, alter the government of the colony, deprive the citizens of their civil rights, and put them under a military government for all practical purposes, including the quartering of troops in private homes. George III had no stomach for any further parley or negotiations with the colonists, was convinced that Massachusetts was the center and core of the rebellious spirit in America, and confidently anticipated that isolating Boston and making an example of Massachusetts would be all that was necessary to right the wrongs of colonial misconduct in the New World. And this is how the war of George III against Massachusetts had its inception.

Massachusetts refused to bend or break from the successive blows of the British hammer, and the other colonies, much to the surprise of the authorities in England, were just as determined to come to her support. Had it not been for these two developments -- there would not have been any reason for the resistance movement in America to escalate to the point it did and the September 1774 meeting of the Congress in Philadelphia would not have been held. As it was, the First Continental Congress, as the gathering was known in history, was an altogether different body from the Stamp Act Congress. In the first place, its name was a misnomer, since the Congress of 1765 had been continental in scope, and probably deserved to be known as the first continental congress. To be sure, the 1774 one had delegates from all the colonies except Georgia. An important difference between the two

bodies, however, was in the credentials of the delegates. The delegates to the Stamp Act Congress had
bona fide credentials in the sense that they had been
selected by the legislatures of the colonies they represented, whereas this was not the case with respect
to the delegates in the 1774 Congress. Pennsylvania
alone used its legislature to select its delegates in
1774, and all the other colonies used extralegal
bodies such as Virginia's "convention" of the colony's
counties to select their delegates. Thus the 1774 Congress was one outside the law at best, or at worst contrary to the law. Thus unlike the Stamp Act Congress,
which was a duly constituted body, the Congress of
1774 was a revolutionary body.

At the outset, the members of the revolutionary
Congress of 1774 decided to call their assembly "the
Congress," and its chairman "the President." There was
no doubt in anyone's mind that this was a diplomatic
congress in the European sense of a meeting of full-
powered delegates. It was not a government or a congress in the legislative sense at all. Thus the first
business of the Congress was to examine the credentials of the delegates. This revealed no surprises of
any kind, for none of the delegates had been empowered
to go beyond a general discussion of the state of the
colonies. How could they? With the exception of the
host state, Pennsylvania, the authorities giving the
delegates their full powers had no authority themselves except that which was self-generated. However,
following the formality of the credentials, the next
question was one of voting procedures. This launched
the first debate in the Congress. Should the voting
be proportinate to the size and population of each
colony, or should each be entitled to one vote? Patrick Henry quickly proposed that each colony should
possess "a just Weight in our deliberations in proportion to its opulence and number of inhabitants, its
Exports and Imports."[30] The small states would not
consent to anything less than absolute equality, and
as a result the principle of one-state-one-vote was
adopted, no matter what common sense had to say about
it. Following this compromise, it was agreed that the
proceedings of the Congress would be secret, unless a
majority decided otherwise. Secrecy is a rule of diplomatic procedure followed the world over in international conferences and congresses.

As to the work in the Congress of 1774, it was
very much like that of the Stamp Act Congress except

that it was more specific in certain areas. One of
these was the passage of five resolutions concerning
the resistance of Massachusetts to the Coercive Acts.
The Congress condemned these Acts for being unconstitutional, and urged the citizens of the Bay Colony to
set up their own civil government, to have no commercial intercourse with the mother country, and to look
to their own defense, even to the raising of troops.
In addition, the Congress approved on October 14 a
Declaration of Rights and Grievances that was a re-
statement of the colonial position on the fundamental
rights of free Englishmen to life, liberty, and property, rights that could not be abridged or taken away
from them without their express consent. Within the
framework of these rights they professed their loyalty
to the King, but at almost the same time, October 20,
they approved an economic warfare plan whereby each
colony would pledge itself to strictly enforce a ban
on imports from England, coupled with a non-consump-
tion and non-exportation agreement. Following this
little coercive act of their own, called the *Association*, the Congress struck off a whole series of petitions and memorials to everybody they could think of,
including the King, the people of England, the resi-
dents of Canada, the British West Indies, and so forth.
However, the Association was the crowning work of the
Congress of 1774. Having approved it on October 20,
the delegates voted to adjourn on October 25, confident that they had done their job, and that the total
economic boycott would quickly bring the mother country to her senses. In case they were mistaken, however,
the delegates did not adjourn sine die, but left the
door open for a resumption of their work, resolving
that another Congress should assemble on May 10, 1775,
"unless the redress of grievances, which we have desired, be obtained before that time.[31]

The last resolve of the Congress of 1774 was in
the nature of an ultimatum to the mother country, and
the answer was short in coming. More troops were dispatched to America, and the government tightened the
screws on Massachusetts by denying her the right to
fish off the Great Bank. This order was extended to
include all the colonies of New England, and even for-
bade them to trade with each other. The London government, with the exception of a few notable exceptions,
had made up its mind by this time that the use of
force would be necessary to restore the authority of
Britain in North America, and the King's Gauleiter for

82

the province was General Thomas Gage, newly appointed governor of Massachusetts. Backed by four regiments of regular troops, it was his unpleasant duty to enforce the Coercive Acts, including the one closing the port of Boston. He was also given the authority to fire on the people of the city if necessary, to arrest the leaders of the rebellion, and to send them to England for trial. All did not go well, and in the execution of these gauletier duties General Gage inadvertently set off the explosion that was heard round the world. This happened just as the members of the second Continental Congress were on their way to Philadelphia to resume their duties.

When General Gage arrived in Boston in May 1774 as the new royal governor of the colony he had 4,000 regulars under his command. At that time it was believed that a force of this size would be more than adequate to re-establish the authority of the Crown in the rebellious colony. When this did not happen, and as the relations with Massachusetts worsened, General Gage came under increasing pressure to exercise the authority of his command. Accordingly, on the night of April 18, 1775, the general dispatched a force of 800 troops to Concord to confiscate the military stores that had been deposited there, and with a secondary objective of picking up two of the rebel leaders the British wanted the most, Sam Adams and John Hancock. The troops reached Lexington as the sun rose, and there the first blood of the Revolution was drawn as eight Americans were killed and 10 wounded. Then the British moved on to Concord where there was another skirmish. Meanwhile the alerted minutemen were assembling fast, and the British began their retreat to Boston. The retreat was nearly turned into a rout, and the only thing that saved the British force was the timely arrival of 1,200 troops sent out from Boston by General Gage. As it was, the British lost 273 as opposed to the American loss of 95 in this first engagement of the war. General Gage also had to settle for the loss of his objectives: the military stores at Concord were not captured, and as the battle progressed Sam Adams and John Hancock made their way to Philadelphia to attend the second Continental Congress.

When this Congress convened in Philadelphia on May 10, 1775, all the colonies were represented, including Georgia, and there were also several new faces

83

in the gathering, the most notable of which was Benjamin Franklin, America's only world figure. He had
arrived back from England only four days before, and
the fact that he was there, after serving nearly 15
years as a colonial Agent at the Court of St. James,
meant that the cause of the British Empire was hopeless on any terms that were acceptable to Americans.
Franklin was the most imperially minded of all the
Americans at the time, and was far out in front of the
little-Englanders that were in the saddle in the
mother country at this time. The friends of America
in England had sought to have him invited to present
the colonial case before the House of Commons as he
had done with the Stamp Act in 1766, but the request
had been refused. "Now in March, 1775," John Fiske
relates, "seeing clearly that he could be of no further use in averting an armed struggle, he returned to
America. Franklin's return was not, in form, like
that customary withdrawal of an ambassador which her-
alds and proclaims a state of war. But practically it
was the snapping of the last diplomatic link between
the colonies and the mother-country."[32]

Upon his return to America, Franklin at long last
broke his silence on the subject of independence, and
the die was cast on June 7, 1776, when Richard Henry
Lee of Virginia rose in Congress to present his famous
tripartite resolution: that these United Colonies are,
and of right ought to be free and independent States;
that it is expedient forthwith to take the most effectual measures for forming foreign alliances; and that
a plan of confederation should be prepared and transmitted to the respective colonies for their consideration and approbation. This was followed by a spirited
debate on the merits of the three proposals and it was
finally decided that a three-week cooling-off period
should be ordered to give the members time to iron out
their differences, but in the meanwhile committees
should be formed to draft a document justifying the
case for independence, and to do some of the preliminary work on a plan of confederation, as well as on
foreign alliance.

The committee chosen to work on a plan of confederation consisted of a member from each colony, and
was headed by John Dickinson of Pennsylvania. The
committee, appointed on June 12, began its labors at
once, and after considerable discussion, submitted to
Congress on July 12 the draft of a plan of union.

84

Intermittently between July 15 and August 20 Congress was engaged in desultory debate, and made some changes in the Dickinson draft. The stumbling blocks were representation, expenses, and western lands. Nevertheless, on August 20 Congress ordered the admittedly imperfect and uncoordinated draft printed. Discussion was resumed in May 1777, but no real progress was made, and when the British entered Philadelphia on September 26, Congress was forced to flee to York, which put an end to the discussion at least for the moment. However, the surprise American victory at Saratoga on October 13 suddenly built a fire under the plan because of its value in connection with the French alliance. Considering this objective, the pressure was to get some kind of plan of union approved quickly, no matter how much opposition to it existed. Forgotten, therefore, were all the arguments about representation, expenses, and western lands, and on November 15, 1777, Congress gave its approval to an emasculated version of the Dickinson plan. Three hundred copies of the Articles were printed, and on November 17 the copies were sent to the 13 states for acceptance or rejection. The issue was now in the hands of the Lord.

The time between June 12, when the committee on the plan of confederation was activated, and November 15, when Congress sent the plan of confederation to the states, was nearly a year and a half. Why did it take so long? What was accomplished? The long delay was occasioned by the fact that when the original report was submitted (July 12) the last thing on the minds of most of the delegates was what would be called today post-war planning, and this is what a plan of confederation looked like at that time. Winning the war was what mattered to Congress. Post-war planning would be an exercise in futility if the war could not be won, or at least a crushing defeat averted. However, some of the problems of confederation surfaced anyway, and when they did the delegates made half-hearted attempts to solve them if they were not too difficult. The tough ones, those that were likely to cause a rupture between the states such as representation, expenses, and western lands, were given temporary solutions or simply put on the back burner for consideration at a later date. On the other hand, one of the major problems of a confederacy of states, indeed the major problem, was raised by a newly arrived delegate from North Carolina, Thomas Burke. This problem was met head-on, and solved in a very forthright manner. It was a problem in political

85

philosophy or constitutional law, and the question was, in the present relationship between Congress and the States, where was the locus of sovereignty? Where should it be in the future? Was it in the Congress or the States?

This question was the fundamental one in the conduct of the war, in the relations between the States and Congress, and in the management of our treaty relations with allies, whether these relations involved direct military aid on the battlefield, commerce among the allies, or the huge loans that were necessary to finance the war. Moreover this question, the point of sovereignty, had been the central question in the dispute with the mother country, whether any authority in London, King or Parliament, could exercise sovereign powers over the colonies, such as the power of taxation. In the political thinking of the day sovereignty was the one distinguishing characteristic of the State, and it went without saying that there could be no such thing as a state within a state, that this was not only a solecism in politics, but a flat contradiction in terms. That being so, the most crucial question that could be asked about a confederation of States was the one as to the location of sovereignty, did it reside in and from the central body, or in and from the component States? This question of political philosophy was infinitely more profound, more important, and more practical than how many angels could dance on the head of a pin, or what authority could be invoked to support the self-evident truths of the Declaration. Yet when Burke raised the question in Congress it did not even provoke a discussion of any kind among these philosopher-kings. Instead, Burke's solution found instant acceptance.

Burke's solution to the problem of sovereignty was precise and unambiguous. He put it in the form of a proposed amendment to Article III of the Dickinson draft. This was a mealy-mouthed statement about the police powers of the States being subordinate to the Articles of Confederation in some undefined cases. Instead of this, Burke proposed that the Congress adopt the following language: "each State retains its sovereignty, freedom and independence, and every power, jurisdiction and right, which is not by this confederation expressly delegated to the United States, in Congress assembled."[33] Burke's amendment became Article II of the Articles of Confederation. It was adopted by a vote of 11 to one, with New Hampshire divided. Virginia was the only state that voted against it.

The Articles did not become effective until March 1, 1781, when Maryland, being satisfied with the disposition of the western lands, empowered her delegates to subscribe and ratify the Articles. The key words in the Burke amendment were "retained" and "expressly delegated." Obviously, no state could retain something it never possessed, sovereignty, for example, and the words "expressly delegated" specifically excluded from Congress all implied powers. This made it clear, as Merrill Jenson said, "the states retained for themselves that vast area of unspecified, unenumerated powers, the twilight zone wherein constitutional governments function most largely."[34] By virtue of the Xth amendment to the Constitution of 1787 Burke's amendment was made part of the present organic law, "the powers not delegated to the United States by the Constitution, nor prohibited by it to the States, are reserved to the States respectively, or to the people."[35]

There is another important point in the first constitution that needs to be stressed. Unlike the Mayflower Compact, for example, where the people under God covenanted and combined themselves together to form "a civil Body Politick"[36] the high contracting parties for the constitutions of 1781 and 1787 were 13 states of America, not the people. This was also true for the Declaration of Independence. It was adopted not by the body of the people of America, but by "the thirteen united (with a small u) States of America."[37] In the case of the constitutions of 1781 and 1787 the same thing is true. The Preamble to the former describes the Confederacy as a "perpetual Union between the States,"[38] and the Preamble to the latter uses the more familiar phrase, "We the People of the United States." Is there a difference? Does this mean that the people, not the States, were the high contracting parties in the Constitution? Apparently not, but the first person to raise the question was Patrick Henry in the Virginia ratifying convention.

The radical leader of the Revolution was a fierce opponent to the Constitution. In making his attack on the great charter of liberty he led off with the Preamble, and he could not have picked a better or more vulnerable place to start. "That this is a consolidated Government," he thundered, "is demonstrably clear, and the danger of such a government, is, to my mind, very striking. I have the highest veneration for those Gentlemen,--but, Sir, give me leave to demand, what right had they to say, 'We, the people?' My political curiosity, exclusive of my anxious solicitude for the public welfare, leads me to ask, who authorized them to speak the language of We, the *people*, instead of, We, the *States*? States are the characteristics, and soul of a confederation. If the states be not the agents of this compact, it must be one great consolidated, National Government, of the people or all the States."[39]

A strict rule of secrecy was enforced in the Federal Convention, and had not been lifted at this point. Thus it was not possible for the defenders of the Constitution to give a straight answer to Henry's challenging question. However, there was one. When the Constitution came out of the Committee of Detail on August 6, the Preamble read "We the people of the States," followed by a listing of the States beginning with New Hampshire, and ending with Georgia.[40] This was changed by the deft pen of Gouveneur Morris of Pennsylvania in the Committee on Style, and when it came out on September 12, the listing of the States had been eliminated in favor of the more familiar form, "We the People of the United States."[41] Why? No one knew what states would ratify the Constitution, or in what order, nor what the ninth State would be. The new form of the Preamble covered all these contingencies without changing the meaning of anything. The character of the government remained the same. It was still one of States, a Federal Government, and did not become a "great consolidated, National Government" as a result of this change in the Preamble. The change went unnoticed and undebated on the floor of the Convention.

The very vain governor of Virginia, Edmund Randolph, rose after Henry's opening blast against the Constitution, and with a fine sense of the dramatic, dismissed Henry's whoel argument with a single word. Trivial was the word the governor used. He dismissed Henry's whole argument by saying that it was "one of the most trivial that will be made to the Convention,"[42] and then turned to another subject. Trivial was probably the right word to use. The Constitution of 1787 was like the one of 1781, a compact between component States. In this case it was like the Declaration of Independence, an agreement among thirteen States to sever the ties that bound them to the mother country, each State binding all its citizens, and none of those in other States. There was nothing in any of these three great documents to suggest that the transfer of sovereignty was from the English Crown or Parliament to an aggregated mass in the United States called "We the People." As Chief Justice Marshall said in one of his greatest opinions, the case of McCulloch v. Maryland (1819); "no political dreamer was ever wild enough to think of breaking down the lines which separate the States, and of compounding the American people into one common mass. Of consequence, when they act, they act in their States."[43]

[1]Phinizy Spalding, *Oglethorpe in America* (Athens: The University of Georgia Press, 1984), 48-60.

[2]Breckinridge Long, *Genesis of the Constitution of the United States of America* (New York: The Macmillan Company, 1926), 36.

[3]Francis Newton Thorpe, *The Federal and State Constitutions, Colonial Charters, and other Organic Laws* (Washington: Government Printing Office, 1909), I, 81.

[4]*Ibid.*

[5]*Ibid.*, I, 79.

[6]*Ibid.*, I, 78.

[7]*Ibid.*, I, 80.

[8]*Ibid.*, I, 78.

[9]James Brown Scott, "Treaty-Making under the Authority of the United States -- Its Use and Abuse" (Presidential Address delivered at the Twenty-eighth Annual Meeting of the American Society of International Law), 2.

[10]Francis Newton Thorp, *op. cit.*, I, 80.

[11]Thomas Hutchinson, *The History of the Colony and Province of Massachusetts-Bay* (Cambridge: Harvard University Press, 1936), I, 131.

[12]*Ibid.*

[13]*Ibid.*, I, 132-33.

[14]*Ibid.*, I, 132.

[15]*Ibid.*, I, 133.

[16]*Ibid.*,

[17]John Marshall, *A History of the Colonies* (Philadelphia: Published by Abraham Small, 1824), 123.

[18]Thomas Hutchinson, *op. cit.*, I, 155.

[19]*Ibid.*

[20]*Ibid.*, I, 160.

[21]Herbert L. Osgood, *The American Colonies in the Seventeenth Century* (Gloucester, Mass.: Peter Smith, 1957), III, 394-95.

[22]James Brown Scott, *The United States of America: A Study in International Organization* (New York: Oxford University Press, 1920), 476.

[23]Breckinridge Long, *op. cit.*, 177.

[24]Benjamin Franklin, *The Writings of*, Albert Henry Smyth (New York: The Macmillan Company, 1907), III, 40-45.

[25]*Ibid.*

[26]*Ibid.*

[27]Max Savelle, *The Origins of American Diplomacy* (New York: The Macmillan Company, 1967), 539.

[28]Carl Van Doren, *Benjamin Franklin's Autobiographical Writings* (New York: The Viking Press, 1945), 731.

[29]*Ibid.*, 732.

[30]Jack N. Rakove, *The Beginnings of National Politics* (New York: Alfred A. Knopf, 1979), 140.

[31]*Ibid.*, 63.

[32]John Fiske, *The American Revolution* Boston: Houghton Mifflin Company, 1891), I, 114.

[33]Jack N. Rakove, *op. cit.*, 170; Francis Newton Thorpe, *op. cit.*, I, 10.

[34]Merrill Jensen, *The New Nation* (Boston: Northeastern University Press, 1981), 25.

[35]Francis Newton Thorpe, *op. cit.*, I, 30.

[36]The Mayflower Compact.   Henry Steele Commager, *Documents of American History* (New York: Appleton-Century Crofts, 1958), 16.

[37]The Declaration of Independence, *ibid.*, 100.

[38]Francis Newton Thorpe, *op. cit.*, 9.

[39]Helen Hill Miller, *George Mason: Gentleman Revolutionary* (Chapel Hill: The University of North Carolina Press, 1975), 288-89.

[40]Max Farrand, *The Records of the Federal Convention of 1787* (New Haven: Yale University Press, 1923), II, 177.

[41]*Ibid.*, II, 590.

[42]Helen Hill Miller, *op. cit.*, 289.

[43]James Brown Scott, *Sovereign States and Suits* (New York: The New York University Press, 1925), 76.

CHAPTER III

THE MORE PERFECT UNION

The most celebrated document in American history is the Declaration of Independence, and rightly so. Like the Magna Carta, it is a legal indictment of a lawful King for betraying his loyal subjects in his attempt to turn back the clock of English liberties in favor of a system of royal absolutism. The Declaration also molded the future of democracy when it laid down the fundamental principles that all men are created equal; that governments rule by the consent of the governed; and that man is endowed by his Creator with certain unalienable Rights, among which are Life, Liberty and the pursuit of Happiness.

But there is more to the Declaration than the philosophy. The headlines of the famous document describes it as "the unanimous Declaration of the thirteen united States of America," and the high contracting parties are the colonies that became States by this Act, not the signatories who ascribed to the document. When John Hancock signed the Declaration he did so as the President of the Continental Congress, and the other delegates signed on behalf of the States they represented, from New Hampshire to Georgia. By virtue of this Declaration these erstwhile colonies, to use their exact language, declared themselves to be "Free and Independent States," and further declared that "all political connection between them and the State of Great Britain is and ought to be totally dissolved." Lest there be any question about what they meant about the political status of the newly emerging States the Declaration went on to say, "that as Free and Independent States, they have full Power to levy War, conclude Peace, contract Alliance, establish Commerce, and to do all other Acts and Things which Independent States may of right do.[1]

There are several things about the famous Declaration that are notable. The most outstanding one is the transfer of sovereignty from the State of Great Britain to the newly created States of America as they

93

are enumerated on the engrossed copy from New Hampshire to Georgia. There is not even a hint that sovereignty was being transferred from the State of Great Britain to some aggregate called the United States. The reference in the headline is to the "united States" (with a small u), and again in the concluding paragraph, to the united States of America." Also, when the framers referred to themselves they used the plural, as educated men would, "Free and Independent States," and when the reference was to the mother country the singular, "the State of Great Britain." The point would not be made, it being too clear for argument, had it not been argued that the transfer of sovereignty was from the Crown to some aggregate in the United States. The people of the United States as a whole did not constitute a legal entity in 1776, and when the definitive treaty of peace was signed on September 3, 1783, His Britannic Majesty acknowledged that the high contracting parties on the American side were the "free, sovereign, and independent States" named in the treaty from north to south: "New Hampshire, Massachusetts Bay, Rhode Island, Connecticut, New York, New Jersey, Pennsylvania, Delaware, Maryland, Virginia, North Carolina, South Carolina and Georgia."[2]

Midway between the Declaration date, 1776, and the date of the treaty of peace, 1783, two treaties were negotiated with France, one of alliance, and the other of commerce. The date for the two treaties was February 6, 1778. The same formula that was later used for the British treaty in 1783 was employed for the French treaties. The treaties were made between the Most Christian King on the one hand, and the thirteen American States on the other, again listing them from north to south, from New Hampshire to Georgia, Congress ratified the treaties on behalf of the States on May 4, 1778, the day on which they were first presented. What was the effect of this ratification? Did the treaties thereby become binding on all the American States? Apparently not. On June 2, 1779, the House of Delegates of the State of Virginia resolved that the aforementioned treaties "ought to be ratified and confirmed, so far as is in the power of this commonwealth," and therefore, "the same are accordingly hereby ratified, confirmed, and declared binding on this commonwealth."[3] The Senate of Virginia concurred the following day.

On June 8 the act of ratification was conveyed to the French Minister in Philadelphia, who in turn, transmitted it to the Minister for Foreign Affairs of France, with the following note:

> On the 20th of this month the Virginia delegates in a body delivered to me in behalf of their State a package containing a letter from the governor of that Commonwealth and an authentic copy of the Act passed by a unanimous vote of the two legislative branches for the ratification of the treaties concluded between the United States and the King and declaring them binding on the Commonwealth.[4]

The governor of the State of Virginia at that time was Thomas Jefferson. As the principal author of the Declaration of Independence, it can be presumed that he had more than a passing knowledge of its contents, as well as of the effects of the Declaration of the State of Virginia, and of the rights and duties of the State to ratify and conclude the treaties with France.

Again, midway between 1779 when Virginia ratified the treaties with France, and the framing of the Constitution of 1787, there was another example of what the people of that day thought of their States -- at least how the State of Massachusetts reacted to the outbreak of war between two of her neighboring States. The governor at that time was John Hancock, and since he had been President of the Continental Congress when the Declaration of Independence was adopted, it has to be assumed that he had a first-hand knowledge of the relationships among the States, as well as their individual responsibilities and obligations under the Articles of Confederation. In any case, the dispute in question was between the unrecognized State of Vermont and the State of New York. The boundary between New Hampshire and New York had always been in dispute, and the early name for the region that is now Vermont was the New Hampshire Grants. Originally, the dispute was between New York and New Hampshire. A decision in favor of New York was handed down in 1764 in England, but New Hampshire refused to accept it, and in 1777 when Ethan Allen and the Green Mountain Boys declared their independence and proclaimed Vermont to be a new State, Vermont took over the controversy with New York.

Thomas Chittenden was elected the first President of Vermont.

In 1778 New York and New Hampshire entered into a secret agreement to divide Vermont Between themselves.[5] However, the plan was abandoned, and the difficulties with New Hampshire were adjusted in 1782. Massachusetts, meanwhile, had recognized the State of Vermont. This was in 1781, the year Congress became de jure when the 13th State, Maryland, ratified the Articles. In 1784 the imminence of war between Vermont and New York was so great that Massachusetts decided to proclaim its neutrality. Accordingly, on April 1, 1784, Governor Hancock published an announcement in the Independent Chronicle and Universal Advertiser, serving official notice on both parties, New York and Vermont, that Massachusetts would follow a course of strict neutrality in the impending clash. To the citizens of Massachusetts, Governor Hancock said:

> I HAVE therefore, at the request of the General Court, thought fit to issue this proclamation, commanding and enjoining it upon all the citizens of this commonwealth, that in all and every controversy now existing, or that hereafter exist between the citizens of New-York, and the people inhabiting the said State, or between any of them, in whatever form or manner the same may exist, they, the citizens of this commonwealth, conduct themselves according to the strictest rules of neutrality; and that they give no aid or assistance to either party.

Governor Thomas Chittenden of Vermont made the position of his State clear when he made an announcement in the Vermont Gazette (September 6, 1784), "that Vermont does not wish to enter into a war with the State of New York, but that she will act on the defensive; and expects that Congress and the twelve states will observe a strict neutrality, and let the contending states settle their own controversy. As to any allegations of the state of New-York against the conduct of this state in bringing a few mal-contents to justice, and obedience to government, whom they had inspired with sedition, I have only to observe that this matter has been managed by the wisdom of the Legislatures of this State, who consider themselves herein amenable to no earthly tribunal."

Happily, war between Vermont and New York was averted, and New York eventually dropped all claim to sovereignty over the territory of Vermont. The affair was finally settled by the admission of Vermont to the union as the 14th State in March, 1791. The case is cited here only as an example of the situation that existed in America in the period between the Declaration of Independence and the adoption of the Constitution. However, it is by no means an isolated case.

Even after the Articles of Confederation went into effect in 1781, the States were more or less on their own to settle any disputes among them that might disturb the peace. Congress was authorized to intervene only if both sides were willing to submit the dispute to arbitration, and even then there was no way to enforce the decision after it was made. The procedures for such a settlement were outlined in the 9th Article of the Confederation.

Within four weeks of the surrender of Lord Cornwallis at Yorktown on October 17, 1781, Pennsylvania filed a petition "stating a matter of dispute between the said state and the State of Connecticut, respecting sundry lands lying on the east branch of the River Susquehanna, and praying a hearing in the premises, agreeably to the 9th article of the Confederation."[6] Congress acquiesced, and the states agreed upon the appointment of seven judges to hear the case. The place and date for the hearing were set for Trenton, New Jersey, on November 12, 1782.

Pennsylvania and Connecticut had been at loggerheads over the Wyoming Valley for a very long period of time. Connecticut based her claim on the royal charter of 1681. Both colonies claimed to have purchased the land from the Indians. Open warfare broke out in 1769, and carried on until 1771. It was called the First Pennamite War. However, rapid settlement of the area continued, and the Connecticut invaders were soon sending representatives to the Connecticut legislature. War broke out again in 1776, and Congress tried to prevail on the States to observe a truce until after the Revolution. However, the States would not listen to reason, and in 1778 the Connecticut forces under Zebulon Butler were defeated by a party of Tories and Indians under John Butler. The

Wyoming Valley massacre followed the victory of Butler's Rangers.

When Congress's arbitral board met at Trenton on November 18, the court was finally organized, and after a full hearing, in which it was said that the case was well argued by learned counsel on both sides, a judgment or a decision was handed down, "we are unanimously of opinion, that the state of Connecticut has no right to the lands in controversy. We are also unanimously of opinion, that the jurisdiction and preemption of all the territory lying within the charter boundary of Pennsylvania, and now claimed by the State of Connecticut, do of right belong to the state of Pennsylvania."[7]

The decision of the board in this case was unique in a way. It was the only example of the 9th Article, of Confederation being used in order to settle a dispute between States. A number of other serious attempts were made to use the machinery of the 9th Article, but they all broke down before the cases were settled. Nevertheless there were high hopes in 1782 that the example of the Trenton case would catch on, and that all the controversies between the States would be settled this happy way. More than that. Robert R. Livingston was so elated at the turn of events that he was ready to predict that the whole world would follow the American example. Writing on January 10, 1783, to the Marquis de Lafayette, Livingston said, "the great cause between Connecticut and Pennsylvania has been decided in favor of the latter. It is a singular event. There are few instances of independent states submitting their cause to a court of justice. The day will come, when all disputes in the great republic of Europe will be tried in the same way, and America will be quoted to exemplify the wisdom of the measure."[8]

Connecticut disappointed Livingston. She refused to accept the decision, and encouraged her settlers to stay in the disputed land. As a result, the Second Pennamite War broke out in 1784. The issue was not resolved until 1799, and then only as a result of direct negotiations between the States. Congress played a part in these negotiations, and not a very noble one, if we are to believe James Madison's account. He bemoaned the fact that the so-called court of the Confederation had failed in the only important case to come before it, Pennsylvania versus Connecticut, and

said, "have we not seen the public land dealt out to
Cont. to bribe her acquiescence in the decree consti-
tutionally awarded agst. her claim on the territory of
Pena.?-- for no other possible motive can account for
the policy of Congs. in that measure."[9]

At the time of the Confederation, which is when
Livingston wrote, and before that, at the time the
issue of Independence was being debated, there were
eleven important boundary disputes that divided the
States, any one of which, like the one between Pennsylvania and Connecticut, or the one between New York
and Vermont or New Hampshire, could lead to war. These
were the ones that were "outstanding and unsettled."[10]
The side-by-side existence of 13 sovereign states in
North America threatened to Balkanize the whole area,
and this was one of the reasons many Americans were opposed to the idea of declaring our independence until
we were more sure of having a plan of union that would
guarantee against a condition of anarchy after independence had been won. Carter Braxton of Virginia expressed just such a view in a letter to Landon Carter
in Philadelphia on April 4, 1776. He said,

> the Colonies of Massachusetts, and Con-
> necticut who rule the other two, have
> Claims on the Province of Pennsylvania
> in the whole for near one-third of the
> Land within their Provincial Bounds and
> indeed the claim extended to its full
> extent comes within four miles of this
> City. This dispute was carried to the
> King and Council, and with them it now
> lies. The Eastern Colonies unwilling
> they should now be the Arbiter have as-
> serted their Claims by force, and have
> at this time eight hundred men in arms
> upon the upper part of this Land called
> Wyoming, where they are peaceable at
> present only through the influence of
> the Congress. Then naturally there
> arises a heart burning and jealousy be-
> tween these people and they must have
> two very different Objects in View.
> The Province of New York is not without
> her fears and apprehensions from the
> Temper of her Neighbours, their great
> swarms and small Territory. Even Vir-
> ginia is not free from Claim on Pennsy-
> lvania nor Maryland from those on Vir-
> ginia. Some of the Delegates from our

Colony carry their Ideas of right to
lands so far to the Eastward that the
middle Colonies dread their being swallowed up between the Claims of them and
those from the east.[11]

Braxton's long epistle had a point. He made it in
the last paragraph, containing a dire prediction.
"And yet," he said, "without any adjustment of those
disputes and a variety of other matters, some are Lug-
ging us into Independence. But as long as these remain
unsettled and men act upon the Principles they ever
have done, you may rely, no such thing will be generally agreed on. Upon reviewing the secret movements of
Men and things I am convinced the Assertion of Independence is far off. If it was to be now asserted, The
Continent would be torn in pieces by Intestine Wars
and Convulsions."[12]

Alexander Hamilton made the same point in the debate over the ratification of the Constitution. "It is
sometimes asked," he said, "with an air of seeming
triumph, what inducements could the States have, if dis-
united, to make war upon each other? It would be a
full answer to this question to say-- precisely the
same inducements which have, at different times, de-
luged in blood all the nations in the world." He went
on to enumerate some of the causes of war among nations, and to speculate on whether they would apply
among the American States. Heading the list were
boundary disputes. "Territorial disputes," he said,
"have at all times been found one of the most fertile
sources of hostility among nations. Perhaps the greatest proportion of wars that have desolated the earth
have sprung from this origin. This cause would exist
among us in full force." Another probable cause of war
that Hamilton cited was commercial rivalry. He referred to the trade regulations that made some States
tributary to others, as Connecticut and New Jersey
were to New York and Massachusetts, and said, "the in-
fractions of these regulations, on one side, the efforts to prevent and repel them, on the other, would
naturally lead to outrages, and these to reprisals and
wars." Finally, Hamilton raised the question of the
foreign alliances that might be entered into by independent States for commercial, military, or territorial advantage. He said the American States "would, by
the operation of such jarring alliances, be gradually
entangled in all the pernicious labyrinths of European

politics and wars; and by the destructive contentions of the parts into which she was divided, would be likely to become a prey to the artifices and machinations of powers equally the enemies of them all. *Divide et impera* (Divide and command--Publius) must be the motto of every nation that either hates or fears us."[13]

The process is clear. However, it would probably be advisable to invoke the authority of a case or two to further clarify the evolution of the American States from the status of colonies in the British Empire. The decision in the first case, *Penhallow v. Doane*, was handed down by a Justice of the Supreme Court, James Iredell, who had the advantage of having taken part in and lived through the times of which he wrote. Speaking of the first period of our continuous and orderly existence, while for 169 years we lived under the colonial system of England, from 1607 to 1776, Justice Iredell said,

> under the British government, and before the opposition to the measures of the parliament of Great Britain became necessary, each province in America composed (as I conceive) a body politic, and the several provinces were not otherwise connected with each other, than as being subject to the same common sovereign. Each province had a distinct legislature, a distinct executive (subordinate to the king), a distinct judiciary; and in particular, the claim as to taxation, which began the contest, extended to a separate claim of each province to raise taxes within itself; no power then existed, or was claimed, for any joint authority on behalf of all the provinces to tax the whole. There were some disputes as to boundaries, whether certain lands were within the bounds of one province or another, but nobody denied that where the boundaries of any one province could be ascertained, all the permanent inhabitants within those boundaries were members of the body politic, and subject to all the laws of it.[14]

While the passage is too clear to need any comment, it does not cover the revolutionary period in our

101

history, the period from the Declaration of Independence in 1776 to the conclusion of the treaty of peace with England in 1783. The important point here is the fundamental one of sovereignty. Did it pass from the Crown of England to the Congress of the United States, or from the Crown to the individual States in America? The case was *Ware v. Hylton*, and the date was 1796, a year after the Penhallow case. The opinion in this case was handed down by a Justice of the Supreme Court, Salmon P. Chase, who had been a signer of the Declaration of Independence, and presumably knew whereof he spoke. He said,

> in *June*, 1776, the Convention of *Virginia formally* declared, that *Virginia* was a free, sovereign, and independent state; and on the 4th of *July*, 1776, following, the *United States*, in Congress assembled, declared the *Thirteen United Colonies* free and independent states; and that as *such*, they had full power to levy war, conclude peace, &c. I consider this as a declaration, not the the United Colonies *jointly*, in a *collective* capacity, were independent states, &c, but that *each* of them was a sovereign and independent state, that is, that *each* of them had a right to govern itself by its own authority, and its own laws, without any controul from any other power upon earth.[15]

The third case invoked here is from a case decided by our greatest Chief Justice, John Marshall, in 1824. The name of the case is *Gibbons v. Ogden*. The question he addressed here is essentially the one about the political status of the States in the relatively short period between 1781, when the Articles of Confederation became fully operative, and the formation of the Constitution in 1787. "As preliminary to the very able discussion of the constitution, which we have heard from the bar," Marshall said, "and as having some influence on its construction, reference has been made to the political situation of these states, anterior to its formation. It has been said, that they were sovereign, were completely independent, and were connected with each other only by a league. This is true."[16]

102

Thus it seems to be clear beyond the shadow of a doubt that the colonies were autonomous political units within the British Empire; that sovereignty passed from the Crown in England to each of the thirteen American colonies, now States; and that there was nothing in the Articles of Confederation, whether before or after their ratification, that injured or impaired the sovereignty of the States of America. This is the only interpretation that is consistent with the concept that prevailed at the time the Articles were drawn up and the Constitution formulated. Sovereignty was understood to be indivisible and absolute; it was the distinguishing characteristic of the state, the only human association that possessed this unique characteristic. This did not mean that the powers of sovereignty could not be delegated. All states routinely delegated powers of sovereignty, and accepted limitations on their freedom of action in dealing with other states, but such limitations and restrictions were self-imposed, and it did not mean that they could not be changed or even repudiated altogether if the state had the power to do so. John C. Calhoun understood it better than any other American writer.

The Congress of the Confederation was a very ethereal body when it was activated, and up to the time when it destroyed itself in favor of the more perfect union. Our mistake has been to look at it and criticize it from the standpoint of a government. A government it was not. A state it was not. And a sovereign state it certainly was not. James Madison said the Articles of Confederation were nothing more than "a treaty of amity, of commerce, and of alliance between independent and Sovereign States.17 John Adams said the same thing, that the Congress was "not a legislative assembly, nor a representative assembly, but only a diplomatic assembly."18 Congress was flawed as a government for the simple reason that it was not designed to function as a government. The Congress, with or without express authority from the States, was a supreme war council of thirteen allies bent on a single purpose--to win the war against the world's strongest power, Great Britain, and thus to be able to assume for themselves individually "the separate and equal station to which the Laws of Nature and of Nature's God entitle them."

The imperfections and defects of this supreme war council, when looked at from the point of view of a government, were endless. Congress had no authority

103

to compel obedience to any of its resolutions or dictates. Noah Webster, the great lexicographer, said that "a law without a penalty is mere *advice*; a magistrate without the power of punishment is a *cypher*. Here is the *great defect* in the articles of our federal government."[19] A government that cannot command is a government that cannot rule, and Congress was this kind of government. Even if the States gave it all the powers it wanted, including the powers of taxation and the regulation of commerce, it could still not rule until it was also given the power to enforce its laws. Otherwise, Congress's so-called laws were merely gratuitous advice. A law without a sanction is a cypher, and this is what Congress was without any power of coercion.

When the pressure of war was lifted, the influence of Congress began to wane. In this respect it was not unique. Alliances born of war-time conditions are prone to disintegrate when the crisis of war ceases to exist. When Congress convened in 1784, it was to find four States absent altogether, three withdrawing in disgust, and the remaining delegates preparing to go home. The battle was on for trade advantage, and the States were erecting tariff barriers against each other. When Congress asked for authority to pass a navigation act to retaliate against British trade regulations, the States not only refused to grant the authority, but Connecticut, when the other New England States attempted to retaliate on their own, actually discriminated against New England by opening all her ports to English vessels. The public credit was gone, and boundary disputes proliferated. In 1786 civil war broke out in Massachusetts, and threatened to spill over into neighboring States. Would the Continent, as Braxton predicted, "be torn in pieces by Intestine Wars and Convulsions?"[20]

The difficulties men lived with during the last days of the Continental Congress, trying to breathe new life into this dying body, gave a big boost to the movement for a more perfect union. A catalysis of sorts was the boundary dispute between Maryland and Virginia over the Potomac River. The Potomac was a principal artery of trade, and jurisdiction over it was claimed by both States. The southern bank was within the jurisdiction of Maryland according to the charter of 1632, but the mouth of Chesapeake Bay was dominated by Virginia by virtue of her possessing Cape

Charles. Maryland could strangle the commerce of Virginia on the Potomac, and Virginia could hamper ships going to and from Baltimore by denying them free passage through the entrance to the Chesapeake Bay.   The result was to stifle trade, and to set Maryland and Virginia against each other.   The general nature of this problem was commented on by Madison.   "The states," he said, "having no convenient ports for foreigh commerce, were subject to be taxed by their neighbors, thro' whose ports, their commerce was carried on. New Jersey, placed between Phila & N. York, was likened to a cask tapped at both ends; and N. Carolina, between Virga & South Carolina to a patient bleeding at both Arms."[21]

In this instance, Maryland and Virginia were interested in working out a peaceful solution to the problem of commerce and trade in the Chesapeake Bay and its tributaries. Washington had a personal interest in the matter because of its bearing on the related problem of the western lands.   At the time, the Father of his country was president of the recently established Potomac Company, and it could not develop profitably until the interstate complications of access to the western lands were solved.   He and his older brother Lawrence had been actively interested in the old Ohio Company, and in the project to develop lands on the headwaters of the Ohio River.

In 1784 Washington, going back to his surveying days (his first public office was that of a surveyor), embarked on a journey of exploration for the purpose of designating a waterway over the Allegheny Mountains to link up the east with the west in an indissoluble commercial union. It was his firm belief that the commerce of free trade was the only cement that would bind the union together, and that without it the union would break apart. Thus it was that Washington took an active part in the labors of Madison to work out a commercial treaty with Maryland where the Potomac River and the Chesapeake Bay would become open arteries of commerce for Virginia and Maryland. Madison was in an ideal position to do this because he had just been made the head of the Committee on Commerce in the Virginia Assembly.   It was largely through his efforts that a conference was convened in Alexandria with commissioners from the two states to see if they could agree on a plan to reconcile the differences between Maryland and Virginia.

The Alexandria Conference was a diplomatic meeting in every sense of the word. The conference met in 1785 to begin their negotiations. However, it was not a good beginning. Three of the members of the Virginia delegation failed to receive notice of the meeting, and of those who showed up none had the proper credentials or full-powers to negotiate seriously on the matters in dispute. Edmund Randolph and James Madison, upon whom Washington relied heavily, were conspicuous by their absence. As a result, no progress was made, and the convention was about to break up when Washington rode into town, and persuaded the delegates not to adjourn, but to remove themselves to nearby Mount Vernon to continue their discussions. At the Mount Vernon home of Washington, Samuel Chase of Maryland and George Mason of Virginia took the lead in working out a compact or treaty. Considering the plight of Congress at the time, no one noticed or paid any attention to the fact that the Mount Vernon compact was a violation of Article VI of the Confederation requiring the consent of Congress to all agreements between two or more states.

In addition to resolving the issues between the two states on the important matter of the Potomac River and the Chesapeake Bay, the Mount Vernon Compact went on to record favoring tariff uniformity throughout the union, freedom of interstate trade, and annual meetings to extend trade benefits. When the treaty came up for ratification in the Maryland legislature, it was approved, and before the year was out the body went on record favoring the extension of the Compact to include Pennsylvania and Delaware. Virginia went even further. Under the leadership of Madison, she proposed that a special Congress be convened of all the states "at a time and place to be agreed on, to take into consideration the trade of the United States; to examine the relative situation and trade of the said States; to consider how far a uniform system in their commercial regulations may be necessary to their commercial interest and their permanent harmony; and to report to the several states such an act."[22]

Pursuant to this invitation (January 21, 1786), which went to all 13 states, nine states promised to attend, but when the convention met in September 1786, only five states (New York, Pennsylvania, Delaware, New Jersey, and Virginia) showed up. Not even Maryland. None of the New England states put in an appearance.

There was good reason for this in at least one New England state, Massachusetts, for the year of the Annapolis Convention was the one in which Shay's Rebellion occurred. The fact that a large majority of the states stayed away from the Annapolis Convention precluded the possibility of their taking any affirmative action, and after a decent interval had passed the delegates decided to issue a call for another convention to meet at Philadelphia on the second Monday in May next, "to take into Consideration the situation of the United States to devise such further Provisions as shall appear to them, necessary to render the Constitution of the Federal Government adequate to the exigencies of the Union."[23] Alexander Hamilton somehow managed to draft the report, though he was not a member of the committee that prepared it. The report itself was sent to the legislatures of every state and to Congress.

Hamilton's strategy was important and successful. Sending the invitation for the Philadelphia Convention to Congress alone, where it could and probably would have been buried, was to practiclaly guarantee its non-success, but to send it to the several states at the same time gave them an opportunity to force the hand of Congress, if they desired to do so. And they did. Seven states jumped the gun on Congress by naming their delegates to the Philadelphia Convention before Congress acted at all. Then the Congress reacted defensively. The members simply ignored the Annapolis Convention and its report, but they did recommend and say "that, in the opinion of Congress, it is expedient that, on the second Monday in May next, a convention of delegates, who shall have been appointed by the several states, be held at Philadelphia, for the sole and express purpose of revising the Articles of Confederation, and reporting to Congress and the several legislatures such alterations and provisions therein as shall, when agreed to in Congress, and confirmed by the states, render the federal Constitution adequate to the exigencies of government and the preservation of the Union."[24] Thus the Philadelphia Convention was designated as an advisory body subordinate to the Congress. By this imperious gesture, the Congress at least saved face for the Members.

Virginia was the first state to comply with the call for a constitutional convention. This was important because the Old Dominion was the mother state of the entire continent from the English point of view,

and from the American she was the first of the thirteen colonies. Virginia was also the largest of the
states at the time, and her population was at least a
fifth of the whole. In other words, while Virginia
could do without a union, the union had no chance to
succeed without Virginia. Massachusetts, New York, and
Pennsylvania were the other three states about which
the same thing could be said, possibly, however, to a
lesser extent. Virginia was to America in 1787 what
England and France were to the concert of Europe at
the same time in history. Therefore, it was of extreme
importance that Virginia should be the first state to
take up the call of the Annapolis Convention for another meeting of the states to "render the federal constitution adequate to the exigencies of Government &
the preservation of the Union."[25] The leadership that
Virginia gave the other states constituted the standard, as Washington later said, "to which the wise and
the honest can repair."[26]

Not only was the standard that Virginia set impor-
tant--being the first state to respond to the resolution of the Annapolis Convention -- but what was even
more important was the character of the Virginia response. Leading the Virginia delegation was the state's
first son, George Washington, who was also the first
son of America as well. This illustrious son of Virginia, after having publicly renounced any further
participation in public affairs, came out of his self-
imposed political exile at Mount Vernon to head the
Virginia delegation to the Philadelphia Convention.
After it became known that Washington would grace the
Convention by his presence, it added greatly to the
importance of the forthcoming meeting. This is still
the case with international conferences. Their success
or failure can usually be predicted with some degree
of accuracy by the character or stature of the delegates appointed, and the ultimate of course is a sum-
mit meeting. Thus, after it became known that Washington had agreed to be a delegate to the Philadelphia
Convention its success became almost a foregone conclusion, and it became a much coveted honor even to be
nominated to serve in the same body. However, there
were some exceptions to this, and one of them was in
Washington's own state, Virginia. There the popular
firebrand of the Revolution, Patrick Henry, refused to
serve after having been nominated, because as he
later said, somewhat inelegantly, to be sure, but
nevertheless quite clearly, he "smelt a rat."[27] What
he meant, of course, was that his first loyalty went

to the state of his birth, and he was suspicious of any movement that might jeopardize the per-eminence of Virginia.

There were also men in the other states, leading men of great importance, who were like Patrick Henry in that their first loyalty was to their own nation-states, and who took a very jaundiced view of any so-called union that could chip away at the prerogatives of the individual states. One such was George Clinton of New York. He was a leading son of the Empire State with impressive credentials. He had served as a brig-adier general in the Continental Army, was elected to be the first governor of the state, and had served for six successive terms as a reward for his energy and qualities of leadership. Governor Clinton, sometimes called the Father of New York state, had no second loyalties. He was first and last a New Yorker. It was clear to him that his native state had much more to lose than gain from a closer union, and as a result was opposed to the idea from the outset. New York was a natural entrepot for goods imported for use in New Jersey, Connecticut, western Massachusetts, and Ver-mont, and she could support herself very well from the revenue derived from her geographic position. Why should she forego the advantages of such a favorable position by investing the power to tax imports in a Congress representing all the States?

Clinton's ambition was to make New York the great-est and most powerful state in North America. As he saw it, this was her destiny, and his duty as the leader was to keep the state true to its destiny. While all this is understandable, what is not under-standable is why Clinton should be so roundly con-demned by liberal-minded historians. Even the great John Fiske seems to have overlooked or misinterpreted the interests, vital in the opinion of men of that time, that were carrying them in the direction of their own individual nationalism instead of toward a unit crystallization of the states. Fiske castigates Clinton's behavior during the critical period of the nation's history by saying that he was "the most dan-gerous man in America" at the time. Fiske went on to say that under Clinton's guidance "the history of New York, during the five years following the peace of 1783, was a shameful story of greedy monopoly and sec-tional hate. Of all the thirteen states, none behaved worse except Rhode Island."[28] Americans tend to over-emphasize the triumph of America as a unit national

republic. They ignore the two centuries of American
history that alone make the Hartford Convention and
the Confederate States of America intelligible. Only
an intelligent understanding of the background of the
18th century of warfare and the revolution itself
makes the petty bickerings and the shameful sectional
hate which so exasperated John Fiske, understandable.
Fiske's comment on Clinton is surprising, considering
the history of his own commonwealth (Connecticut).

     What Fiske seems to forget is that during the
period in question, which he rightly calls the critical period, Clinton's individual nationalism was a
natural result of a conviction held by men like him in
all the states, a conviction based on the manner in
which each was founded, a conviction that each was a
sovereign state, and that each had the right (and some
the interest) to go on that way without any control
from any other power on earth. It is not easy to remember that these states which seemed so new in 1783
had been tending steadily in that direction for nearly
two centuries, and that it was the same status that
Spain's colonies ·took in other parts of the Western
Hemisphere. The American states were nation-states as
truly as were Chile, Peru, or the Argentine, which
have chosen to remain so. They did not assume this
status suddenly at the stroke of a pen in 1783. Their
whole evolution had been in that direction from their
foundation in the very early part of the 17th Century.
The date 1783 is not a beginning, but a halfway point
in the evolution of America. This is often overlooked
by even the most eminent of our historians. It is a
major shortfall in American history.

     The Federal Convention was scheduled to begin its
deliberations on the second Monday in May of 1787,
which was the 14th. However, as James Brown Scott has
said,

          the second Monday of May came, but the
          delegates did not. On the 14th of the
          month, the Virginia delegation, with
          George Washington at its head, arrived
          at Philadelphia on time, where they
          were met by the Pennsylvania delegates,
          who would have found it difficult to
          be elsewhere. A majority of the States
          was obtained for the first time on
          May 25, 1787. On that day the confer-
          ence held the first of its sessions,

which was not to revise the Articles of
Confederation and to make them adequate
for the purposes of union, but to
create a more perfect Union, the model,
as many think, of organization for the
society of nations.[29]

What happened in the 11 days between the 14th of
May and the 25th? According to George Mason, the delegates from the Old Dominion took advantage of the
opportunity thus presented to "meet & confer together
two or three Hours every Day, in order to form a Correspondence of Sentiments" on the business at hand.
He also said the opportunity was not missed to spread
the word and gain the support of other delegates as
they appeared on the scene. "For Form's Sake," Mason
said, "and to see what new Deputies are arrived & to
grow into some Acquaintance with each other, (we) regularly meet, every Day, at 3 o'clock P.M. at the State-
house."[30] These meetings of the Virginians included
the Pennsylvania delegates, of course, as well as any
others from like-minded States. The idea was to sort
out the views of all the delegates from the large
states, iron out any differences between them, and
package the deal for presentation to the Convention
when and if a majority of states put in their appearance.

The workhorse of the Virginia cabal was the inde-
fatigable James Madison. He had arrived in Philadelphia from his post at the moribund Congress in New
York 10 days ahead of the Washington delegation, and
for 10 days had been hard at work among his books,
notes, and papers, preparing resolutions, motions, and
other papers for submission to the Convention. Madison was known in New York as the stoutest of the Virginia nationalists, and he also had the reputation of
being an excellent scholar, debater, and committeeman.
Clinton Rossiter has speculated that "if all the delegates to Congress from all the states had taken their
work as seriously as did Madison, we might still be
living under the Articles of Confederation."[31] In
other words, Madison, though a relatively unknown and
inconspicuous member of the Virginia delegation, was
nevertheless what the cabal and later the Convention
needed, a spark plug to animate the Convention, to
give it plan and purpose, to provide it with something
it could work with, regardless of any inhibiting restrictions. As a result of his efforts, the Virginia

111

plan or set of resolutions was formulated in the pre-Convention consultations during the 11 days between the 14th of May and the 25th, and as Madison said later in life, this outline of a plan "was laid before the convention by Mr. Randolph, at that time governor of the state, as well as member of the convention. This project was the basis of its deliberations; and after passing through a variety of changes in its important as well as its lesser features, was developed and amended into the form finally agreed to."[32] Thus it is clear that the Virginia plan was "largely a product of Madison's creative genius," as Clinton Rossiter said it was, and that the Virginia plan eventually became the Constitution of the United States, but not until it was "elaborated, tightened, amended, and refined under three months of unceasing pressure--much of which Madison resented at the time."[33]

During the pre-Convention meetings of the Virginia cabal, or the small group of persons joined in a design to scrap the old Articles of Confederation in favor of a truly national government, Gouverneur Morris of Pennsylvania took the lead in proposing that the delegates should make it clear at the outset to the small states that they would not be allowed to stand on an equal footing with the large states, but would have to reconcile themselves to an inferior position in the new government. The same problem was faced up to in the same way by the large powers at the end of each of the two great wars of the 20th Century. At the Peace Conference in Paris at the end of World War I, Premier Georges Clemenceau of France made it clear that the five Great Powers (United States, British Empire, France, Italy, Japan) had twelve million men on the field of battle; that they would decide the fate of the world on their own initiative; and that if the little Powers did not like it they could withdraw. Similarly, at the end of World War II the Great Powers (China, France, Great Britain, United States, and Russia) organized the United Nations, and rigged it in such a way that substantive control would be exercised by themselves. For example, military force can be used against the lesser powers without their consent, but not against any of the permanent members of the Security Council. The real world is still one of large and small states, all the cant to the contrary notwithstanding. This world was the one that Gouverneur Morris called attention to in 1787, when he brought up the issue of the large and small states. Madison agreed with Morris's objectives, but insisted that this was not the time to bring them up. To do so, he said, was likely to "beget fatal altercations between the large and small states." On the other hand, he believed that the small states might be persuaded in the course of debate "to give up their equality, for the sake of an effective government." What he had in mind was proportional representation in the new government, the rule whereby the large states would have more votes than the small states by virtue of their bigness --more people, more wealth, more votes. Consequently, it was decided that for the moment at least this issue would be "discountenanced and stifled."[34]

That done, the Federal Convention could be called to order. However, before any substantive work could be done, it was necessary to organize the meeting in the sense of electing a president of the Convention, adopting some rules of order, and appointing a recording secretary. Of these, the most important from the standpoint of the business at hand was the election of a presiding officer, and Madison had his way there too as the Father of his Country was the unanimous choice. Benjamin Franklin was the only possible alternative, and he graciously led the movement for the selection of Washington. Above everything else, there was the matter of the credentials of the delegates representing independent and sovereign states come together to see if they could agree upon some kind of a union better designed to meet their individual concerns and interests than the old and imperfect, if not outworn, Articles of Confederation. How far would their respective governments allow the delegates to go in making the compromises necessary to render the federal government adequate to the exigencies of the union? The state of Delaware enjoined its delegates not to agree to *any* change in the rule of equal representation of the state in Congress. This was in strict accordance with the 5th of the Articles of Confederation, that each state should have one vote in Congress assembled. It was also in conformity with the 13th, that the Articles of Confederation could not be altered or amended except by the consent of all the states. In other words, the credentials of the delegates were such that there was little or no room to maneuver beyond the narrow confines of the one-state-one-vote rule. Of course, this was based on a fundamental axiom of the law, in this case international law, that all states are equal before the bar of justice. The law makes no distinction between large and small states, between strong and weak states, or between rich and poor states.   They are all equal   before the law.

There was much more   to this than meets   the eye. For nearly   two centuries   the   13 colonies,   later to form 13   sovereign   and   independent states,   had been struggling,   each in its own way,   to establish a body politic that   could stand   on its own against whatever opposition   might   develop.   Final   success   was   not achieved until September 7, 1783,   when their independence was recognized by the mother country,   not their collective   but their separate   independence.   Before this, the de facto independent states had entered into a firm league of friendship   with each other under the Articles   of Confederation,   which legally   recognized the right of each of them   to govern itself by its own authority without any control   from any other power on earth.   Now that they had tasted the fruits of sovereignty they did not want   to surrender it lightly,   no matter how much the exigencies   of the union seemed to require it.   It is   in the   light   of   this that the credentials of the delegates to the Federal Convention should be read, particularly those from Delaware.

Delaware was the smallest of the states attending the Convention,   since Rhode Island failed   to appear, and it was probably for this reason that its delegates were   restricted   in their full   powers   to the extent they were, not being allowed to even discuss any alterations that pertained to the 5th Article of the Confederation which declared that   "in determining Questions in the United States   in Congress Assembled each State shall have one Vote."[35] This was a sacred principle to the little state   of Delaware because   its sovereignty was the only shield it   had against the designs of the large states.   To a   certain extent,   this same thing applied to the other small states,   and it is   in   the light of this consideration that the truly international character of the Federal Convention is so obvious.

As a part of the work   of organizing   the Federal Convention, and before the members could address themselves   to problems   of substance,   the report   of the rules committee   came up   for discussion.   A delegate from   South   Carolina,   Pierce Butler,   observed   that there should be a rule against licentious publication, by which he meant unauthorized disclosure   of the happenings   in the   Convention.   Accordingly,   the rules were amended to include   a gag rule binding on all the members, specifically stating:

114

That no copy be taken of any entry on
the journal during the sitting of the
House.

That members only be permitted to in-
spect the journal.

That nothing spoken in the House be
printed, or otherwise published or communicated without leave.[36]

The rule of secrecy was not a meaningless gesture.
Armed sentries were placed at the doors of the meeting
place to prevent anyone from entering or leaving without proper authority, and the members themselves
helped to enforce the rule, fully realizing that the
seriousness of their work was such that it could not
be done with the members playing to the galleries of
public opinion. George Mason of Virginia wrote to his
son on May 27, saying "It is expected that our doors
will be shut, and communications upon the business of
the Convention be forbidden during its sitting." He
continued by saying, "This I think myself a proper precaution to prevent mistakes and misrepresentation until the business shall have been completed, when the
whole may have a very different complexion from that
in which the several crude and indigested parts might
in their first shape appear if submitted to the public
eye."[37]

Judged by the Wilsonian ideal of open covenants
openly arrived at, the rule of secrecy was a moral disgrace, and it is shocking to discover that the virtue
of the founding fathers was not above that sort of
thing. However, the standards are not always the same
in every age, and this is certainly true of the role
of secrecy in diplomacy. While it may (or may not) be
a fixed standard today, it certainly was not in the
Revolutionary period of our history. The founding
fathers accepted secrecy for what it was worth, a necessary measure designed to facilitate the work of diplomacy. As such, the rule of secrecy was specifically
written into the first Constitution for these united
States. In the 14th of the Articles of Confederation
it was provided that in all matters of national security, such as in treaties, alliances, and military
operations, "secresy" should prevail, depending on the
judgment of Congress. In other words, secrecy was not
a sin in 1787, and most of the delegates to the Federal Convention accepted it for what it was, a normal

115

and useful adjunct to the diplomacy of the period. As such, its application and utility for the work at hand were obvious. The nationalists in the Convention needed all the help they could get in their uphill fight to effect a peaceful revolution in the government of America, and they all agreed that the rule of secrecy was an imperative. For what the nationalists had set as their goal was the peaceful overthrow of an existing constitution, and the substitution of another of their own design. It was a revolutionary objective in every sense of the word.

The constitution that had to be overthrown before the nationalists could proceed with their plans was legally unassailable. It was unassailable because of three provisions, two of which were in Article VIII, and the third in Article V. The former contained the perpetuity clause, saying that the union under the Confederation "shall be perpetual," and that the terms of union could not be altered without the consent of "the legislatures of every state." The perpetuity and unanimity clauses froze the status quo against change not embodying due process, and Article V froze it against change through the amendment process by stipulating that "each state shall have one vote" in determining questions in Congress assembled. What the nationalists in the Convention were determined to propose out of their deliberations was the adoption of a new constitution that would do away with the one state-one-vote rule, and provide instead one that would have proportional representation as the base for representation in the national government. At the same time, the new constitution would eliminate the perpetuity and unanimity rules of the old Confederation.

In the new government, thus instituted, a few large states, notably Virginia, would exercise control because of their larger voting power. Instead of equality, the smaller states would be reduced to satellites. But the problem was how could a revolutionary coup d'etat such as this be effected in a peaceable manner? There was no authority for it in the Articles of Confederation, and it was obviously lacking in due process, but it needed some legal foundation to support it. The question was what. Madison faced the issue squarely in Number XL of the Federalist papers. There he denounced the existing constitution as an "absurdity" because under it one-sixtieth of the people could block the will of fifty-nine

116

sixtieths, and justified its overthrow on the Jeffer-
sonian principle that under certain circumstances it
was the right of the people, if not their duty, to
"abolish or alter their governments as to them shall
seem most likely to effect their safety and happiness."
While this was not an accurate quotation from or cita-
tion of the Declaration of Independence it was close
enough to make the point--the right of revolution!

The fact that most of the members of the Federal
Convention helped to enforce the rule of secrecy did
not mean that they all agreed with it or that they
were all as serious about it as some were. But it was
an important rule, so important that James Madison,
looking back on it in 1830, said without equivocation
that, in his opinion, "no Constitution would ever had
been adopted by the convention if the debates had been
made public."[38] Be that as it may, there were some
inside the Convention, as well as others outside, who
made no secret of the fact that they were opposed to
the rule of secrecy. A leading spokesman of this group
was Luther Martin of Maryland. Of course, he was not
one of the nationalist elite in the Convention, and
never missed an opportunity to inveigh against them in
the Convention. Carrying his vendetta over into the
debates on the ratification of the Constitution, Martin told the Maryland Legislature that at one point in
the Convention he,

> moved for liberty to be given to the
> different members to take correct
> copies of the propositions, to which
> the convention had then agreed, in
> order that during the recess of the
> convention, we might have an opportun-
> ity of considering them, and, if it
> should be thought that any alterations
> or amendments were necessary, that we
> might be prepared against the conven-
> tion met, to bring them forward for dis-
> cussion. But, Sir, the same spirit,
> which caused our doors to be shut, our
> proceedings to be kept secret, -- our
> journals to be locked up, -- and every
> avenue, as far as possible, to be shut
> to public information, prevailed also
> in this case; and the proposal, so
> reasonable and necessary, was rejected

by a majority or the convention; thereby precluding even the members themselves from the necessary means of information and deliberation on the important business in which they were engaged.[39]

William Paterson of New Jersey was among those who
defended the doctrine of state equality in the Convention, and while he respected the rule of secrecy, was
not above making light of it in his private correspondence with another sitting member, Oliver Ellsworth of
Connecticut, who was his colleague in the fight
against the steam-roller tactics of the ardent nationalists. Paterson left the Convention around July 23,
and on August 23, just about the time Ellsworth was
also leaving, wrote to him about the progress of work
in the Convention. It was at this time that Paterson
poked some good-natured fun at the rule of secrecy. He
said,

What are the Convention about? When
will they rise? Will they agree upon a
System energetick and effectual, or
will they break up without doing any
Thing to the Purpose? Full of disputa-
tion and noisy as the Wind. it is said,
that you are afraid of the very Windows,
and have a Man planted under them to
prevent the Secrets and Doings from fly-
ing out.[40]

Outside the Convention, the rule of secrecy was
accepted almost without question. There were no inves-
tigative reporters in those days to make a scandal of
the rule, and public and press alike seemed to understand and respect the need for the same. The character of the leading delegates to the Convention undoubtedly had much to do with this feeling of confidence.
No one could imagine a Washington or a Franklin being
engaged in any kind of a plot under a mask of secrecy
to sell his country short for personal gain, nor could
any reasonable man think that a gathering of such men
as were at the Convention could be anti-Republican in
spirit or purpose. Nevertheless, many on the outside
felt left out and frustrated by the rule of secrecy.
It was enforced by the members against each other,
against their closest friends in the political community, and even against members of their own families.
James Madison wrote to his father on September 4, 1787,

118

telling him that the proceedings were "still under the injunction of secrecy," but promising that he would tell him something "as soon as the tie of secrecy shall be dissolved."[41] Earlier than this, on June 15, William Blount of North Carolina met William Pierce of Georgia in New York, and while both were members of the Federal Convention, Blount had not yet taken his seat. He took advantage of the chance meeting with Major Pierce to bring himself up to date on what had transpired thus far in Philadelphia. However, he was in for an unexpected disappointment. Instead of bringing him up to date, the Major evidently invoked the rule of secrecy, and told him nothing. "I have not learned from him," Blount complained, "what in particular is done but he says in general Terms very little is done and nothing definitive indeed I suppose he would not like to descend to particulars even to me who am a Member as I have not taken my seat for the Members are under an Injunction not to disclose by writing or otherwise any part of their proceedings to any Persons but sitting Members."[42] Thomas Jefferson, on the other hand, was not as quiescent as William Blount and others on being told that he could not be let in on what was going on in the Federal Convention. Jefferson was the American minister to France at the time, and finally unburdened himself on the rule of secrecy in a letter to John Adams from Paris on August 30, 1787.

> I have news from America as late as July 19, nothing had then transpired from the Federal convention. I am sorry they began their deliberations by so abominable a precedent as that of tying up the tongues of their members. Nothing can justify this example but the innocence of their intentions, & ignorance of the value of public discussions. I have no doubt that all their other measures will be good & wise. It is really an assembly of demigods.[43]

Jefferson's remark about demigods applies to at least two of the delegates present at Philadelphia-- Washington and Franklin. Whatever can be said of the other delegates, and much has been said, for the gathering had many outstanding men, the two luminaries were Washington and Franklin. Oddly enough, these two were both involved in incidents related to the rule of secrecy, each in his own way. The many-sided Franklin at age 81 was the acknowledged dean of the delegates at Philadelphia, and probably the only real world-figure in America at the time, but he was so relaxed about the rule of secrecy that the other delegates took it upon themselves to watch the world-patriarch when he attended convivial dinners at which non-members were present. The idea was to protect Franklin against any accidental slip of the tongue. It was at one such affair that Franklin related the story of the two-headed snake until a member reminded him of the rule of secrecy, which annoyed the guest by depriving him of the story Franklin was about to tell.

The occasion for this close call from the point of view of secrecy was the chance visit to Philadelphia of Manasseh Cutler of Massachusetts. Having credentials of the highest order, he sought out the Massachusetts delegates to the Federal Convention, and they introduced him to the delegates from Virginia, New York, South Carolina, and so forth. But the one figure Cutler wanted to meet most of all was Franklin, "this great man," Cutler said, "who has been the wonder of Europe as well as the glory of America."[44] Elbridge Gerry of Massachusetts accommodated the distinguished visitor by taking him to call on Franklin at tea time. The two had many things in common, one of which was the fact that Cutler was a scientist of note, and a member of the American Philosophical Society, while Franklin was its president. Thus it was that Franklin launched into the story of the two-headed snake. The story probably had reference to Franklin's known preference for a unicameral legislature, and in the story he compared a legislature of two houses with a snake with two heads. He said that the snake had to choose whether to go on the right or the left side of an obstacle in the woods, and before the two-headed creature could make up its mind, it died with thirst. However, Cutler never did hear the end of the tale because of the security interruption. As Cutler related the incident in his Journal, he said that Franklin showed him a curiosity he had just received, a snake with two heads preserved in a large vial. Cutler continued,

> the Doctor mentioned the situation of this snake, if it was traveling among bushes, and one head should choose to go on one side of the stem of a bush and the other head should prefer the other side, and that neither of the

heads would consent to come back or
give way to the other. He was then going to mention a humorous matter that
had that day taken place in Convention,
in consequence of his comparing the
snake to America, for he seemed to forget that everything in Convention was
to be kept a profound secret; but the
secrecy of Convention matters was suggested to him, which stopped him and deprived me of the story he was going to
tell.[45]

Washington was the opposite of Franklin from the
point of view of being security conscious. Perhaps it
was his military background and upbringing, but whatever the reason, he was a veritable martinet when it
came to matters of security, and this applied particularly to the rule of secrecy in the Convention. To
him, there was no such thing as an accidental slip of
the tongue, or a minor infraction of the rule, because
he considered any deviation as an unpardonable sin,
the sin of not being able to take orders, of insubor-
dination. Thus it was that William Pierce of Georgia
had a great scare in the early days of the Convention.
The members were allowed to make notes of some of the
proceedings for personal use, and one day at the close
of business, but before the adjournment, General Washington shocked the delegates by addressing them, according to Pierce, as follows:

Gentlemen, I am sorry to find that some
one Member of this Body, has been so
neglectful of the secrets of the Convention as to drop in the State House a
copy of their proceedings, which by accident was picked up and delivered to
me this morning. I must entreat Gentlemen to be more careful, least our transactions get into the News Papers, and
disturb the public repose by premature
speculations. I know not whose Paper
it is, but there it is (throwing it
down on the table) let him who owns it
take it.

Major Pierce continued his account by saying that
at this point Washington "bowed, picked up his Hat,
and quitted the room with a dignity so severe that

121

every Person seemed alarmed; for my part I was extremely so, for putting my hand in my pocket I missed my
copy of the same Paper, but advancing up to the Table
my fears soon dissipated; I found it to be the hand
writing of another Person. When I went to my lodging
at the Indian Queen, I found my copy in a coat pocket
which I had pulled off that Morning. It is something
remarkable that no Person ever owned the Paper."[46]

The rule of secrecy was carried to its logical
conclusion on September 17, 1787, when the elected
Secretary of the Convention, William Jackson of South
Carolina, surrendered the *Journal* he had kept to Washington, and then proceeded to burn "all the loose
scraps of paper which belong to the Convention."[47] To
this day, no one knows what was consumed in that fire,
and efforts are still being made to repair the damage
by diligent research into all possible sources of information. The unfortunate decision to burn all the
Convention papers, except the official *Journal*, was
one that was first made in the Convention. However,
it was not explicit. The President had asked the Convention what "should be done with the Journals &c,
whether copies were to be allowed to the members if
applied for?" The Resolution that was approved was
"that he retain the Journal and other papers, subject
to the order of Congress, if ever formed under the
Constitution."[48] Therefore, it seems clear that the
decision to burn "all the loose scraps of paper" was
one that was made by the Secretary of the Convention,
William Jackson.

Washington complied with the order, and transferred the Journal Jackson gave him to the State Department in 1796, and in 1818 Congress ordered that
the Journal be published under the direction of the
President of the United States. John Quincy Adams was
Secretary of State at the time, and he found that the
so-called Journal was a joke. Instead of being a co-
herent Journal, Adams said it was "no better than the
daily minutes from which a regular journal ought to
have been, but never was, made out."[49] Even a cursory
examination revealed that the papers were disorderly,
incomplete, and full of errors. After the expenditure
of considerable time and much labor, Adams finally got
the papers into some kind of order, but he was still
not satisfied with the results. Consequently, he
called on some of the surviving members of the Convention for help, including the errant William Jackson.
When asked to explain the condition of his papers,

122

Jackson confessed that "he had no recollection of them which could remove the difficulties arising from their disorderly state, nor any papers to supply the deficiency of the missing papers."[50] Despairing of getting anything better, Adams decided to go ahead with what amounted to a patchwork version of an official Journal, figuring that what he had would give posterity a "tolerably clear"[51] view of the proceedings of the Convention. Consequently, the result was the publication of the *Journal, Acts and Proceedings of the Convention* at Boston in 1819. The best that can be said of this publication is that it made the record "tolerably clear," but not tolerably accurate, nor tolerably complete. Nevertheless, the publication of the *Journal* broke the veil of secrecy on the proceedings of the Convention, and two years later, in 1821, another inaccurate, and this time self-serving, account of the proceedings was published by Robert Yates and John Lansing, both of New York. Yates and Lansing both left the Convention long before the debates ended, and the apparent purpose of their publication was to discredit the role of James Madison in the Convention. Thus the *Secret Proceedings and Debates* is also a very unreliable source of information on the Convention, probably even more incomplete and unreliable than the official *Journal* by William Jackson.

Madison's *Notes* were not published until 1840. He died in 1836, and it was in accordance with his wish that the posthumous publication took place. Shortly after the publication of the *Secret Proceedings* took place Madison explained why he was not willing to rush how own *Notes* into publication. He said he thought it was best "to let the work be a posthumous one; or at least that its publication be delayed till the Constitution should be well settled by practice, & till a knowledge of the controversal part of the proceedings of its framers could be turned to no improper account."[52] At the same time, Madison advanced a novel theory of constitutional interpretation, that "the legitimate meaning of the instrument must be derived from the text itself; or if a key is to be sought elsewhere, it must be not in the opinions or intentions of the Body which planned & proposed the Constitution, but in the sense attached to it by the people in their respective State Conventions where it recd. all the authority it possesses."[53] Finally, in connection with Yates's *Secret Proceedings*, Madison said that it was "not only a very mutilated but a very erroneous edition of the matter to which it relates."[54]

Against this background of the *Secret Proceedings*
and the earlier *Journal*, it is amazing to learn that
over the years from 1819 to 1836 Madison made many
changes in his original *Notes* in order to reconcile
them with entries in the printed *Journal*. He did the
same thing when other writings from Convention members
began appearing. The notes kept by William Pierce of
Georgia were published in 1828, and Madison may have
seen some of the other notes that the members kept,
such as those by Rufus King of Massachusetts, James
McHenry of Maryland, William Paterson of New Jersey,
Alexander Hamilton of New York, and George Mason of
Virginia.

Madison obviously would not have made all these
changes to his original *Notes* if he had been sure of
himself in the first place. Another factor may have
been his age. Madison was 68 at the time the *Journal*
was published, and 85 when he died. His powers of
discrimination, and his passion for accuracy, had to
be reduced in his 70s and 80s. More important than
anything else, however, was the fact that Madison's
original task was something that no man could accomplish. Madison meant to take an active, if not a leading, part in the work of the Convention, and he did
so in good measure. In fact, measured by a crude statistical yardstick, the number of times each member
spoke in the Convention, Madison was near the top.
Gouverneur Morris of Pennsylvania spoke 173 times,
James Wilson of Pennsylvania 168 times, James Madison
161 times, Roger Sherman of Connecticut 138 times,
George Mason of Virginia 136 times, and Elbridge Gerry
of Massachusetts 118 times. In addition to this, Madison took on the responsibility of maintaining a running record of everything that transpired in the Federal Convention, all the speeches, the plans presented,
the important votes, and everything else that would be
of historic value. In order to do this, Madison said,

> I chose a seat in front of the presiding member, with the other members, on
> my right and left hand. In this favorable position for hearing all that
> passed I noted in terms legible and in
> abbreviations and marks intelligible
> to myself what was read from the Chair
> or spoken by the members; and losing
> not a moment unnecessarily between the
> adjournment and reassembling of the
> Convention I was enabled to write out

my daily notes during the session of
within a few finishing days after its
close.[55]

Madison's record was maintained, as he said, in
terms and abbreviations legible to himself, that is
legible at the time, but not necessarily 40 or 50
years later, which was when he began revising his
Notes for publication. In addition to all the difficulties inherent in this process, Madison had been
very casual about his reporting in the first place,
particularly about the names of some of the elegates.
Some of the most outstanding and distinguished delegates to the Convention have their names spelled wrong
by Madison, not excluding the great Franklin (Frank-
lyn), Paterson (Patterson), Dickinson (Dickenson),
Carroll (Carrol), Ingersoll (Ingersol); Pinckney
(Pinkney), Broom (Broome), Sherman (Sharman), and Rutledge (Rutlidge). On the other hand, Madison had his
own name mangled by some of his colleagues, who knew
him only as Maddison. In addition to these discrep-
ancies, Madison's *Notes* contain the shorthand, abbreviations, and marks that were written in great haste
and were intelligible when he jotted them down, even
though some of them were unintelligible 30 or 40 years
later when he began to edit them for publication. The
process of unediting them to get back to the originals
has been a major undertaking for serious scholars over
the years. After all Madison's *Notes*, for all their
deficiencies and shortcomings, outline the boundaries
of our knowledge of the secret proceedings of 1787.

The *Notes* make it clear that the rule of secrecy
worked, and that the members had confidence in it.
Their debates were open and forceful, and they made no
effort to hide anything, not their passions, and certainly not their prejudices. What they said and did
was designed to impress and persuade their fellow
delegates, not to promote their political careers in
their home constituencies, and certainly not to carve
out places for themselves in the annals of history.
The extent to which the members felt free to vent
their emotions and even their passions came out in
the debate over representation in the national government. The small states had their backs against the
wall on this issue, and felt that if they did not succeed in blocking the Virginia steamroller they would
be swallowed up by the large states. Thus it was that
on June 30 Gunning Bedford of Delaware stunned the Convention by raising the issue of foreign aid for the

small states as a measure of last resort. As a pre-
face to his remarks on foreign aid he made it clear to
his colleagues in the large States that he did not
trust them. "I do not, gentlemen," he said, "trust
you. If you possess the power, the abuse of it could
not be checked, and what then would prevent you from
exercising it to our destruction?"[56] He then said,
"sooner than be ruined, there are foreign powers who
will take us by the hand."[57] In short, Bedford bluntly
accused the nationalists of threatening the use of
force to gain their unworthy objective of destroying
the smaller states. "The small states," he said,
"never can agree to the Virginia plan, and why then is
it urged? But it is said that it is not expected that
the state governments will approve the proposed system,
and that this house must directly carry it to THE
PEOPLE for their approbation. Is it come to this,
then, that the sword must decide this controversy, and
that the horrors of war must be added to the rest of
our misfortunes?"[58]

Bedford said that the simple alternative to this
mad scheme to destroy the small states, which was his
characterization of the Virginia plan, was to do what
the people had already said they wanted done, which
was to amend and enlarge the confederation by giving
it the powers to regulate trade, to collect taxes, and
the means to discharge the foreign and domestic debt.
"Can we not then, as their delegates, agree upon these
points? As their ambassadors, can we not clearly grant
these powers?"[59] However, there was one point on which
Bedford would not yield. This was that the little
states give up their idea of equality. "The little
states," he said, "are willing to observe their engagements, but will meet the large ones on no ground but
that of the Confederation."[60]

Gunning Bedford was criticized, as he should
have been, by his colleagues for his intemperate remarks on foreign aid. Rufus King of Massachusetts took
him to task on the same day. "He could not sit down,"
he said, "without taking some notice of the language
of the honorable gentleman from Delaware (Mr. Bedford).
It was not he that had uttered a dictatorial language.
This intemperance had marked the honorable gentleman
himself. It was not he who with a vehemence unprecedented in that House, had declared himself ready to
turn his hopes from our common Country, and court the
protection of some foreign hand -- This too was the
language of the Honbl member, himself. He was grieved

126

that such an expression had dropped from his lips.
(The gentleman can only excuse it to himself on the
score of passion. For himself whatever might be his
distress, he wd. never court relief from a foreign
power.)"61

Madison also took exception to the idea of appeal-
ing to foreign powers to protect the independence of
the small states. As a practical matter, he said that
"he could not suspect that Delaware would brave the
consequences of seeking her fortunes apart from the
other States, rather than submit to such a Govt: much
less could be suspect that she would pursue the rash
policy of courting foreign support, which the warmth
of one of her representatives (Mr. Bedford) had suggested, or if she shd. that any foreign nation wd. be
so rash as to hearken to the overture."62 On the other
hand, Gouverneur Morris of Pennsylvania did not rule
out the use of force in the controversy between the
large and small states. In the final analysis, he said,

> This Country must be unified. If persua-
> sion does not unite it, the sword will.
> He begged that this consideration might
> have its due weight. The scenes of
> horror attending civil commotion can
> not be described, and the conclusion of
> them will be worse than the terms of
> their continuance. The stronger party
> will then make traytors of the weaker;
> and the Gallows & Halter will finish
> the work of the sword. How far foreign
> powers would be ready to take part in
> the confusions he would not say.
> Threats that they will be invited have
> it seems been thrown out. He drew the
> melancholy picture of foreign intru-
> sions as a standing lesson to other na-
> tions. He trusted that the Gentlemen
> who may have hazarded such expressions,
> did not entertain them till they
> reached their own lips.63

Bedford defended himself on the foreign aid issue
by saying it was the large states that seemed bent on
a revolutionary secession from the Articles of Confederation, and in that case the consequence would be
"that foreign nations having demands on this Country
would find it their interest to take the small States
by the hand, in order to do themselves justice. This

was what he meant. But no man can foresee to what extremities the small States may be driven by oppression. He observed also in apology that some allowance ought to be made for the habits of his profession in which warmth was natural & sometimes necessary. But is there not an apology in what was said by (Mr. Govr. Morris) that the sword is to unite: by Mr. Ghorum that Delaware must be annexed to Penna. and N. Jersey divided between Pena. and N. York. To hear such language without emotion, would be to renounce the feelings of a man and the duty of a citizen."[64] Elbridge Gerry of Massachusetts expressed agreement with Bedford. "We were," he said, "in a peculiar situation. We were neither the same Nation nor different Nations. We ought not therefore to pursue the one or the other of these ideas too closely. If no compromise should take place what will be the consequence. A secession he foresaw would take place; for some gentlemen seem decided on it; two different plans will be proposed, and the result no man could foresee. If we do not come to some agreement among ourselves some foreign sword will probably do the work for us."[65]

All the while this threatening language was being heard in the Convention, the delegates from the small states had been arriving in driblets, but not until June 14 were there enough of them to put up a real resistance to the steamroller tactics of the Virginians. On this date, however, they coalesced around a leader, William Paterson of New Jersey, and he immediately moved an adjournment until the following day in order to give the small states enough time to prepare a "purely federal" plan to oppose the "purely nationalist" plan of the Virginians. The request was granted.

The New Jersey plan, as it came to be called, was no more a plan, in the strict sense of the word, than the original Virginia plan was, but like it it was a series of resolutions. The 15 resolutions of the Virginia plan represented the views of the large states, particularly Virginia, and the nine resolutions of the New Jersey plan represented the views of the small states, particularly New Jersey. The essence of the New Jersey plan was that the Convention should address itself to proposing amendments to the Articles of Confederation, not to devising a new Constitution, contrary to the will of Congress, and to the authority of the delegates. As for the shortcomings of the Confederation, it was well recognized what they were.

128

Amidst the plentitude of powers there was no power to
raise money by taxation, no power to regulate foreign
and domestic commerce, and no coercive power. The New
Jersey plan sought to remedy these defects, but to do
so within the framework of the Articles of Confederation. James Wilson of Pennsylvania stated that the
differences between the two plans were as follows:

> Virginia plan proposed two branches in
> the legislature. Jersey a single legis-
> lative body.
>
> Virginia, the legislative powers de-
> rived from the people. Jersey, from
> the states.
>
> Virginia, a single executive. Jersey,
> more than one.
>
> Virginia, a majority of the legislature
> can act. Jersey, a small minority can
> control.
>
> Virginia, the legislature can legislate
> on all national concerns. Jersey, only
> on limited objects.
>
> Virginia, legislature to negative all
> state laws. Jersey, giving power to
> the executive to compel obedience by
> force.
>
> Virginia, to remove the executive by
> impeachment. Jersey, on application of
> a majority of the states.
>
> Virginia, for the establishment of in-
> ferior judiciary tribunals. Jersey,
> no provision.[66]

But to revert to the period of sword rattling
(June 20-July 16), the basic point at issue was proportional representation, whether voting should be by
states, or by some other formula, such as population
or wealth. The growing opposition to the idea of proportional representation manifested itself as early as
June 11, when the small states acted together to almost defeat the proposal for proportional representation in the upper house of the legislature. The vote
was six to five. Now on June 15, when the New Jersey

plan was presented to the Convention, it was clear
that the small states were at last effectively organized in opposition. It was also at this point that
John Dickinson of Delaware said to Madison, "you see
the consequence of pushing things too far. Some of the
members from the small states wish for two branches in
the General Legislature, and are friends to a good
National Government; but we would sooner submit to a
foreign power, than submit to be deprived of an equality of suffrage, in both branches of the legislature,
and thereby be thrown under the domination of the
large States."[67] Finally, it was at this point that
Charles Pinckney, a large-state man from South Carolina, carried Dickinson's point to its logical conclusion by saying that the great concern over credentials
from the small-state men was nothing but a smoke
screen, "the whole comes to this, as he considered.
Give N. Jersey an equal vote, and she will dismiss her
scruples, and concur in the Natl. system."[68]

There was not much evidence on the floor of the
Convention that Dickinson and Pinckney were right
about the small states rolling over and playing dead
if they were only given an equal voice in a nationalist government. Certainly, this is not the way it appeared to Alexander Hamilton. This luminary from New
York delivered himself of a speech on June 18 that
left no doubt where he stood in the Convention. He
opened up by denouncing both the Virginia and the New
Jersey plans, and said that the people were beginning
"to be tired of an excess of democracy." More than
that, "what even is the Virginia plan," Hamilton said,
"but pork still with a little change of the sauce?"[69]
The kind of government he favored was clearly a monarchy on the British model. However his ideas did not
make much of an impression on the delegates. William
Samuel Johnson of Connecticut summed it up by saying
that the gentleman from New York "has been praised by
everybody, he has been supported by none."[70] In any
case on June 19, in a choice between the Virginia and
New Jersey plans, the vote was seven to three in favor
of the Virginia plan, with the vote of Maryland
divided. In other words, the fight continued, and
Virginia continued to dominate the Convention, with no
sign that it would retreat from its original position.
The invitation held out by Dickinson, and the easy
course recommended by Pinckney, had not as yet picked
up any support in the Virginia delegation. The momentum of its advance carried it forward.

If anything, the easy victory of June 29 emboldened the nationalists, and encouraged them to make some concessions to the small-state men for the sake of harmony. One of these was to back-pedal on the issue of nomenclature, or as Rufus King of Massachusetts called it "phraseology." In particular, "he conceived that the import of the terms 'States', 'Sovereignty', 'national', 'federal', had been often used & applied in the discussion inaccurately & delusively."[71] Later, Madison clarified the point by explaining that in the original Virginia resolutions the word National was used not "to express the extent of power, but the mode of its operation, which was to be not like the old Confederation operating on States, but like that of ordinary Governments operating on individuals; & the substitution of 'United States' for 'National' noted in the journal, was not designed to change the meaning of the latter, but guard agt. a mistake or misrepresentation of what was intended."[72] Thus, when the word National was eliminated from the Virginia resolutions on June 30 it was nothing but a gesture of good will, and did not represent a concession of any consequence to the small-state men.

On June 27 the delegates quit beating around the bush, and got down to the business at hand, which was the split over proportional representation. Should voting in the upper and lower houses be according to the rule of state sovereignty, as in the Congress, or should it be changed to proportional representation, as the large-state men demanded? This was the question, and everything else was secondary. But before the voting could begin, Luther Martin of Maryland got the floor. He held it for the rest of the day, and then to the disgust of nearly everybody, announced that he would continue the next day. Later, Oliver Ellsworth of Connecticut wrote to the long-winded Marylander, saying, "you opened against them in a speech which held during two days, and which might have continued two months, but for those marks of fatigue and disgust you saw strongly expressed on whichever side of the house you turned your mortified eyes."[73]

When the Convention finally got around to the real issue, it took the members three weeks before they could agree on a compromise solution. This was the most critical period of the Convention, and the crisis came to a head on July 2 when the vote was taken on

131

whether each state should have an equal vote in the upper house. This was also the period during which the small states threatened to withdraw if they were not given an equal voice in the upper house. Finally, this was the period in which the question of foreign aid came up, and the large state men began making noises about uniting the country by the sword, if all else failed. The vote on July 2 was a tie, and Gouverneur Morris of Pennsylvania probably did not exaggerate when he said that "the fate of America was suspended by a hair."[74] Nevertheless, the large-state men stood by their guns, and stubbornly refused to budge an inch. They still had not the wisdom to see that Dickinson and Pinckney were right, that the way to get their nationalist government was the way of compromise on this one issue.

The July 2 stalemate in the Convention was not broken utnil July 16, when the stubborn nationalists finally gave in to the even more stubborn small-state men. It was better this than have the Convention break up with nothing to show for its pains. The small-state men got exactly what they wanted, an equal vote in the upper house, or second branch of the legislature. This satisfied them, and they proceeded to do exactly what Dickin son and Pinckney had said they would do, come out for a strong national government. However, before this happened a spirited debate broke out on another matter. This was whether the Constitution should be rigged so that the original states would not lose control of the government by being outvoted by the new states that might be admitted from out of the western territory.

It was only fitting and proper that the delegates should concern themselves with the admission of new states. The membership problem is one that can be the death of any international organization, ours included. The old League of Nations died because of this problem; in its case it was the problem created by the empty chair reserved for the United States. Later, the United Nations suffered the same fate, the only difference being that its problem was one of the crowded vestibule. It got out of hand in the 1960s when all the mini-states of the so-called Third World took their seats as members. They soon transformed the world body into a forum of futility and hubbub of anti-American, anti-European, and anti-Western propaganda.[75] This is exactly what the framers of the American Constitution were seeking to avoid in 1787 when

132

they had their spirited debate on the admission of new states.

In 1787 the problem of letting the membership get out of hand was one of liberals versus conservatives more than the present problem of the haves and the have-nots. What the framers were concerned about was an excess of democracy, and governemnt by frontier types who were not accustomed to the restraints and responsibilities of older societies. In other words, great dangers of a levelling nature were apprehended from the admission of new states carved out of the western territory. Conservative propertied men of the east, including Nathaniel Gorham of Massachusetts, Gouverneur Morris of Pennsylvania, and John Rutledge of South Carolina, felt that something should be written into the Constitution to protect the Atlantic states from losing control of the government. Pierce Butler of South Carolina, as early as July 13, made a very prophetic observation when he noted that "the people & strength of America are evidently bearing Southwardly & S. Westwdly."[76] In this connection, Elbridge Gerry of Massachusetts, on July 14, asked the members to consider his views on admitting new states. He said he was:

> for admitting them on liberal terms, but not for putting ourselves into their hands. They will if they acquire power like all men, abuse it. They will oppress commerce, and drain our wealth into the Western Country. To guard agst. these consequences, he thought it necessary to limit the number of new States to be admitted into the Union, in such a manner, that they should never be able to outnumber the Atlantic States. He accordingly moved "that in order to secure the (liberties of the) States already confederated, the (number of) Representatives in the 1st branch (of the States which shall hereafter be established) shall never exceed in number, the Representatives from such of the States (as shall accede to this confederation.)[77]

Rufus King of Massachusetts seconded Gerry's motion, and when it was put to a vote the motion failed to carry by a vote of five to four. It is not surprising that the vote was so close. If anything, the surprise is that the motion failed to carry. Over the course of nearly 200 years there had grown up a profound difference between the coastal fringe of society and the frontier outposts. The cities and counties had held the power in their own hands right up to the time of the Revolution, and had refused to share it in any reasonable way with the "back counties" or the up county settlements. However, with the coming of the Revolution and the writing of new constitutions all this began to change. And to change for good. To the dismay of the seaboard cities, it was soon apparent that there was no going back. South Carolina is a good example. Before the Constitution of 1776, which was adopted before Independence was declared, "Charleston District had elected 75 percent of the colonial Commons; it chose 48 percent of the new representatives (96 to 202). The backcountry, which had elected six percent of the old Commons, chose 38 percent of the new lower house (76 representatives)."[78] In 1786, as part of this movement away from the seacoast, the capital itself was moved from Charleston to Columbia, even though the new site was then almost in primeval forest. The only way to prevent power from completely draining away from the Atlantic States, it seemed to some at the time, was to put safeguards in the new Constitution itself.

Prior to Gerry's motion of July 14, in fact on July 5, Gouverneur Morris of Pennsylvania said he also,

> looked forward to that range of New States which wd. soon be formed in the west. He thought the rule of representation ought to be so fixed as to secure to the Atlantic States a prevalence in the National Councils. The new States will know less of the public interest than these, will have an interest in many respects different, in particular will be little scrupulous of involving the Community in wars the burdens & operations of which would fall chiefly on the maritime States. Provisions ought therefore to be made to prevent the maritime States from being hereafter outvoted by them. He thought

134

this might be easily done by irrevoc-
ably fixing the number of representatives which the Atlantic States should
respectively have, and the number which
each new State will have. This wd. not
be unjust, as the western settlers wd.
previously know the conditions on which
they were to possess their lands. It
would be politic as it would recommend
the plan to the present as well as future interest of the States which must
decide the fate of it.[79]

Rufus King of Massachusetts agreed. On July 6, he
provided the Convention with some statistics. "With
regard to New States," he observed, "there was something peculiar in the business which had not been
noticed. The U.S. were now admitted to be proprietors
of the Country, N. West of the Ohio. Congs. by one of
their ordinances have impoliticly laid it out into ten
States, and have made it a fundamental article of compact with those who may become settlers, that as soon
as the number in any one State shall equal that of the
smallest of the 13 original States, it may claim admission into the Union. Delaware does not contain it
is computed more than 35,000 souls, and for obvious
reasons will not increase much for a considerable time.
It is possible then that if this plan be persisted in
by Congs. 10 new votes may be added, without a greater
addition of inhabitants than are represented by the
single vote of Pena."[80]

Three days later, on July 9, Nathaniel Gorham of
Massachusetts took the floor to explain why a committee of which he was a member had proposed what it did
with respect to the actual number of representatives
each state should have in the first Congress. The cal-
culation did not correspond with any rule of numbers,
and the question was what had been the basis? Gorham
said,

two objections prevailed agst. the rate
of 1 member for every 40,000 unhts. The
1st, was that the Representation would
soon be too numerous; the 2d. that the
Westn States who may have a different
interest, might if admitted on that
principal by degrees out-vote the Altan-
tic. Both these objections are removed.
The number will be small in the first

instance and may be continued so, and
the Atlantic States having ye. Govt. in
their own hands, may take care of their
own interest, by dealing out the right
of Representation in safe proportions
to the Western States. These were the
views of the Committee.[81]

The idea of dealing out the right of representation to the Western States in safe proportions came up
again on August 29. Gouverneur Morris restated his
reservations about the New States. Saying that he
"did not mean to discourage the growth of the Western
Country" because he knew that would be impossible,
nevertheless argued that he "did not wish however to
throw power into their hands." John Langdon of New
Hampshire agreed, saying he "did not know but circumstances might arise which would render it inconvenient
to admit new States on terms of equality." Hugh Williamson of North Carolina supported him by arguing
that the New States would be on a different footing
from the original states. "The existing small States,"
he said, "enjoy an equality now, and for that reason
are admitted to it in the Senate. This reason is not
applicable to (new) Western States."[82] Madison, on the
other hand, was not among those who were caught up in
the wave of fear that admitting the New States on a
plane of equlaity would cause the Atlantic States to
lose their grip on the government. In fact, as early
as June 30 Madison had argued that the whole controversy bordered on the ridiculous. He accepted the idea
that geopolitics was a factor in the equation of power,
but argued that it was not the East-West axis that prevailed here, but the North-South. It was his conten-
tion that,

> the States were divided into different
> interests not by their difference of
> size, but by other circumstances; the
> most material of which resulted from
> climate, but principally from (the ef-
> fects of) their having or not having
> slaves. These two causes concurred in
> forming the great division of interests
> in the U. States. It lay between the
> Northern & Southern, and if any defen-
> sive power were necessary, it ought to
> be mutually given to these two inter-
> ests.[83]

The only concession Madison made to the idea of the New States being a threat to the original 13 was on June 19. It was part of Madison's argument that proportional representation should be the basis of voting rights in both houses of the legislature. If not, ran the argument, "the prospect of many new States to the Westward was another consideration of importance. If they should come into the Union at all, they would come when they contained but few inhabitants. If they shd. be entitled to vote according to their proportions of inhabitants, all would be right & safe. Let them have an equal vote, and a more objectionable minority than ever might give law to the whole."[84]

James Wilson of Pennsylvania took the high road in the debate over admission of new states. If the balance of power shifted to the New States he would not argue with it. Going back to the great Declaration, he rested his case on the proposition "that all men wherever placed have equal rights and are equally entitled to confidence." He went on to say that,

> he viewed without apprehension the period when a few States should contain the superior number of people. The majority of people wherever found ought in all questions to govern the minority. If the interior Country should acquire this majority they will not only have the right, but will avail themselves of it whether we will or no. This jealousy misled the policy of G. Britain with regard to America. The fatal maxims espoused by her were that the Colonies were growing too fast, and that their growth must be stinted in time. What were the consequences? first, enmity on our part, then actual separation. Like consequences will result on the part of the interior settlements, if like jealousy & policy be pursued on ours.[85]

Roger Sherman of Connecticut sided with Wilson in the great debate. First, he disparaged the debate, calling the whole thing a tempest in a teapot, because he did not think there was any "probability that the number of future States would exceed that of the Existing States." However, he went on to say, "if the event should ever happen, it was too remote to be taken into

137

consideration at this time. Besides We are providing
for out posterity, for our children & our grand Children, who would be as likely to be citizens of new Western States, as of the old States. On this consideration alone, we ought to make no such discrimination as
was proposed by the motion."[86]

Elbridge Gerry of Massachusetts gave Sherman his
answer. He said that,

> if some of our children should remove,
> others will stay behind, and he thought
> it incumbent on us to provide for their
> interests. There was a rage for emigra-
> tion from the Eastern States to the
> Western Country and he did not wish
> those remaining behind to be at the
> mercy of the Emigrants. Besides for-
> eigners are resorting to that Country,
> and it is uncertain what turn things
> may take there.[87]

Madison should have had the last word in the debate over the admission of new States. It should have
been his as a result of the debate with Gouverneur
Morris on July 11. In this debate, Morris supported
his earlier position by again predicting that "if the
Western people get the power into their hands they
will ruin the Atlantic interests."[88] Madison simply
could not be certain of this. With regard to the Western States, he said "He was clear & firm in opinion
that no unfavorable distinctions were admissible
either in point of justice or policy." As a clincher,
he said he could not imagine it would be possible, as
Morris apparently did, to determine "the human character by the points of the compass."[89] On the other hand,
Madison did not reckon with what a determined, if not
slippery, character he was dealing with in Gouverneur
Morris. On September 8 a committee of five was appointed, and charged with the task of producing a constitution out of the agreed resolutions of the Convention. Morris was a member of this group, called a Committee of Style, as were William Samuel Johnson of Connecticut, Alexander Hamilton, James Madison, and Rufus
King of Massachusetts. Morris was selected to do the
writing for the Committee, and as Madison said, "a
better choice could not have been made, as the performance of the task proved." He also said that in the
performance of the task of actually drafting the finished Constitution "there was sufficient room for the

talents and taste stamped by the author on the face of it."[90]

Gouverneur Morris himself later explained how he managed to stamp his talents and taste on the part of the Constitution dealing with the admission of new states. The Constitutional provision simply says that "new states may be admitted by the Congress into this Union," and there is no mention of equality or inequality. At the time of the Louisiana Purchase the question was put to Morris as to "whether the Congress can admit, as a new State, territory, which did not belong to the United States when the Constitution was made?" His answer was no. Morris went on to explain,

> I always thought that, when we should acquire Canada and Louisiana it would be proper to govern them as provinces, and allow them no voice in our councils. In wording the third section of the fourth article, I went as far as circumstances would permit to establish the exclusion. Candor obliges me to add my belief that had it been more pointedly expressed, a strong opposition would have been made.[91]

The admission of new states, while important as an issue in the framing of the Constitution, was probably not as important as some of the other issues such as proprotional representation, which pitted the large states against the small, and the secrecy rule, which so infuriated Thomas Jefferson, and caused trouble with the likes of Luther Martin of Maryland and Ben Franklin of Pennsylvania. There was still another issue, however, that was not highlighted in the debates, but was of overwhelming importance. This was the use of force. The Congress of the Confederation is said to have had a plentitude of powers, but no real power. How could this defect be remedied? What was the proposal of the founding fathers? This was far more important than anything else in the Constitution. If the problem could not be solved it would make a mockery of the Constitution.

To the founding fathers it was axiomatic that the sanction of coercive force of the government should operate against the states. Accordingly, this was provided for in both the Virginia and New Jersey plans. The former stipulated that the new government should

139

have the power "to call forth the force of the Union agst. any member of the Union failing to fulfill its duty under the articles thereof," and the latter in its Article 6 provided that the federal executive should be authorized "to call forth ye power of the Confederated States, or so much thereof as may be necessary to enforce and compel obedience to such Acts, or an observance of such Treaties."[92] This was not a new line of reasoning for Madison. In a letter to Jefferson on April 16, 1781, he referred to sanctions against a state, and made the naive suggestion "that the imposition of simple naval blockades against recalcitrant states would render any exertion of force relatively painless."[93]

The use of force against a state as a remedy for the "great defect" of the Confederation was not an idea that prevailed for very long in the Virginia delegation. Introduced on May 29 as part of the original package, George Mason of Virginia struck it down on May 30. He differentiated between a federation of states and a confederation by pointing out that in the latter it was permissable to use force against a state, but in the former it was not, that in that case the force of law, i.e. the sanction, would be against the individuals who broke the law, not against the state. What Mason said was "that the present confederation was not only deficient in not providing for coersion & punishment agst. delinquent States; but argued very cogently that punishment could not in the nature of things be executed on the States collectively, and therefore that such a Govt. was necessary as could directly operate on individuals, and would punish those only whose guilt required it."[94]

This was a wholly new concept of governemnt, and the following day (May 31) Madison himself embraced it. When the "use of force" provision in the original Virginia plan came up for consideration, Madison said,

> that the more he reflected on the use
> of force, the more he doubted the prac-
> ticability, the justice and the effi-
> cacy of it when applied to people col-
> lectively and not individually. -- A
> Union of the States (containing such an
> ingredient) seemed to provide for its
> own destruction. The use of force agst.

140

a State, would look more like a declaration of war, than an inflicting of punishment, and would probably be considered by the party attacked as a dissolution of all previous compacts by which it might be bound. He hoped that such a system would be framed as might render this recourse unnecessary, and moved that the clause be postponed. This motion was agreed to nem. con.[95]

A week later, to be exact on June 8, Madison again found occasion to comment on the impracticality of a sanction that involved the use of force against a state. "Was such a remedy eligible? was it practicable?" he asked. "Could the national resources, if extended to the utmost enforce a national decree agst. Massts. abetted perhaps by several of her neighbours?" His answer was, "It wd. not be possible. A: small proportion of the Community in a compact situation, acting on the defensive, and at one of its extremities might at any time bid defiance to the National authority. Any Govt. for the U. States formed on the supposed practicability of using force agst. the (unconstitutional proceedings) of the States, wd. prove as visionary & fallacious as the Govt. of congs."[96]

Madison never changed his view that the use of force against a state would not be practical. After the adjournment of the Convention, he wrote to Thomas Jefferson (October 24, 1787), telling him of his thoughts on the subject. "A *voluntary* observance of the Federal law by all the members," Madison said, "could never be hoped for. A *compulsive* one could evidently never be reduced to practice, and if it could, involved equal calamities to the innocent & the guilty, the necessity of a military force both obnoxious & dangerous, and in general a scene resembling much more a civil war than the administration of a regular Government. Hence was embraced the alternative of a Government which instead of operating on the States, should operate without their intervention on the individuals composing them; and hence the change in the principle and proportion of representation."[97]

Madison had a strong supporter in the Convention on the use of force against a state, or rather on the impracticality of such use, in the person of Alexander Hamilton of New York. In the delivery of his plan of union on June 18, he began by ticking off a list of

the great and essential principles he considered necessary in any good government. Number 4 of these (it
should have been higher) was the element of force. On
this subject, Hamilton said,

> 4. *Force* by which may be understood a *coer-
> tion of laws* or *coertion of arms.*
> Congs. have not the former except in a
> few cases. In particular States, this
> coercion is nearly sufficient; tho' he
> held it in most cases not entirely so.
> A certain portion of military force is
> absolutely necessary in large commu-
> nities. Massts. is now feeling this
> necessity & making provision for it.
> But how can this force be exerted on
> the States collectively. It is impos-
> sible. It amounts to a war between the
> parties. Foreign powers also will not
> be idle spectators. They will inter-
> pose, the confusion will increase, and
> a dissolution of the Union will en-
> sue.[98]

Hamilton not only gave Madison strong support in
the Federal Convention, but also in the bitter fight
over the ratification of the Constitution. And in a
pivotal state--New York. Accordingly, in number XVI of
The Federalist papers, Hamilton argued,

> whoever considers the populousness and
> strength of several of these States sin-
> gly at the present juncture, and looks
> forward to what they will become even
> at the distance of half a century, will
> at once dismiss as idle and visionary
> any scheme which aims at regulating
> their movements by laws to operate upon
> them in their collective capacities,
> and to be executed by a coercion appli-
> cable to them in the same capacities.

Hamilton went on to appeal to history, and particularly to the history of confederations, to support
his argument that laws could not be enforced by taking
action against states. "The principle of legislation
for sovereign states, supported by military coercion,"
he said, "has never been found effectual. It has
rarely been attempted to be employed, but against

weaker members; and in most instances attempts to coerce the refractory and disobedient have been the sig-
nals of bloody wars, in which one-half of the confederacy has displayed its banners against the other half."

George Mason of Virginia was not content with leading the way in the Federal Convention on the vital issue of sanctions, that is in opposition to the use of
force against a state, and on June 20, after the presentation of the New Jersey plan, took issue with the
provision in the plan for the use of force against
states that failed to live up to their federal obligations. Referring to the author of the plan, William
Paterson, Mason said,

> it was acknowledged by (Mr. Patterson)
> that his plan could not be enforced
> without military coertion. Does he con-
> sider the force of this concession. The
> most jarring elements of nature, fire &
> water themselves are not more incompat-
> ible than such a mixture of civil liber-
> ty and military execution. Will the
> militia march from one State to another,
> in order to collect the arrears of
> taxes from the delinquent members of
> the Republic? Will they maintain an
> army for this purpose? Will not the
> citizens of the invaded State assist
> one another till they rise as one Man,
> and shake off the Union altogether. Re-
> bellion is the only case in which (the
> military force of the State can be
> properly) exerted agst. its Citizens.
> In one point of view he was struck with
> horror at the prospect of recurring to
> this expedient. To punish the non-pay-
> ment of taxes with death, was a sever-
> ity not yet adopted by despotism itself;
> yet this unexampled cruelty would be
> mercy compared to a military collection
> of revenue, in which the bayonet could
> make no discrimination between the inn-
> ocent and the guilty.[99]

Oliver Ellsworth of Connecticut was not one of the
like-minded when it came to the establishment of a
strong central government at the expense of the states,
but he was also not part of the lunatic-fringe in the

Convention opposed to everything the nationalists wanted. In fact, he was very much of a nationalist on the basic issue of coercion, and supported the Constitution in the fight over ratification. He said that no man could deny that a coercive principle was necessary in a government, and the only question was whether it should be "a coercion of law, or a coercion of arms?" Continuing, he allied himself with the nationalists, and said, "I am for a coercion of law --that coercion which acts only upon delinquent individuals. The Constitution does not attempt to coerce sovereign bodies, states, in their political capacity. No coercion is applicable to such bodies, but that of an armed force. If we should attempt to execute the laws of the Union by sending an armed force against a delinquent state, it would involve the good and bad, the innocent and guilty, in the same calamity."[100] To illustrate the point, which was a key one in the debate over the ratification of the Constitution, he took issue with Luther Martin of Maryland, one of the leading anti-nationalists, and said that the principle he espoused was "tyrannic," namely "that where a State refused to comply with a requisition of Congress for money, that an army should be marched into its bowels, to fall indiscriminately upon the property of the innocent and the guilty, instead of having it collected as the Constitution proposed, by the mild and equal operation of laws."[101]

Madison was very wrong on May 30 when he thought he had disposed of the "use of force" issue in the deliberations of the Convention. The argument on this occasion was with the small-state men who thought they should have an equal voice in the upper house in order to protect themselves in cases where the central government would act on them instead of on individuals. Madison denied there were any such cases. He challenged the small-state men to cite "a single instance in which the Genl. Govt. was not to operate on the people individually," and said "the practicality of making laws, with coercive sanctions, for the States as political bodies, has been exploded on all hands."[102] However, the last word on this important subject was probably spoken by Oliver Ellsworth when he observed that "if the United States and the individual states will quarrel, if they want to fight, they may do it, and no frame of government can possibly prevent it."[103]

The sovereign and independent States of America were hard to convince that the diplomatic union of the Articles was not the safest and best for them in the long run. Under it a hard war had been won, and a generous peace secured that was still lasting. Many feared the proposed new Constitution because of the centralization of power in a federal government, all of which would be at the expense of the States, and the absence of anything remotely resembling a Bill of Rights. After all, the Revolution had been fought to free the American people from the arbitrary rule of a King and Parliament, neither of which had ever had the power that the proposed Constitution would vest in the President and Congress, to say nothing about how the new Federal Judiciary might operate against the States. On the other hand, with a Washington and a Franklin giving their full support and endorsement to the new order of things, how could any reasonable man doubt that the proposed Constitution would be an improvement over the Articles of Confederation. Anyway, wasn't it time for a change? Wasn't it almost silly to view with alarm the motives of Washington and Franklin?

Unless the words of John Dickinson of Delaware and Charles Pinckney of South Carolina are forgotten, that the small states will dismiss their scruples and concur in the national plan, if given an equal voice in the new government, the outcome of the ratifying conventions was something of a surprise. The small states did not hang back as they had done in the Convention prior to July 16, but took the lead in ratifying conventions in a way to put the large states to shame. Delaware, the smallest state to be represented in the Convention, acted first, and unanimously ratified the Constitution on December 7, 1787. Eleven days later, on December 18, New Jersey concurred with another unanimous vote. Two weeks later, Georgia cast the third unanimous vote, and on January 9, Connecticut swung into line with the other small states, voting to ratify by an impressive majority of 128 to 40. This was followed by Maryland's vote of 63 to 11 in favor of the Constitution. However, all this proved was that Dickinson and Pinckney had been right. It did not prove that the small states could force the large ones to give the new government a fair trial. And without the large states, particularly Virginia, and to a lesser extent, but not much, New York, Massachusetts, and Pennsylvania, the union would have been a hollow shell. How did the voting go in the large states?

145

It started off well in Pennsylvania. Well, that is from the point of view of the Federalists, as the nationalists now called themselves, but not so well from the point of view of the Anti-federalists, which was what the opposition came to be called. The Constitution had been signed on September 17, and had been transmitted to Congress on the same day by letter from the President of the Federal Convention. On September 20 the proposed new Constitution was laid before Congress. It considered it on the 26th and 27th, and on the 28th resolved to send it to the States. The following day an express rider arrived in Philadelphia, and the Federalists were waiting for him. They demanded that a state convention be called immediately to act on the subject. The Anti-federalist minority objected to being rushed, and when they saw they were getting nowhere, some of the members absented themselves so there would not be a quorum. This didn't work either, however, because a Federalist mob dragged enough of them to the State House to make a quorum, and kept them there by force until an act had been passed calling for a state convention. At the convention, the Federalists also had their way, and Pennsylvania became the first large state to ratify the Constitution. This was December 15. The vote was 46 to 23.

The next large state to vote on the Constitution was Massachusetts. Its convention met on January 9, 1788, and on January 25 one of the delegates, Amos Singletary spoke for the Anti-federalists when he said, "these lawyers, and men of learning, and monied men, that talk so finely and gloss over matters so smoothly, to make us poor illiterate people, swallow down the pill, expect to get into Congress themselves; they expect to be the managers of this constitution, and get all the power and all the money into their own hands, and then they will swallow up all uf little folk, like the great *Leviathan*, Mr. President: yes, just as the whale swallowed up *Jonah*."[104] He was answered by a farmer delegate, Jonathan Smith, obviously with Federalist sympathies, who said he was not of that mind concerning "monied men, and men of learning." Delegate Smith continued,

> I dont think the worse of the constitution because lawyers and men of learning, and monied men are fond of it. I dont suspect that they want to get into congress and abuse their power. I am

not of such a jealous make. They that are honest men themselves are not apt to suspect other people. I dont know why our constituents have not as good a right to be jealous of us, as we seem to be of the congress; and I think those gentlemen who are so very suspicious that as soon as a man gets into power he turns rogue, had better look at home.[105]

This little dispute aside, in Massachusetts all the big guns were on the side of the Federalists, including a former governor, James Bowdin, three judges of the supreme court, 15 members of the senate, and three generals of the Continental Army, as well as three delegates to the Federal Convention. But a majority of the delegates, including those from Maine, probably belonged to the Anti-federalists, and as a result the Federalists played for time to give them an opportunity to pick up more votes. Two of the big names that were won over during the course of debate were Samuel Adams and John Hancock. The latter was governor of the state at the time, and what may have persuaded him was the prospect that he might be the logical candidate for President, if Virginia did not ratify the Constitution. In any case, when it came down to a vote on February 6, the Federalists won by a majority of 187 over 168. There was nothing comfortable about this margin, but it was an important victory, nevertheless. The second large state was now in the Federalist fold, and with the six small states; the stage was now set for New Hampshire (another small state) to click in the Constitution by becoming the ninth State.

While this issue lay suspended, the next big state to vote on the Constitution was Virginia, and there it was nip and tuck all the way. The legislature had called for elections to a convention in March 1788, and had set the date for the convention as June 2, 1788. Previously, in the Pennsylvania convention, James Wilson had told the delegates that the choices before them were several. They could consolidate the whole under a unitary government, which would mean lumping the American people into one solid mass, after the fashion of a government Hamilton and some others had favored in the Convention; they could let the Confederation die a natural death as it was on the verge of doing, which would have the effect of Balkanizing

147

the entire continent; they could erect two or more confederacies in accordance with the interests of the great sections of the country, on any kind of an axis they desired, East-West, North-South, or the more traditional one of New England, Southern, and Middle states; and they could ratify the Constitution presented to them, which would give the federal principle an opportunity to unify the continent. Now that the Virginia convention was met to debate the Constitution the issues were essentially the same, the only difference being that it was now apparent a race was on to be the ninth state. The New Hampshire convention had reconvened on June 17, and it was altogether possible that it would be the ninth state. Even if it turned out to be this way, it would still leave the question open, could a Union survive that did not include Virginia and New York, to say nothing of North Carolina and Rhode Island?

Looking at the geography of the 13 states, it almost goes without saying that New York and Virginia were essential elements of any kind of an effective Union, and that without them no continental union could hope to survive. But it was not at all certain at this time that either one or both would ratify the new Constitution. The governors of both states were opposed to it, though not in the same degree. New York's Governor George Clinton had been an Anti-federalist from the beginning, having done everything he could to sabotage the Federal Convention, and Governor Edmund Randolph of Virginia was so dissatisfied with the Constitution as it came out of the Federal Convention that he refused to sign it. Added to this was the fact that many other leading Virginians, including the lordly George Mason and the popular Patrick Henry, were also opposed to the Constitution. The reasons the two governors were opposed to the Constitution were not the same, but they agreed on the essentials, that the proposed new government should not be put into effect until a series of amendments had been added, or better still, a second convention convened to take into consideration all the objections to the Constitution that had come up in the State conventions.

In the Virginia convention, Patrick Henry led the attack on the Constitution. Following his opening blast, Governor Randolph surprised everybody, including George Mason, his fellow non-signer, by coming out in favor of the Constitution. He said, "as with me the only question has ever been, between previous and

148

subsequent amendments, so will I express my apprehensions that the postponement of this Convention to so late a day, has extinguished the probability of the former without inevitable ruin to the Union, and the Union is the anchor of our political salvation."[106]

The impact of Randolph's volte-face was like a bombshell in the Convention. After making allowances for the weight of Madison's influence, and for his skills as a debater and as a manager, there is still not much doubt that Governor Randolph's shift of position was the decisive factor in determining the outcome of the Virginia convention. The governor was a very popular and influential figure in the state, and had a host of friends in all walks of life and in all geographic localities. His sudden switch to the Federalist ranks offset Henry's enormous eloquence, and robbed the Anti-federalists of the majority position they undoubtedly held at the opening of the Convention. More than that. Randolph was a towering influence in the continuous lobbying that went on behind the scenes, and was the point man for the contacts with Robert and Gouverneur Morris of Pennsylvania, who were in Richmond to help with the Federalist cause. Randolph was also the point of contact with his opposite number in New York, Governor Clinton, who, before it was known that Randolph would switch sides, had made a formal written proposal, in diplomatic language, that the two states act together to demand that a second convention be called, or at least that their conditional amendments be accepted in advance. Randolph deliberately suppressed the letter until it was too late to have any effect on the voting in Virginia. Accordingly, it changed no votes, and when the final tally was taken the Federalists won by a margin of 89 to 79. The vote was taken on June 26.

The New York convention met on June 17. By this time it was clear that eight states had already ratified the Constitution, and that only one more was needed to bring the new government into effect. It was also clear that this could take place any time, since the New Hampshire convention was reconvening that very day, and the Virginia convention was already in session, having been convened on June 2. Under the new circumstances, what was the proper policy for the Empire State? Up to this time, policy had not been difficult, but now was it complicated by the ninth State problem? At first, George Clinton was not willing to admit that this was so. He had been governor for 11 years, and for 11 years he had been opposed to any kind of a "more perfect union." His hand-picked delegates to the Federal Convention had followed his lead in that body, and when they failed to halt the Virginia steamroller, had reported to the governor, disregarding the rule of secrecy, exactly what he wanted to hear, that the drift in the Dark Conclave was toward a consolidated government with the complete annihilation of the states as a primary objective. Armed with this knowledge, Clinton refused to change his policy, and therefore when the New York convention met on June 17, it is not surprising that it was packed by an Anti-federalist majority of at least three to two among its membership of 64. Which raises an interesting question: what was the miracle of delivery whereby between June 17 and July 26, this huge majority was changed into a minority of 30 to 27?

The miracle of delivery was the march of events. Anti-federalist strength in New York lay in the entire mass of interior counties, and the Federalist strength was in New York City, and certain strips radiating from that center. Alexander Hamilton took the lead in opposing the Clinton machine in New York, and was ably supported by James Madison in Virginia and also by John Jay in New York. Together, Hamilton, Madison, and Jay were the authors of 85 articles and essays on federalism that appeared in certain New York journals from the fall of 1787 to the spring of 1788, and they undoubtedly had some impact on the voters between June 17 and July 26. But this was not all, by any means. The most critical new issue during the period was first the imminence and then the certainty of the ratification of the Constitution, with or without New York. Robert Livingston, an ardent Federalist, sounded a warning in his opening speech to the New York convention on June 19. He did not tell the delegates anything they did not know, but pointed out very clearly that the New York ports were on islands close to New Jersey and Connecticut, which might be unfriendly to New York in the event of war, and to the northeast lay Vermont which was already unfriendly. He then mentioned the British posts to the northwest, and the hostile Indians. Finally, he "shewed that in the case of domestic war, Hudson River, that great source of our wealth, would also be that of our weakness; by the intersection of the state, and the difficulty we should find in bringing one part to support the other."[107] This took on a new importance on June 24, when news of New Hampshire's ratification reached New York, and really peaked when the news of Virginia's ratification reached New York on July 2. At the same time there were rumors that if Clinton persisted in his folly of holding out against what was now the certainty of union, the southern counties might break away from the north, in order to avoid being left out of the union.

These, then, were the reasons for the dramatic change in the voting in the New York Convention between July 17 and July 26. The New York state legislature, on February 5, 1789, explained the *volte-face* by saying that "an invincible reluctance to separate from our sister states" was the basic reason for agreeing to the ratification "without stipulating for previous amendments."[108] Thus it was that the new ship of state was launched without any dragging anchors, save only for Rhode Island and North Carolina. It was a fitting climax for 148 years of straining to effect "a more perfect union" in this part of the world.

The American solution to the problem of *e pluribus unum* had its beginning in 1639 because that was the year in which three towns on the western bank of the Connecticut River established the Fundamental Orders of Connecticut, which lay the basis in a written covenant for the state of that name, and the year 1787 is appropriate for the climax of the movement because it was the year in which the 13 sovereign states of America entered into another written covenant transforming their league of friendship into a more perfect union that was appropriately styled the United States of America. During this period of a century and a half the relations of colony to colony and of state to state were of an international character. Those men were diplomats who were formed in that century and a half of negotiations to settle boundary disputes, to reach some *moduc vivendi* on conflicting trade interests, and to negotiate leagues of offense and defense. Every international problem that faced the United States in the period after the adoption of the Constitution had been dealt with in one form or another during the first period of the national existence. Even the methods used were never fundamentally changed. Americans continued under the Constitution in the same ways they had used while they were colonies, in the same ways they had used as representatives of separate and independent states.

None of this was lost on the more thoughtful members of the Federal Convention. That is why Benjamin

151

Franklin, the acknowledged dean of the delegates, and probably the wisest man in the Convention, said what he did about the prospects for the future on the last day of the Convention. According to Madison's *Notes*,

> The members then proceeded to sign the instrument. Whilst the last members were signing it, Doctr. Franklin looking towards the Presidents Chair, at the back of which a rising sun happened to be painted, observed to a few members near him, that Painters had found it difficult to distinguish in their art a rising from a setting sun. I have, said he, often and often, in the course of the Session, and the vicissitudes of my hopes and fears as to its issue, looked at that behind the President without being able to tell whether it was rising or setting. But now at length I have the happiness to know that it is a rising and not a setting Sun."[109]

But this was not all. On October 22, 1787, Franklin penned a note to Ferdinand Grand saying, "I send you enclos'd the propos'd new Federal Constitution for these States. I was engag'd 4 Months of the last Summer in the Convention that form'd it. It is now sent by Congress to the several States for their Confirmation. If it succeeds, I do not see why you might not in Europe carry the Project of good Henry the 4th into Execution, by forming a Federal Union and One Grand Republick of all its different States & Kingdoms; by means of a like Convention; for we had many Interests to reconcile."[110] James Wilson, also of Pennsylvania, was of the same mind. Speaking on the floor of his State Convention on December 11, he also referred to the grand project of the good King Henry IV of France, and said that now is accomplished what was only in contemplation by the French monarch--"a system of government for large and respectable dominions, united and bound together, in peace, under a superintending head, by which all their differences may be accommodated, without the destruction of the human race."[111]

152

FOOTNOTES -- CHAPTER III

[1]Francis Newton Thorpe, *The Federal and State Constitutions, Colonial Charters, and Other Organic Laws* (Washington: Government Printing Office, 1909), I, 5-6.

[2]James Brown Scott, *Sovereign States and Suits* (New York: The New York University Press, 1925), 39.

[3]*Ibid.*, 55.

[4]*Ibid.*

[5]James Brown Scott, *The United States of America: A Study in International Relations* (New York: Oxford University Press, 1920), 219.

[6]*Ibid.*, 231.

[7]*Ibid.*, 233.

[8]*Ibid.*, 234.

[9]Max Farrand, *Records of the Federal Convention of 1787* (New Haven: Yale University Press, 1923), I, 316-17.

[10]James Brown Scott, *The United States of America: A Study in INTERNATIONAL Relations, op. cit.*, 231.

[11]Paul H. Smith, ed., *Letters of the Delegates to Congress* (Washington, D.C., 1976-), 523.

[12]*Ibid.*

[13]*The Federalist*, No. VII (Hamilton).

[14]James Brown Scott, *Sovereign States and Suits, op. cit.*, 42.

[15]*Ibid.*, 46-47.

[16]*Ibid.*, 58.

[17]James Brown Scott, *The United States of America: A Study in International Organization* (New York: Oxford University Press, 1920), 55.

[18]Jack N. Rakove, *The Beginnings of National Politics* (New York: Alfred A. Knopf, 1979), 383.

[19]Homer Carey Hockett, *The Constitutional History of the United States 1776-1826* (New York: The Macmillan Company, 1939), 185-86.

[20]Paul H. Smith, *op. cit.*, 523.

[21]James Brown Scott, *The United States of America: A Study in International Organization*, *op. cit.*, 55.

[22]*Ibid.*, 56.

[23]Homer Carey Hocket, *op. cit.*, 198.

[24]James Brown Scott, *The United States of America: A Study in International Organization*, *op. cit.*, 57-58.

[25]*Ibid.*, 147

[26]John Corbin, *Two Frontiers of Freedom* (New York: Charles Scribner's Sons, 1940), 144.

[27]James Brown Scott, *The United States of America: A Study in Interantional Organization*, *op. cit.*, 312.

[28]John Fiske, *The Critical Period of American History* (Boston: Houghton Mifflin Company, 1888), 146.

[29]James Brown Scott, *The United States of America: A Study in International Organization*, *op. cit.*, 147.

[30]Helen Hill Miller, *George Mason: Gentleman Revolutionary* (Chapel Hill: The University of North Carolina Press, 1975), 234.

[31]Clinton Rossiter, *1797-- The Grand Convention* (New York: The Macmillan Company, 1966), 124.

[32]Max Farrand, *op. cit.*, 409.

[33]Clinton Rossiter, *op. cit.*, 161.

[34]James Brown Scott, *The United States of America: A Study in International Organization, op. cit.*, 148.

[35]Max Farrand, *op. cit.*, 575.

[36]*Documents Illistrative of the Formation of the Union of the American States* (Washington: Government Printing Office, 1927), 114.

[37]Max Farrand, *op. cit.*, 28.

[38]*Ibid.*, 479.

[39]*Ibid.*, 191.

[40]*Ibid.*, 73.

[41]*Ibid.*, III, 76.

[42]*Ibid.*, IV, 65.

[43]*Ibid.*, III, 76.

[44]Carl Van Doren, *The Great Rehearsal* (New York: The Viking Press, 1948), 129.

[45]Max Farrand, *op. cit.*, III, 59.

[46]*Ibid.*, III, 86-87.

[47]*Ibid.*, III, 82.

[48]*Ibid.*, II, 648.

[49]*Ibid.*, I, xii.

[50]*Ibid.*, III, 426.

[51]*Ibid.*, I, xii.

[52]*Ibid.*, III, 447.

[53]*Ibid.*, III, 447-48.

[54]*Ibid.*, 448.

[55]*Ibid.*, I, xvi.

[56]*Ibid.*, I, 500.

[57]*Ibid.*, 501.

[58]*Ibid.*

[59]*Ibid.*, I, 501.

[60]*Ibid.*, 492.

[61]*Ibid.*, I, 493.

[62]*Ibid.*, 528.

[63]*Ibid.*, I, 530.

[64]*Ibid.*, 531.

[65]*Ibid.*, I, 532.

[66]*Ibid.*, I, 260.

[67]*Ibid.*, I, 242.

[68]*Ibid.*, I, 255.

[69]*Ibid.*, I, 301.

[70]*Ibid.*, 89.

[71]*Ibid.*, I, 323.

[72]*Ibid.*, III, 474-75.

[73]*Ibid.*, III, 272.

[74]*Ibid.*, 94.

[75]John Lukacs, *Outgrowning Democracy* (New York: Doubleday & Company, 1984), 251.

[76]Max Farrand, *op. cit.*, I, 605.

[77]*Ibid.*, III, 2-3.

[78]Jerome J. Nadelhaft, "The Democratization of Revolutionary South Carolina," in Ronald Hoffman and Peter J. Albert's *Sovereign States in an Age of Uncertainty* (Charlottesville: The University Press of Virginia, 1981), 68.

[79]Max Farrand, *op. cit.*, I, 541.

[80] *Ibid.*, xx.

[81] *Ibid.*, 559-60.

[82] *Ibid.*, I, 454.

[83] *Ibid.*, I, 486.

[84] *Ibid.*, I, 322.

[85] *Ibid.*, I, 605.

[86] *Ibid.*, III, 3.

[87] *Ibid.*, II, 3.

[88] *Ibid.*, I, 583.

[89] *Ibid.*, 584.

[90] *Ibid.*, III, 499

[91] Homer Carey Hockett, *op. cit.*, 185-86

[92] Max Farrand, *op. cit.*, I, 245.

[93] Jack N. Rakove, *op. cit.*, 293.

[94] Max Farrand, *op. cit.*, I, 34.

[95] *Ibid.*, I, 54.

[96] *Ibid.*, I, 164-65.

[97] James Brown Scott, *The United States of America: A Study in International Organization, op. cit.*, 204.

[98] Max Farrand , I, 284.

[99] *Ibid.*, I, 399-40.

[100] *Ibid.*, III, 241.

[101] *Ibid.*, III, 272.

[102] *Ibid.*, II, 9.

[103] *Ibid.*, III, 241.

[104] Carl Van Doren, *op. cit.*, 197-98.

157

[105]*Ibid.*, 199.

[106]Helen Hill Miller, *op. cit.*, 289.

[107]Carl Van Doren, *op. cit.*, 2331

[108]Charles A. Beard, *An Economic Interpretation of the Constitution of the United States* (New York. The Macmillan Company, 1936), 230.

[109]Max Farrand, *op. cit.*, II, 648.

[110]*Ibid.*, II, 131.

[111]James Brown Scott, *Sovereign States and Suits*, *op. cit.*, 80.

Book Two

THE STRATEGIC HERITAGE

CHAPTER IV

THE INDIAN NATIONS

The subject of Indians is as remote from the
average American city-dweller today as the subject of
the manners and social customs of any of the strange
beings of Alice in Wonderland or Grimm's Fairy Tales.
Some picture may arise in his mind of a train of covered wagons plodding wearily westward to the strains
of "Oh Susannah!" plunked from a banjo by some small
tow-headed boy with freckles. He may see a tall, hawk-
faced scout, with an antiquated long rifle, shading
his eyes against the setting sun, wheeling his incon-
gruous pinto cow-pony suddenly to give the alarm of
"Injuns," upon which the covered wagons wheel about into a close circle, with the cattle, women and children
inside, while bearded pioneers open a dropping fire on
the war-whooping dusky demons of the Plains. Others
will think of Indians as people living in adobe
pueblos, performing Zuni, Hopi, or Navajo ritual cere-
monies or snake dances; or they may think of them in
connection with the survival of Mexican art. Some will
remember comic stories of a bewildered Indian owner of
an Oklahoma oil well, buying himself a Packard or
Rolls Royce, running out far and fast across the
plains, to walk back and buy another when his gasoline
gives out. Perhaps someone remembers the tales of
Fenimore Cooper. None, surely remembers William Gil-
more Sims and his fascinating romances of early Carolina days, broken, dog-eared and yellow with much read-
ing before they got fully into circulation over a hundred years ago.

If anything in particular is known about our Indian relations in the early days of our history it is
probably the story about Captain John Smith and John
Rolfe, that Smith was saved by "Princess" Pocohontas,
daughter of the "King" or "Emperor" "Powhatan, and
that all or most of the "First Families of Virginia"

159

are descended from Pocohontas' marriage to John Rolfe in 1614. The efforts to debunk the dramatic rescue of Captain Smith by the Indian princess have themselves been largely discredited. By Indian custom, adoption into a tribe was quite a regular procedure. Francis Parkman recalled the fate of a pious Frenchman, Rene Cuillerier, who, though a captive of the Iroquois, refused to be intimidated by the torture death of one of his companions, and "declared that they could wring from him no cry of pain, but that throughout he ceased not to pray for their conversion. The witness himself expected the same fate, but an old squaw happily adopted him, and thus saved his life."[1] One thing that is so generally and firmly accepted as to defy contradiction is that we behaved like beasts to the Indians, cheated them, debauched them and murdered them atrociously, and that our relations with them show no redeeming act anywhere. The purchase of Manhattan Island from the Indians for about $24.00 in trinkets to found the settlement of New Amsterdam is often cited as a case in point. Actually, the Director-General of the Dutch company was the one who got swindled in this instance. Peter Minuit bought the land from a tribe of Indians, the Manhates, who laid no claim to the land in question. However, it is true, of course, that the Indians were defrauded on many occasions, and cheated out of what rightfully belonged to them, but the full implication of that fact does not follow, that chicanery, malice, and greed characterized all our relations with the Indians.

In the beginning, the leading men in nearly all the various English colonies in America were divided in their attitude toward the original inhabitants. The division was one of principle, not merely one of expediency. The same problem with the same division was present in Mexico. Las Casas, the Dominican Monk, and Don Antonio de Mendoze, the first civilian viceroy, saw desirable qualities in the Indians which should be assimilated into the body politic, not annihilated. Las Casas, in his state papers, left on record his positive conviction that the Christian religion could not be developed on a sound basis in Mexico unless a native clergy were established into which the survivors of the Aztec and other tribal nobility could be assimilated by careful university training. On the other hand, the conquering military chiefs and feudal lords of the Spanish advocated the incorporation of the docile Indians as slave labor, and the complete annihilation of the hostile tribes.

In the early North American colonies a theory similar to the enlightened perspective of Las Casas and Don Antonio Mendoza held intermittent sway. The foundation of the oldest American colleges shows nearly everywhere some trace of this thought. Harvard College was founded in 1636, and one of the ideas underlying it was that it could be effective in convdrting and educating the Indians. One of the stated reasons for the founding of the College of William and Mary in 1693 was to provide free education for the Indians. As late as 1769 Dartmouth was founded with the idea of being instrumental in converting and educating Indians, and preaching the gospel to the Indians was one of the primary reasons for the founding of Georgetown College in 1789.

Intermarriage between whites and Indians was not a disgrace. It was encouraged as late as 1784 in the State of Virginia through the efforts of no less a personage than Patrick Henry who, as his biographer tells us:

> proposed to encourage, by a system of pecuniary bounties, the practice of marriage between members of the two races, believing that such ties, once formed, would be an inviolable pledge of mutual friendship, fidelity, and forbearance, and would gradually lead to the transformation of the Indians into a civilized and Christian people. His bill for this purpose elaborately drawn up, was carried through its second reading and "engrossed for its final passage," when, by his sudden removal from the floor of the House to the governor's chair, the measure was deprived of its all-conquering champion, and, on the reading, it fell a sacrifice to the Caucasian rage and scorn of the members[2]

Many other plans were bruited about in the search for a solution to the Indian problem. One of the most imaginative of these was the Fundamental Constitutions of Carolina--1669, a document drawn up by John Locke. This would have recreated in America the vanishing feudal world of England. It comtemplated drawing in the Indian population as partly free but with provision for permanent slavery. Slavery, however, was not

161

to be confined to Indians. White men and women might also be "leet-men" and "leet-women," and their children should be leet-men "to all generations." Locke even took an Indian title (cazique) as one of the titles of the English territorial nobility to be instituted in Carolina. Pertinent articles of the Fundamental Constitutions were:

> Twenty-two. In every signiory, barony, and manor, all the leet-men shall be under the jurisdiction of the respective lords of the said signiory, barony, or manor, without appeal from him. Nor shall any leet-man or leet-woman have liberty to go off from the land of their particular lord and live anywhere else, without license obtained from their said lord, under hand and seal

> Twenty-three. All the children of leet-men shall be leet-men, and so to all generations.[3]

Meanwhile, it was from their Indian neighbors that these first Englishmen learned to plant corn as it is still planted, to raise the various vegetables the Indians cultivated, and to plant and use the native tobacco. However, even before the development of the great staple products (tobacco, naval stores, rice, indigo, and later cotton), and in the very first place of importance, came the fur trade. The Indians were the source of that trade. Colonial founders, whether as Lords Proprietary, groups of religious dissenters, or chartered trading companies, were very much alike in that respect. All sought the conservation and extension of the fur trade. Friendly, stable relations with the native Indian nations were essential for that purpose alone, if for no other.

George Washington, later, knew and visited the "Queen Aliquippa," whose tribe lived on the banks of the "Yaghyaughane" River. He knew "Shingiss," the "King of the Delawares," and "Tanacharisson," "Half-King" of the Senecas, "so named because his sway over his subjects was not total, the Six Nations being their sovereign."[4] In other words, Tanacharisson was a vassal lord -- something that Englishmen of this period still understood. All those titles, "Queen," "Half-King," and "Emperor," all in current use since

162

the first formal settlements, should indicate that the newcomers were aware of some form of political organization among the natives of the continent not too dissimilar from those European forms they knew so well. Had they not recognized some native dignity and organized power, some visible though perhaps faint analogy to European ideas, they would hardly have troubled to apply and to record such definitely European titles.

One outstanding obstacles to the maintenance of friendly relations with the Indians lay in our manner of creating new settlements, and of throwing out protective frontiers beyond them. Even in those colonies where this was an orderly process, hostilities were likely to occur, and where it was conducted in a haphazard fashion or with cynical disregard of consequences it led to hostilities unavoidably. This was the case with the settlement of Jamestown in 1607.

Originally, the Indians were friendly, and willingly gave food to the needy settlers of Jamestown, but they gradually became less friendly, and then turned to open hostility. Apparently, the reason for this was the result of a decision on the part of the acting governor, Captain John Smith, to throw out two protective frontiers. He had on his hands a very unruly group of new settlers who, as John Marshall said, "were much fitter to spoil and ruin a Commonwealth, than to help to raise or maintain one." In any case, to continue from Marshall's account, Smith:

> after imprisoning the chief promoters of sedition, and thereby restoring regularity and obedience, he, for the double purpose of extending the colony, and of preventing the mischiefs to be apprehended from so many turbulent spirits collected in Jamestown, detached one hundred men to the falls of James River, under the command of West, and the same number to Nansemond, under that of Martin. These persons conducted their settlements with so little judgment, that they soon converted all the neighboring Indians into enemies. After losing several parties, they found themselves in absolute need of the support and direction of Smith. These were readily afforded.[5]

In Maryland, the first group of English settlers
obtained the cession of half an Indian village, moved
in, and lived over the first winter with reasonable
comfort until, in the following spring, the Indians
ceded the rest of the place, and moved back further.
The manor system of land division in Maryland provided
a more orderly system of frontier planning than in
many other colonies. The manor was the old English and
French unit of feudal land distribution. It was a
tract of six thousand acres, and in the Old World was
the Knight's Fee, the parcel of land from which a
Knight could maintain himself and a sufficient number
of armed men to perform his required duty to his overlord from whom he held the land. The Maryland manor
lord, with sufficient capital to develop such a tract,
was required to bring over or to send for settlers. He
brought farmers, skilled artisans, and mechanics to
make it self-sustaining, and brought them under contract or indenture, to work for him for a specified
number of years, without pay, in return for their passage money. At the end of that contract, he was obliged to grant a parcel of two hundred acres to each
of them, and to give to each a full supply of clothes,
weapons, tools, food, seed, and stock to see him
through until his first crop on his own land. That is
the reason the early Maryland records speak of colonists and settlers. There was a distinction: the settlers constituted the colonial frontier elements, but
the colonists were the founders.

In other colonies on the Atlantic seaboard, such
as Virginia, the frontiers were formed by the erection
of block houses and stockades from 25 to 50 miles out
beyond the settlements. These were not garrisoned nor
provisioned, but were built and left as rallying
places for the safety of the neighboring isolated
traders and adventurers. A new and dangerous element
of frontier building now entered the picture as foreigners were imported to settle along the fortified
line and bear the brunt of Indian attacks. The system
contained the origin, not only of continual disorders
between settlers and Indians, but of why it becams so
easy to detach frontiersmen from the later United
States. The intrigues of James Wilkinson and the so-
called conspiracy of Aaron Burr are cases in point.
The West was ripe for secession in the early days of
the Republic.

The foreigners we imported and settled on the frontiers were the ones who would be scalped and toma-hawked while the counter-attack was being prepared. Such strategy is an age-old custom of warfare, but it is not conducive to close harmony and brotherly love between those sacrificed and the general staff which directs the campaign from a safe distance. Nor is the bitterness likely to vanish even after a successful counter-attack wins the victory over the mutilated bodies of the sacrificial elements on the original frontiers. It is to this system that we should look for our tradition of ill treatment of the Indians. To the frontiersman, the only good Indian was a dead one. It was the statesman and the diplomat behind the lines who could afford other policies towards the Indians. The system of frontier-building really marked the beginning of the end of the planned population that Washington, Franklin, Jefferson and other early Americans had hoped and planned to establish.

An example showing the difference between these two attitudes can be drawn from the records of Pennsylvania in the year 1763. There, to quote Franklin, on the night of Wednesday, December 14, 1763, a band of fifty-seven men:

> came, all well mounted, and armed with Firelocks, Hangers, and Hatchets, having travelled through the Country in the night, to Conestogo Manor. There they surrounded the small Village of Indian Huts, and just at Break of Day broke into them all at once. Only three Men, two Women, and a young Boy, were found at home, the rest being out among the neighbouring White People, some to sell the Baskets, Brooms and Bowls they manufactured, and others on other Occasions. These poor defence-less creatures were immediately fired upon, stabbed, and Hatcheted to Death![6]

The Indians thus massacred were the ones who, on the first arrival of the English in Pennsylvania, had welcomed William Penn with presents, "and the whole Tribe entered into a Treaty of Friendship with the first Proprietor, William Penn, which was to last 'as long as the Sun should shine, or the Waters run in the Rivers.'" Consequently, the Governor of Pennsylvania issued a proclamation ordering the capture of the perpetrators of the crime and removing the remaining Indians to a place of greater safety. Less then two weeks later, however, the Paxton Boys, as they were called,

> again assembled themselves, and hearing that the remaining fourteen *Indians* were in the Workhouse at *Lancaster*, they suddenly appeared in that Town on the 27th of *December*. Fifty of them, armed as before, dismounting, went directly to the Workhouse, and by Violence broke open the Door, and entered with the utmost Fury in their Countenances. When the poor Wretches saw they had *no Protection* nigh, nor could possibly escape, and being without the least Weapon for Defence, they divided into their little Families, the Children clinging to the Parents; they fell on their Knees, protested their Innocence, declared their Love to the *English*, and that, in their whole Lives, they had never done them Injury; and in this Posture they all received the Hatchet! Men, Women, and little Children were every one inhumanly murdered in cold Blood![7]

The defense of the frontiersmen, as in countless other cases, was very simple; they had suffered horrible crimes at the hands of Indians, and to them a dead Indian was much safer than an uncertain Indian ally. The trouble with the system of justice was that local justices and juries were sympathetic toward the actions of the frontiersmen, and would not find them guilty. In this case, Franklin was outraged:

> If an *Indian* injures me, does it follow that I may revenge that Injury on all Indians? It is well known, that *Indians* are of different Tribes, Nations and Languages, as well as White People. In Europe, if the *French*, who are White People, should injure the Dutch, are they to revenge it on the *English*, because they too are White People? The only Crime of these poor Wretches seems to have been, that they

166

had a reddish-brown Skin, and black Hair; and some people of that Sort, it seems, had murdered some of our Relations. If it be right to kill Men for such a Reason, then, should any Man, with a Freckled Face and red Hair, kill a Wife or Child of mine, it would be right for me to revenge it, by killing all the freckled red-haired Men, Women, and children, I could afterwards anywhere meet with.[8]

The issue between the frontiersmen and the interior statesmen and diplomats on the subject of Indian policy was never resolved to the satisfaction of either. Franklin's view was representative of the establishment or the governing elite in the coastal colonies, that the people who "inhabit the frontiers are generally the refuse of both nations, often the worst morals and the least discretion, remote from the eye, the prudence, and the restraint of government."[9] George Mason of Virginia looked beyond the unsettled border problems with the Indians that the frontiersmen kept in such an uproar, and speculated on the role of the frontiersmen in disturbing our relations with the rival European claimants to empire in America, particularly on the southern and southwestern borders. Writing in 1784, he said that "we are every day threatened by the eagerness of our disorderly citizens for Spanish plunder and Spanish blood." Six weeks later he complained that there was no concealing the danger "of our being speedily embroiled with the nations contiguous to the United States, particularly the Spaniards, by the licentious and predatory spirit of some of our Western people."[10]

Going all the way back to the earliest days of the Virginia colony, the leading men had the same misgivings about the frontier elements of society. In 1612, Sir Thomas Dale punished those who "did Runne Away unto the Indjans" in a most severe manner. His punishments were: "Some he apointed to be hanged. Some burned. Some to be broken upon wheles, others to be staked and some to be shott to deathe." And even in Puritan Massachusetts, Increase Mather warned his flock about the frontier settlements, saying in his election sermon on May 23, 1677, that they were partially to blame for the Indian wars, since the frontier inhabitants "lived like Heathen, without Sabbaths, without the word and Prayer, which are moral duties

167

that all are bound to attend; and it is therefore in-
cumbent on the Magistrates to see that they do. People
are ready to run wild into the woods again, and to be
as heathenish as ever, if you do not prevent it."[11]

The frontier, then, was the one outstanding obstacle to friendly and orderly relations with the Indians.
But there was more at stake than that. Even if there
had been no conflict over policy toward the Indians,
our very existence could be threatened by the fact
that the Indians were always on the war-path against
each other, and the struggling English colonies could
be caught in the middle. These warring tribes were
knitted by kindred or common interest into allied
groups or nations. Indian nations occupying the same
general vast territory were linked into confederations
and even federations. These federations (and even the
confederations) were hostile to each other, and engaged constantly in age-old insatiable feuds with mere
intervals of peace (burying the hatchet) for trading
purposes. Such a condition was sufficiently similar to
the Europe the colonists knew to be clearly intelligible to them. But above all, it was not long before
the colonists felt the effects of Spanish intrigue behind these confederations to the south and west. To
the west and north, they gradually perceived another
powerful influence behind the Indians, the imperial
projects of the French empire and the machinations of
the French Jesuits. Indians, therefore, were not only
of primary commercial importance to the colonies, but
their private warfare might be a menace to their very
existence, and the danger was even more real if they
permitted the Indians to be used as pawns or allies
against them by the great European rivals of England,
in whom Americans recognized more quickly than Englishmen at home, the imperial rivals to the possession of
the continent.

With the realization that the Indians were important factors in the imperial rivalry for the possession of the American continent, colonial diplomacy entered another important field, American-Indian relations. A very real question, however, arises: were
these relations, in fact, diplomatic, considering the
accepted definitions of diplomacy? Bernard Fay expresses a general impression, and raises a legitimate
question, whether American-Indian relations could be
called diplomatic, in any proper use of the word, when
he says:

The agreements with the Indians were

168

made verbally over the peace pipe. Mere smoke! And the wind dissipated it all the more quickly, as, on these most important occasions, the Indians were given over to strong drink. On such occasions they became so thoroughly drunk that they had no idea what they were doing. It would have been a simple matter to persuade them to sign a treaty, but alas! they could neither read or write, which made the possibility of their observing a written covenant extremely uncertain.[12]

Benjamin Franklin is often used to confirm such opinions by his biting cynicism in speaking of an Indian apology for a breach of the peace caused by rum. "And, indeed," Franklin said, "if it be the design of Providence to extirpate these savages in order to make room for cultivators of the earth, it seems not improbable that rum may be the appointed means. It has already annihilated all the tribes who formerly inhabited the sea-coast."[13]

A Doctor's treatise might perhaps be written on the use of rum as an adjunct to American diplomacy. There was at least one celebrated Anglo-American treaty floated to success upon a sea of champagne, and Commodore Perry carried many barrels of whiskey with which to negotiate a treaty with Japan. The Congress of Vienna set such a standard of splendor in that respect that it led many a young man into the career in the hope that some day he might attend such another. But a treatise of that nature is not our point here. We are concerned only with the fact of a real American diplomacy, according to the established and recognized rules, which we practiced with the Indian nations.

The French and the Spanish were ever in the background in that continental field -- great explorers, great warriors and great empire builders, whom we did not fear at sea, but respected greatly on land. It was for our own empire building in the first place that we wanted written (not verbal) treaties with the Indians who could not read and write. We wanted them set down carefully according to the accepted rules, to produce if necessary to rivals who could read and write and who knew the rules. We wanted them also to use, on occasion, against our own sovereign who, still unaware of the full implications of the imperial game we were

169

playing, might yield something here that we did not
want to yield as a move in the narrow national game he
was playing in Europe. It is not to be supposed too
lightly that the Indians did not know what was in such
treaties, or that we simply made casual groups of Indians drunk and wrote down something to which we held
them pledged when they woke up with a splitting head-
The evidence is all against any such supposition.

The best evidence of what our ancesters did, and
why they did it, comes from themselves. While Franklin
records his cynically pious observations with regard
to the providential mission of rum, he also records in
his own treaty negotiations that the Indians were not
permitted to drink during the sessions and that they
understood very well what was being discussed and written down. What Franklin said was:

> As those people are extremely apt to
> get drunk, and when so, are very quar-
> relsome and disorderly, we strictly
> forbade the selling any liquor to them;
> and when they complain'd of this res-
> triction, we told them that if they
> would continue sober during the treaty,
> we would give them plenty of rum when
> business was over. They promised this,
> and they kept their promise, because
> they could get no liquor, and the trea-
> ty was conducted very orderly, and con-
> cluded to mutual satisfaction.[14]

In June, 1744, a very important Indian conference
was held at the frontier town of Lancaster, Pennsylvania, and a detailed Journal of the proceedings was
maintained by the Secretary of the Maryland delegation,
Witham Marshe. His account is both an official record
of the proceedings of the Conference, and a good narrative of the customs of the time, including some shrewd
and enlightening comments on the leading personalities
among the Indians, as well as the highly civilized manner in which we treated them, not as masters but as
negotiators, as diplomats. He also meets the issue of
rum head on, and comments on the point raised by Bernard Fay, whether the Indians had any idea what they
were doing in the give and take of treaty negotiations.
Marshe also had some unflattering things to say about
the conference site, the frontier outpost of Lancaster.
He said the town had been built only about 16 years
ago, and that:

170

the inhabitants are chiefly High-Dutch, Scotch-Irish, some few English families, and unbelieving Israelites, who deal very considerably in this place. The spirit of cleanliness has not as yet in the least troubled the major part of the inhabitants; for, in general, they are very great sluts and slovens. When they clean their houses, which, by the bye, is very seldom, they are unwilling to remove the filth far from themselves, for they place it close to their doors, which, in the summer time, breeds an innumerable quantity of bugs, fleas, and vermin.[15]

On the subject of rum and treaty-making, Marshe said that "the chiefs, who were deputed to treat with the English by their different nations, were very sober men, which is rare for an Indian to be so, if he can get liquor."[16] That last sentence is important. It is good evidence that while it might have been very easy to get what we wanted by making the Indians drunk, we kept them sober so that they would understand what they were doing. Marshe continued by saying:

They behaved very well during our stay amongst them, and sundry times refused drinking in a moderate way. Whenever they renew old tresties of friendship, or make any bargain about lands they sell to the English, they take great care to abstain from intoxicating drink for fear of being over-reached; but when they have finished their business, then some of them will drink without measure.[17]

Proceeding to communications and the language barrier, Marshe made it clear that at Lancaster the negotiations were not carried on in a lanugage the Indians did not understand. Nor were the negotiations carried on only by colonial interpreters with no check on them by the Indians. There were white men and white women too whose interests with the Indians were as important to them as their interests with the whites. There were also white men and white women who were full members of some Indian tribe and yet preserved their equally full contacts with the best colonial society. Catharine Montour is one of many such. She figured very

171

largely in the history of Pennsylvania, New York, and Canada. The village in which she lived was called French Catharine's Town, and her name is still preserved in Mountoursville in the State of Pennsylvania. Of this lady, Francis Parkman said she "still held the belief, inculcated by the guides of her youth, that Christ was a Frenchman crucified by the English."[18] It is of Catharine Montour that Marshe writes in his diary:

> and then I went to a cabin, where I heard the celebrated Mrs. Montour, a French lady (but now, by having lived so long among the Six Nations, is become almost an Indian), had her residence. When I approached the wigwam, I saluted her in French, and asked her whether she was not born in Canada? Of what parents? and whether she had not lived a long time with the Indians? She answered me in the same language very civilly, and after some compliments were passed betwixt us, told me, in a polite manner, "That she was born in Canada, whereof her father (who was a French gentleman) had been Governor; under whose administration, the then Five Nations of Indians had made war against the French, and the Hurons in that government (whom we term the French Indians, from espousing their part against the English, and living in Canada), and that, in the war, she was taken by some of the Five Nations' warriors, being then about ten years of age; and by them was carried away into their country, where she was habited and brought up in the same manner as their children; That when she grew up to years of maturity, she was married to a famous war captain of those nations, who was in great esteem for the glory he procured in the wars he carried on against the Catawbas, a great nation of Indians to the southwest of Virginia, by whom she had several children; but about fifteen years ago, he was killed in a battle with them; since which, she had not been married; That she had little or no remembrance of the place of her birth, nor indeed of her parent, it

172

being near fifty years since she was
ravished from them by the Indians.[19]

Of this somewhat mysterious lady, Marshe records
that she was a lady in the accepted meaning of the
term. He made an emphatic distinction between a "lady"
and the local society of the frontier outpost of Lancaster who were invited to the grand ball with which
the treaty conference closed; of these local "ladies"
he notes that many were more savage than the Indians.

Marshe continued by saying that Catharine Montour
"has been a handsome woman, genteel, and of polite address, notwithstanding her residence has been so long
among the Indians; though formerly she was wont to accompany the several chiefs, who used to renew treaties
of friendship with the proprietor and governor of Pennsylvania, at Philadelphia, the metropolis of that province, and being a white woman, was there very much
caressed by the gentlewomen of that city, with whom
she used to stay for some time. She retains her native
language, by conversing with the Frenchmen who trade
for fur, skins, etc. among the Six Nations; and our
language she learned at Philadelphia, as likewise of
our traders, who go back into the Indians' country."[20]

Catharine Montour was one of the best known of all
those who merged with the Indian peoples without losing their European identity. This anecdote of her may
serve to show that the Indian nations were not wholly
deprived of counsel from people who knew and understood both sides. The fact that such people were so
often called "renegades" might indicate that they were
not always on the side of the whites. Bernard Fay
spoke of the French renegade who called himself Captain Montour, and who served the interests of the English with a perfect knowledge of expert Indian lore.
Parkman said he was an excellent interpreter "held in
high account by his Indian kinsmen."[21] Captain Montour
was Catharine Montour's son.

The French, the English, and the Indians, all had
their experts in each other's languages and customs,
though it is probably true that the French had more
such experts than we had, and the French also had
their Jesuits, missionary priests whose whole lives
were spent with the Indian tribes, lives dedicated not
only to converting them, but to promoting the French
policy among them, even to the point of inciting the
Indian tribes to go on the war-path against the English.

173

Whatever provincial commissioners and negotiators may have expected written treaties to do in the way of binding Indians to peace, we may concede that the principal value of such treaties lay in their potential use with the imperial rivals of England. It was necessary, therefore, that they be negotiated and drawn with strict conformity to European usage.

A good example of the way treaties negotiated on the frontier could affect European diplomacy is the Treaty of Utrecht in 1713. According to the terms of the treaty, England and France recognized the fact that there were French-Indians and English-Indians in North America, and each signatory promised not to interfere with the Indians under the other's jurisdiction. This made it imperative that the territories of the Indian nations be defined, and defined according to European diplomatic usage.[22] It also raised difficult questions for the Indians. If the Treaty of Utrecht called the Iroquois, for example, subjects of the British crown, what did the word "subjects" mean? As Francis Parkman said, the English told the Iroquois that the word "subjects" meant that they were the "children" of the English; the French, on the other hand, told the Iroquois that the word "subjects" meant that they were "dogs and slaves"[23] of the English.

The diary of Witham Marshe describes the plenary sessions between the delegates of the Six Nations and the delegates from Pennsylvania, Maryland and Virginia, each group sitting together as a "block"; it describes then the separate sessions of the Indian delegates as a "bloc" with each of the American groups in matters affecting the special interests of each province; and it describes the secret sessions from which all but commissioners and their special experts were excluded -- to the intense disgust of the younger gentlemen of Maryland and Virginia who had been permitted to accompany the delegates as an adventure. A very rigid code of private behavior was also enjoined on those same young gentlemen, lest anything occur to warrant suspicion of those very malpractices of which we read today in reference to such formal diplomatic conferences.

Marshe also describes the social formalities of the Lancaster Conference:

> The twenty-four chiefs of the Six Nations, by invitation of yesterday from

174

the honourable commissioners of Maryland, dined with them in the courthouse; when were present, at other tables, his Honour the Governor of Pennsylvania, the Honourable commissioners
of Virginia, and a great many gentlemen of the three colonies. There were
a large number of the inhabitants of
Lancaster present to see the Indians
dine. We had five tables, great variety of dishes, and served up in very
good order.[24]

Diplomatic precedence was carefully observed as
it was in all the conferences, both for Indians and
for the white delegates:

The sachems sat at two separate tables;
at the head of one, the famous orator,
Cannasateego, sat, and the others were
placed according to their rank. As
the Indians are not accustomed to eat
in the same manner as the English, or
other polite nations do, we, who were
secretaries on this affair, with Mr.
Thomas Cookson, prothonatary of Lancaster county, William Logan, Esq., son
of Mr. President Logan, and Mr. Nathaniel Rigbie, of Baltimore county in
Maryland, carved the meat for them,
served them with cider and wine, mixed
with water, and regulated the economy
of the two tables.[25]

Throughout his narrative, Marshe writes often of
the Maryland delegates to the Conference as "their Embassy." He is thinking of them as ambassadors, in
terms of European diplomacy. And on the last day, he
records, "this morning, Mr. Peters, secretary of the
Governor (of Pennsylvania), Mr. Black, secretary to
the honourable commissioners of Virginia, and myself,
examined the whole treaty, and finished all matters
any way relating to it."[26]

This is no isolated description of procedure on
such occasions. It is chosen here because it is des-
criptive and full, and also because it brings out numerous examples of how well the Indians understood and
practiced the principles of international law, as we
understood them, in their relations with other Indians.

175

Marshe relates that a body of Indians he called Shawa-
nese had come down to the Eastern Shore of the Province of Maryland in 1742, two years before the present conference, and had stirred up a tributary of the
Six Nations, the Nanticokes, to an attack on the English, to recover lands formerly ceded to Lord Baltimore "by treaty." Sixty-eight Nanticoke chiefs had
been arrested by the colonial militia, "with old Pan-
quash, their emperor," and had been tried at Annapolis,
but were set at liberty. Marshe continued:

> The commissioners took an opportunity,
> in private conference with them this
> afternoon "to ask them the reason of
> the Shawnesse's procedure, and whether
> they had any countenance from other
> nations, and also desired the Chiefs,
> then present, to search this business
> fully, and reprimand the criminal Shaw-
> nese, who were more blameable than the
> deluded Nanticokes. The Six Nations,
> by their orator, said, "that they were
> heartily sorry for what the Shawnese
> had done; but on their return to Onon-
> dago, they would make a strict inquiry
> of the whole affair; and if they found
> them so culpable as we alleged they
> were, then they would severely repri-
> mand them for their treacherous behav-
> ior, contrary to the faith of trea-
> ties."[27]

Marshe describes Gachradodon, the spokesman for
the delegates of the Six Nations, as "about forty
years of age, tall, straight-limbed, and a graceful
person, but not so fat as Connasateego. His action,
when he spoke, was certainly the most graceful, as
well as bold, that any person ever saw; without the
buffoonery of the French, or over-solemn deportment of
the haughty Spaniards." He was complimented by the
Governor who said: "that he would have made a good figure in the forum of old Rome." And "Mr. Commissioner
Jenings declared, 'that he had never seen so just an
action in any of the most celebrated orators he had
heard speak.'"[28]

There is a mass of evidence that we Americans respected the chiefs of the Indian nations with whom we
came in contact in war or in diplomatic conference. We
realized that they were formidable in themselves as

176

well as because they lay as buffer nations between us and the French and Spaniards. Our diplomacy with them followed the accepted diplomatic forms and usage. Indeed there are other examples of the observance of diplomatic principles in the relations of the Indian nations between themselves. Benjamin Franklin observed one such relation when he said: "when six *Catawba* Deputies, under the Care of Colonel *Bull*, of *Charlestown*, went by Permission in-to the *Mohawk* Country, to sue for and treat of Peace for their Nation, they soon found the *Six Nations* highly exasperated, and the Peace at that time impracticable; They were therefore in Fear for their own Persons, and apprehended that they should be killed in their way back to *New York;* which being made known to the *Mohawk Chiefs* by Colonel *Bull*, one of them, by Order of the Council, made this Speech to the *Catawbas:*

'Strangers and Enemies--

> While you are in this Country, blow away all Fear out of your Breasts; Change the black Streak of Paint on your Cheek for a red One, and let your Faces shine with Bear's Grease: You are safer here than if you were at home. The *Six Nations* will not defile their own land with the Blood of Men that came unarmed to ask for Peace. We shall send a Guard with you, to see you safe out of our Territories. So far you shall have Peace, but no further. Get home to your own Country, and there take Care of yourselves, for there we intend to come and kill you.'[29]

The Catawbas came away unhurt accordingly.

The Indians were not unaware of themselves as buffer nations between the rival European claimants to empire in America. In a bibliography of the English colonial treaties with the Indian nations (which Bernard Fay should have noted), the author claims that "the Iroquois played a more important part than the Eastern Indians and finally came to be regarded by the British colonies as a 'buffer state' between them and the French. The Iroquois were well aware of their importance to both sides and the treaties with them show what astute politicians they were."[30]

177

Another book was published in London (1727) the very title of which throws light on our early American-Indian relations: "The History of the Five Nations of Canada, which are dependent on the Province of New York, and are a barrier between the English and the French in that part of the world."[31] On page 10 of this book is an amusing anecdote of a three-cornered conflict between the English Five Nations on one side and the French Hurons on the other. The English Five Nations, who were apparently unable to cope with the firearms of the French, "amused the Adirondacks and their allies, the Quatoghies (called by the French, Hurons), by sending to the French and desiring Peace." The French, as a condition of peace, required the Five Nations to receive some priests among them. The Five Nations "readily accepted the Offer (of the French) and some Jesuits went along with them." As soon as the Jesuits were safely within their control, the Five Nations turned on the French Hurons with redoubled vigor. The French themselves and their firearms were held helplessly neutral lest the Five Nations kill the Jesuits, and the Five Nations then roundly defeated the French Hurons, whose "amusement" no doubt ceased abruptly when the survivors saw the meaning of the strategem.

What was at stake in American-Indian realations? In one word--survival. This was true of all the parties concerned, for the English, the French, the Spanish to a lesser degree, and for the Indians themselves. The problem can be seen in its full clarity only with the benefit of hindsight, of course, but the broad outlines of the problem began to emerge about the middle of the 17th Century, more particularly in March 1649, when a thousand Iroquois warriors began a war of extermination against the Hurons in Canada. The former were under the English influence, and the latter the French.

The fierce Iroquois--the Mohawks, Oneidas, Onondagas, Cayugas, and Senecas-- were the indispensable key to the dominion of North America. The Homer of the American wilderness saga, Francis Parkman,[32] said of these New York Indians:

> among all the barbarous nations of the
> continent, the Iroquois of New York
> stand paramount. Elements which among
> other tribes were crude, confused, and
> embryotic, were among them systemat-
> ized and concreted into established

polity. The Iroquois were the Indian
of Indians. A thorough savage, yet a
finished and developed savage, he is
perhaps an example of the highest el-
evation which man can reach without
emerging from his primitive condition
of the hunter.[33]

As to why this was so, and what the consequences
were, Parkman went on to explain:

a geographical position, commanding on
one hand the portal of the Great Lakes,
and on the other the sources of the
streams flowing both to the Atlantic
and the Mississippi, gave the ambitious and aggressive confederates advantages which they prefectly understood, and by which they profited to
the utmost. Patient and politic as
they were ferocious, they were not only conquerors of their own race, but
the powerful allies and the dreaded
foes of the French and the English colonies, flattered and caressed by both,
yet too sagacious to give themselves
without reserve to either. Their organization and their history evince
their intrinsic superiority.[34]

The Founding Father of the great Indian confederacy of the Five Nations, according to Iroquois legend,
was Longfellow's Hiawatha, who "lived by the shore of
Gitche Gumee, by the shining Big-Sea-Water." Hiawatha
was, of all things, a kind of peacnik among these ferocious Indians, one who dedicated his life to the
ideal of a Great Peace among the kindred tribes. This
was in the late 1400s or the early 1500s. By virtue
of Hiawatha's efforts the great confederacy was born,
and the People of the Long House came into existence.
Of the original Five Nations, the Mohawks were the
guardians of the eastern door, the Senecas the guardians of the western door, and the Onondagas in the
middle were the keepers of the council fire. The
Oneidas and Cayugas were also in the middle. The Tuscarors were added to the confederation in 1715, and
the Five Nations became the Six Nations, but it was in
name only as the Tuscarors never attained full status
with the original nations. Dr. Ruth Murray Underhill
said of the great confederacy and the role it played
in determining the fate of North America:

The Iroquois are some of the most famous Indians in American history and
justly so. Their government was the
most integrated and orderly north of
Mexico, and some have even thought it
gave suggestions to the American Constitution (Lee, Franklin, Jefferson,
and Washington were quite familiar
with the League). They developed what
came close to an empire, with conquered nations paying tribute and taking their orders. For over a hundred
years they held a pivotal position in
America between the French and the English. It seems very possible that,
except for the Iroquois, North America
at this day might have been French.[35]

North of this great union of civilization and
power, variously called the Five Nations, the Six Nations, and the People of the Long House, were the people of a loose union of widely scattered tribes called
the Algonquin (also called Algonkian and Algonquian).
These tribes originally controlled Canada, the New
England region, most of the Ohio Valley, and had scattered offshoots in eastern Pennsylvania, New Jersey,
Maryland, and parts of Virginia. Between the Algonquin
and the Iroquois there was a bitterness and an enmity
that was so deep it probably had no equal in history.

The French, without realizing what they were doing, picked sides in the feud between the Algonquins
and the Iroquois. They allied themselves with the
former, and thus forced themselves to accept a permanent state of war with the latter. Since the Iroquois
were destined to become the most powerful Indian Confederacy in North America, and also the pivot in the
balance of power between the French and the British,
the mistake probably cost France her empire in the
long run.

Samuel de Champlain got France off on the wrong
foot in America in the early days of the 17th Century.
The first encounter with the Iroquois under the terms
of the Algonquin alliance, however, was something of a
disaster for the Iroquois. Cadwallader Colden described it by saying that the French "kept themselves
undiscovered, till the Moment they began to join Battle; and their Fire-arms surprised the Five Nations so
much, for, before that Time, they had never seen such

Weapons."[36]   The result was an Iroquois defeat.   This
was in 1613.   Afterwards, the Iroquois fled to the
forests of central New York, where they remained in
isolation until they were inadvertently rescued by the
Dutch.

In 1609 an Englishman, Henry Hudson, in the service of a Dutch trading company entered the Delaware
Bay and explored the Hudson River to Albany.   During
the course of the exploration Hudson met and entertained some Iroquois chieftains in the cabin of his
ship, the *Half Moon*. Following company policy, he established, and later Dutch settlers maintained,
friendly relations with the Indians. This ripened into the formal treaty of 1618.   However, even before
this time the Dutch merchants had become excited by
the potential of the fur trade with the Indians, particularly when they considered the high prices they
had to pay to obtain furs from Russia, as opposed to
the baubles, firearms and rum that would satisfy the
Indians.   To the Dutch trading post at Albany, Dr.
Underhill said,

> the Iroquois paddled their elm-bark
> canoes, loaded with beaver furs, one
> trader calculating that the Mohawk
> could bring four thousand a season. In
> return, they wanted guns, and the
> Dutch were willing to supply them.
> Here the remote position of the Five
> Nations stood them in good stead, for
> the Hollanders were afraid to arm
> their closer neighbors, the Algonkian.
> An armed group of Iroquois, however,
> seemed to them an excellent device for
> keeping those same Algonkian in order.
> Moreover, it would form a buffer
> against the French, who, otherwise,
> might have streamed down into New York
> State. The French, too, went slowly
> in the arming of their Algonkian al-
> lies. So the Iroquois, by a stroke of
> geographical good luck, were raised
> to a position of potential mastery.[37]

The key factor in the "mastery" the Iroquois
sought to establish was the fur trade. To a lesser extent (but not much) the fur trade was the basis of
policy for the other Indian tribes and nations in
North America. Why was this so? It was all part of a

catch-up game the Indians were forced to play with their white rivals for possession of the continent. Prior to the establishment of the European beachheads in North America, the Indians were living in a period of human culture not much advanced from the Stone Age. In fact, the Indians had no iron tools among them when the Europeans arrived. As Lawrence H. Gipson said, "a people still living on the level of the culture of the Stone Age was suddenly elevated vicariously, as it were, into that of the Iron Age."[38]

The confrontation was on a fifteen-hundred-mile front, and was moving swiftly and relentlessly forward. A tribe that had the weapons of the white man and the steel tools, as well as the luxuries (such as cloth, blankets, beads, rum, and so forth) was suddenly elevated into a new way of life, and the one thing that made all the rest possible was the fur trade. According to the values of the white man, he would trade anything he had for an adequate number of beaver skins, or other appropriate products of the forest, such as the skins of the racoon, fox, muskrat, marten, otter, mink, wolf, wildcat, bear, and deer. But the beaver was king. With an adequate number of beaver skins, the Indian could trade his way out of the Stone Age and buy his way into the new age. Without them, he had to face a grim future. At best, the prospect was to return to the Stone Age ways of his forefathers, and at worst it was to face annihilation at the hands of the white men, or what was worse, at the hands of other Indians armed with the white man's weapons. It was, in truth, a Hobson's choice. The beaver skin was the key to future and power, if not the key to survival for the Indians.

None of the Indian tribes was ahead of the Iroquois in recognizing the fact that the beaver was king. The only trouble was that the Iroquois also began to recognize that there was a shortage of beaver in their hunting country. This happened about the middle of the 17th Century. It was also happening in other parts of eastern Canada at the same time, and consequently the fur trade was moving west, leaving poverty-stricken and degenerate tribes behind it. However, these tribes, as Dr. Underhill pointed out,

> were not organized in a league and were vulnerable accordingly. The Five Nations, instead of pulling apart, had been slowly cementing their alliance.

Perhaps they actually thought of it as
the Great Peace which their speeches
proclaimed. Certainly they had kept
their people together except for a few
scattered episodes, and now they had a
united force with which to fight for
commercial advantage. This they did
with as single-minded a purpose as any
modern nation. Since they had no furs,
they had either to loot furs directly
from other Indians or to force those
others to trade through them as middlemen.[39]

The Iroquois decision was to fight their way out
of the impasse brought on by the dwindling supply of
beaver. As a result, between 1649 and 1656 the Five
Nations systematically destroyed the Huron, Petun,
Neutral, and Erie nations. These were the Beaver Wars,
and their purpose was to rid the Iroquois of their
rivals in the fur trade.[40] The conflict began on a
March dawn when the Iroquois surprised the Hurons with
a massive assault against that nation. This was a logical first step because the Hurons were one of the
richest Indian nations in the west, and owed their
prosperity to the fur trade, not to the fact that the
Huron hunting grounds abounded in beaver, but to the
skill of the Hurons in exploiting the northern and
western tribes where the beaver were still in plenti-
ful supply. In other words, the Hurons were the rich
middlemen between the northern and western tribes and
the French at Montreal, Three Rivers, and Quebec. The
Iroquois tried to muscle in on that organization by
the peaceful methods of diplomacy, and when that
failed resorted to the cruder methods of war.

The war that the Five Nations waged against the
Hurons, the Petuns, the Neutrals, and the Eries, was
not the usual kind of Indian warfare. Ordinarily, warfare to the Indians was a kind of sport with religious
overtones. It was usually confined to a few dozen
braves who decided to go on the warpath to avenge themselves for a real or an imagined injury, and in the
process to cover themselves with glory by taking a few
scalps. It was highly personalized, even to the point
of torturing captives in order to make the hereafter
more comfortable for the slain warriors of their own
tribe. On the other hand, the Beaver Wars were truly
national affairs for the Five Nations. Still operating on the political principle of unanimity in the making of basic decisions, and of one war at a time
against all their enemies, wars became national in

183

scope for the Five Nations. It was a turning point in Iroquois history.

Dr. Underhill underscored the importance of this turning point in Iroquois history when she said of the wars of the Five Nations that henceforth they:

> gradually ceased to be commando attacks, made by a few dozen men whose aim was glory and captives. The torture of a few captives would hardly alter the course of the fur trade. Therefore, the Five Nations began to send out armies of from five hundred to over a thousand men. Their aim was complete annihilation of tribes handling the fur trade or else conquest and tribute. In the former case, they could hunt the abandoned territory themselves. In the latter, they could collect a toll of furs from the hunters. With this in view they forged west, wiping out Huronia from 1648 to 1649, liquidating the Neutral Nation by 1651, the Erie Nation in 1654, and the Susquehannock of Pennsylvania in 1653. For some years their attacks were carried on with such violence that sometimes not one canoe-load of furs came to Montreal, and the shores of Lake Huron, once populous, harbored not a single Indian. Even Montreal was attacked (between temporary treaties of peace) and for the trading post of Three Rivers "it was evil upon evil and sorrow upon sorrow."[41]

The Mohawk power came to be such a legend that when Cadwaller Colden wrote his history of the Five Nations in 1737 he said that he had been told "by old Men in New England, who remembered the Time when the Mohawk was discovere'd in the Country, their Indians raised a Cry from Hill to Hill, A Mohawk! A Mohawk! upon which they all fled like Sheep before Wolves, without attempting to make the least Resistance, whatever Odds were on their Side."[42]

The Five Nations did not succeed in taking over the role of middleman from the Hurons. Enough of the refugee Indians escaped to the northern and western tribes and countries to keep up their organization and their trade, and they still brought their beaver fleets down the Ottawa to the French on the St. Lawrence. Not even a blockade of all the trade routes succeeded in completely eliminating the traffic. The French did their part by invading the Iroquois country twice in 1666, but could not win a complete victory, and still had to face another obstacle to their trade, the fact that the Indians could get much better prices for their furs from the English at Albany than from the French on the St. Lawrence. In other words, one beaver skin at Albany would buy two or three times as much quality merchandise as it would from the French on the St. Lawrence.

The Albany price differential was a powerful bargaining chip the Iroquois had in their fight to win over the northern and western tribes from their trade with the French. By the same token, it meant that the French would have to outdo themselves in the fight to prevent this from happening. For if France lost the trade with the northern and western tribes she would go bankrupt in the New World. The fur trade was practically the only source of income France had from her American possessions on the mainland. Take that away, and France's mainland colonies lost almost the only excuse for their existence. Thus the French had no choice but to defend themselves against the Iroquois even to the last drop of French blood. It was that vital.

For the Iroquois, the crisis was almost as bad. By this time, the huge debt that had been piling up against the great union of civilization and power, the Five Nations, was nearing a breaking point. The victories they had won in their bid for supremacy in North America, beginning with the Beaver Wars, had exacted a toll in an area where it could not be tolerated--manpower. According to some estimates, the steep decline in the Iroquois population over a period of only 10 years from 1689 to 1698, was of the order of nearly 50 percent. This meant there was a corresponding drop in the number of fighting men, from "2,500 Iroquois warriors in 1689" to "only 1,230 in 1698."[43] It is no small wonder that the Five Nations drew in their victorious horns at this time, and began to explore the possibilities of peace, more specifically neutrality in the hostilities between England and France. The result was "The Grand Settlement of 1701."[44]

A spectator at the treaty-council that produced the Grand Settlement, Bacqueville de La Potherie, commented on the haughty behavior of the Iroquois, and the subservience of the French and their numerous Indian allies. "Strange," he exclaimed, "that four or five thousand should make a whole new world tremble. New England is but too happy to gain their good graces; New France is often wasted by their wars, and our allies dread them over an extent of more than fifteen hundred leagues."[45] Nevertheless, there was no denying the fact that the Iroquois struck terror into the hearts of the other Indians, and gave pause to the whites, French and English, but particularly the French.

In this case, the treaty the Iroquois came away with was a very favorable one from their point of view. They gained what they wanted most, a surcease from war at the present time, to give them an opportunity to build up their manpower strength, the better to fight the next time. In return, they agreed to follow a course of neutrality the next time England and France crossed swords. In addition, the Iroquois won valuable hunting rights in the west, a long sought objective, and the right of profitable trade with the western tribes going to sell their furs at Albany. Finally, the Iroquois were given free access to the markets in New France. In other words, the treaty guaranteed economic stability for the Iroquois over the foreseeable future.

At the same time, to protect their flanks, the Iroquois negotiated a treaty with the English at Albany, telling them to ignore the simultaneous parleys in Montreal, assuring them of their fidelity, and giving the English a clear title to any western lands they might gain from the French or their Indian allies. Anthony F.C. Wallace said of these two "neutrality" treaties, that they inaugurated a new era of Iroquois policy, "a policy of peace toward the Far Indians, of political manipulation of nearby tribes, and of an armed neutrality between contending Europeans. This policy led to commercial profit and to the seizure of a balance of power between the French and English."[46] This is the kind of diplomatic "sport" that Machiavelli would have applauded. The English were held at arm's length, and the French were royally duped. The secrets of the white man's diplomacy were being bent to serve the needs of the red man for survival.

186

The Treaty of Ryswick was signed in 1697. It put an end to King William's War, and it was four years later that the Iroquois negotiated their Grand Settlement treaties with England and France. England declared war on France in May 1702, within a year of the Grand Settlement, and this put it to a test. It was quickly found wanting from the English piont of view, but not from the French. Canada reversed its previous strategy, and avoided the Iroquois country, which shielded New York. Instead, she launched attacks on a wide front from Maine through New Hampshire and into western Massachusetts. New York refused to come to the aid of New England, as did Pennsylvania and Virginia, and New England had to go it alone. The worm did not turn until 1709-11, when New York and the Five Nations too joined in two abortive attempts to invade Canada. Both failed because the promised British naval support did not materialize. It was diverted to Portugal in the first instance, and was turned back in the second because of the cowardice of an incompetent British commander. Iroquois relations with the English began to chill after the debacle of these two failures, and the Indian relations with France slipped back to where they had been before the Grand Settlement. The Treaty of Utrecht brought peace to all in 1713, and trade flourished again between the Iroquois and the western Indians.

The next great conflict between England and her rival European claimants to empire in America broke out in 1739. It was with Spain, and the conflict bore the undignified name of the War of Jenkins' Ear. By 1744 England and France were at war again. The broader conflict became known in America as King George's War. The European belligerents paid little attention to the American phase of the war, and in the treaty of peace between France and England in 1748, the Treaty of Aix-la-Chapelle, the belligerents agreed to return all territory captured during the wa . As far as the Indians were concerned, the Mohawks made a half-hearted effort to engage the French in Canada, but felt they had been double-crossed by the failure of the mother country and the American colonists to back them up with the massive support they had promised.

On the other hand, among the western Indians, particularly those in the Ohio Basin, there was a definite shift away from their French trading partners to the English. The cause was the working out of the economic law of supply and demand. The French were always willing, or more accurately, eager partners in the Indian trade, but their prices were high, and their supply of goods short. The longer the war lasted the worse the disadvantages got for the French. Britain's superiority on the seas began to pay off in a big way. As a result, the French began to lose out in the competition for the Indian trade. In 1748 a treaty was signed at Logstown, downstream from the forks of the Ohio, by which the Indians formerly allied with France opened their markets to the English. All things considered, this treaty was probably more important to the English colonies than the Treaty of Aix-la-Chapelle.

The period between Aix-la-Chapelle and the French and Indian War is sometimes called the Battle of the Maps. And rightly so. There were at least three critical zones in North America, any one of which could lead to war, and one real flash-point that was almost certain to lead to hostilities. The former were Nova Scotia, the Albany-Montreal corridor, and the Great Lakes region; the latter was the Ohio River Valley. The importance of the Ohio was stressed by Francis Parkman when he said that the French empire in America "had two heads, --one among the snows of Canada, and one among the cane-brakes of Louisiana; one communicating with the world through the Gulf of St. Lawrence, and the other through the Gulf of Mexico. These vital points were feebly connected by a chain of military posts, --slender and often interrupted, -- circling through the wilderness nearly three thousand miles. Midway between Canada and Louisiana, lay the valley of the Ohio. If the English should seize it, they would sever the chain of posts, and cut French America asunder. If the French held it, and entrenched themselves well along its eastern limits, they would shut their rivals between the Alleghanies and the sea, control all the tribes of the West, and turn them, in case of war, against the English borders,--a frightful and insupportable scourge."[47]

The ultimate clash of empire came over the debatable land at the forks of the Ohio River. In 1753 the new governor of Canada, Marquis Duquesnne de Menneville, sent out an army of 2,000 soldiers and Indian allies to occupy the upper reaches of the Ohio, and to secure the passes with forts and garrisons. He managed to build forts at Presque Ile, and at Le Boeuf and Venango, but long before the expedition had completed its work an epidemic broke out among the soldiers, and it was forced to turn back to Montreal. The expedition aroused the English to the danger of having France join hands, as it were, behind their backs, and cooping them up on a narrow Atlantic strip.

The newly arrived governor of Virginia, Robert Dinwiddie, took a dim view of the invasion of the Ohio lands claimed by Virginia, and sent George Washington, then twenty-one, to inform the French that they were poaching on lands belonging to England, and that they would have to get out. The French were not impressed. While Washington was very cordially received at a conference at Fort Le Boeuf, he was also told that the French would not turn back, and that they would proceed next spring with the construction of a major fortification at the forks of the Ohio.

Dinwiddie was enraged at this defiance, and proceeded to send a small workforce into the wilderness, to begin the construction of an English fort at the same site. As part of this plan to get ahead of the French at the forks of the Ohio, Dinwiddie sent Washington back into the wilderness, this time with two companies of troops. His orders were to protect the workforce. However, the orders came a little late, for by the time he was on the scene the English workforce had already been displaced by the French. Thus it was that the French began the construction of Fort Duquesne.

Not knowing all this, Washington proceeded on his mission, and on May 28, 1754, after a night's march, came up to a small French force under Coulon de Jumonville. A battle (or rather a skirmish) ensued, and as a result de Jumonville and nine of his men were killed, with 21 taken prisoner. To the English there was nothing remarkable about the action, a routine encounter in the wilderness, but to the French it was an act of treachery, for they asserted that de Jumonville was protected by his status as a diplomat when he was assassinated. Washington, of course, denied this, and the de Jumonville incident has little importance except in retrospect. "A trifling action," Horace Walpole called it, "but remarkable for giving date to the war."[48] However, it was not until May 18, 1756, that England got around to declaring war on France, and the French did not reciprocate until the following month, when they declared war on the English. The real significance of the de Jumonville incident, what made it truly remarkable in history, as Voltaire said, was that a "torch lighted in the forests of America set all Europe in conflagration."[49] Europeans called the conflict the Seven Years' War, and in America it was known as the French and Indian War.

The death of de Jumonville was not the end of the incident. By this time, two things were clear to both the French and the English. One was that the debatable land over which they were quarreling, the Ohio Valley, was the key to the control of the American west, and that as between the French and the English that side which could get the support of the Indian nations would probably triumph. To this end, the French sent strong reinforcements to Fort Duquesne, and began making preparations to advance against Washington at Great Meadows. Here Washington had decided to make his stand, and had thrown up what defenses he could, aptly calling them Fort Necessity. True to expectations, the French attacked the so-called fort in overwhelming strength, with 500 French soldiers and 400 Indians. The Father of his country was forced to surrender on July 4, 1754. Thus the first round of the French and Indian War went to the French. It meant that France was now in undisputed control of the Ohio Valley. It also meant two other things. One was that not a single English flag now flew beyond the Alleghanies, and that, as Francis Parkman said, "when, in the next year. the smouldering war broke into flame, nearly all the western tribes drew their scalping knives for France."[50]

Before the blow fell at Fort Necessity, a call went out from London to the governor of New York, Sir Danvers Osborne, advising him of the London government's "displeasure and surprise that the provincial authorities had permitted a serious misunderstanding to develop between themselves and the Mohawks and calling upon him to take immediate steps to restore the former friendship by means of a conference with the whole Confederation, to which the governments of Virginia, Maryland, Pennsylvania, New Jersey, New Hampshire, and Massachusetts Bay were to be invited to send commissioners and presents and for the furtherance of which presents from England were also to be sent in the name of His Majesty."[51]

The incident to which the London government alluded was the one involving the Iroquois reaction to the expedition Duquesne sent out to the Ohio in the spring of 1753. King Henrdick of the Mohawks was so outraged at the failure of the English to use counterforce against the French that he led a Mohawk delegation to New York for the purpose of laying down the law to the English. Hendrick told Governor Clinton and his Council that because of a long train of abuses and usurpations, including the failure of the British to persevere in the last war, "the covenant chain is broken between you and us. So, brother, you are not to expect to hear of me any more, and, brother, we desire to hear no more of you."[52]   What this meant was that the great weight of the powerful Iroquois could not only be denied to the English, but might be thrown into the war on the side of the French. This would tip the balance in favor of the French, and might mean that the whole of the North American continent would become part of New France.   It is no wonder that the imperialists in the London government demanded that immediate steps be taken to restore the former friendship with the Five Nations by means of an intercolonial conference. Out of this fear, out of this clear and present danger, came the Albany Congress of 1754. In our history the real significance of the Albany Congress has been somewhat obscured by the famous Plan of Union that Franklin presented at the conference.   At the time though, it was not the Plan of Union but the treaty-alliance with the Five Nations that mattered. As the century-old struggle with France for the North American continent approached its violent climax in the French and Indian War nothing was more important than the long-established alliance with the great Indian Confederacy. Survival itself was at stake for the English colonies.

The Albany Congress opened on June 19, 1754. This was three weeks after the de Jumonville incident, and two weeks before the fall of Fort Necessity.   Of the colonies invited to attend, including the host New York, of course, New Hampshire, Massachusetts, Pennsylvania, and Maryland sent delegates. New Jersey failed to answer the summons, and Virginia was represented by James DeLancey, governor of New York and presiding officer of the meeting.   Connecticut and Rhode Island also sent delegates, though they were not specifically invited to do so.   Altogether, 23 official delegates attended.   It was a very distinguished gathering of Americans, and included such outstanding personalities as Benjamin Franklin of Pennsylvania, William Johnson of New York, and Judge Thomas Hutchinson of Massachusetts.

There was never any doubt about the Albany gathering being a Congress in the European diplomatic sense. Before the proceedings even opened, the "powers" the colonial delegates brought were produced and recorded.

It was proposed and agreed "that to avoid all disputes about precedency of the Colonies (an old diplomatic sore among nations) they should be named in the minutes according to their situation from north to south."[53] This was not an idle precautionary measure, for there had been disputes concerning the rank and precedence of the envoys of participating colonies at other colonial conferences. The official Journal of the proceedings of the Congress at Albany is full of incidents to show the independence of the Indians, their ability to meet the colonial spokesmen in equal debate, their full realization of the nature of the conflict between the French and the English, as well as their own relation to it. Their speeches are forceful and to the point; their recommendations solid; and their accusations and criticism of policy fearless.

The first order of business at the Albany Confress was, from the English point of view, to do something, if possible, to heal the rift that had opened up between the English and their Indian allies. The object, of course, was to gain the support of the Five Nations in the war that was already upon the English colonies. However, the Indian delegates were all slow to arrive, and what was worse the Mohawks arrived last, though they lived only forty miles distant. The Mohawks were famous among the confederations for their love of Machiavellian artistry in negotiation and in warfare, and all their moves and coups were quite like their counterparts in European diplomacy. In this instance, their late arrival at the conference was an augury that they were not too interested in the outcome. Some imputed the delay to fear that the French would fall upon their countries in their absence; others to art, that the Mohawks did not want to be taken for granted in their alliance with the English. In any case, when they arrived one of their notables, Sachem Hendrick declared the delay to have been intentional because at a previous conference it had been said that the Mohawks had come first in order to make sure that they were favored in the welcoming address. "This is our reason," Hendrick said, "for staying behind; for if we had come first the other nations would have said that we made the Governor's speech; and therefore, though we were resolved to come, we intended the other nations should go before us, that they might hear the Governor's speech, which we could hear afterwards."[54]

The complaints of the Iroquois were that the English had neglected them for the past three years,

that they had taken advantage of them on numerous occasions, particularly when land transactions were involved; and that the English had not been vigorous
enough in protecting the legitimate interests of the
Indians against encroachments by the French. Referring
to King George's War and the shameful Treaty of Aix-
la-Chapelle which ended it, Hendrick said

> 'Tis your fault, bretheren, that we
> are not strengthened by conquest; for
> we would have gone and taken Crown
> Point, but you hindered us. We had
> concluded to go and take it, but we
> were told it was too late, and that
> the ice would not bear us. Instead of
> this, you burnt your own fort at Sara-
> toga, and ran away from it, which was
> a shame and a scandal to you. Look
> about your country, and see you have
> no fortifications about you; no, not
> even to this city. 'Tis but one step
> from Canada hither, and the French may
> easily come and turn you out of your
> doors. [55]

Hendrick was not willing to leave it at that.
Looking at the chain of forts the French were con-
structing to link Lake Erie with the forks of the Ohio
and at the lack of such activity on the part of the
English, the Mohawk Chief said, "brethren, you were
desirous that we should open our minds and our hearts
to you. Look at the French; they are men; they are
fortifying everywhere. But we are ashamed to say it,
you are all like women, bare and open, without any
fortifications." [56]

on the face of it, the Albany Congress failed in
the accomplishment of its primary objective, which was
to rescue and revive the offensive and defensive alliance with the Five Nations. It could not have been
otherwise because the English did not have anything to
offer other than wordy promises, and the Indians, after the misrepresentations that brought them into King
George's War in 1746, namely that thousands of British
soldiers had already arrived from England to fight the
war, were not of a mind to be deceived a second time.
The best thing that can be said about the Albany Congress is that it was at least an answer to the armed
might the French were demonstrating in the Ohio Valley.

As such, it was important, for, as the Albany delegates warned the Crown, if the Iroquois joined the enemy "there is the utmost danger that the whole continent will be subjected to the French."[57]

But the Iroquois didn't. Thanks to colonial diplomacy in general, and to William Johnson in particular, the Five Nations continued to respect the English alliance, and did not throw in their lot with the French, even when English fortunes were at their lowest ebb. This descent into the anarchy of feebleness and ineptitude began with the arrival of Major General Edward Braddock in early 1755. He came at the head of some 1,400 British regulars, and proceeded to make his headquarters at Alexandria, Virginia. Here a council of war was held, and there it was decided that four campaigns would be undertaken almost simultaneously, the most important being the one against Fort Duquesne, which Braddock would lead personally. The other three campaigns were the ones against Niagara and Frontenac, led by Governor William Shirley; the one against Crown Point, led by William Johnson; and the forth led by Robert Monckton against Nova Scotia. None of these plans were successfully executed except the one against Nova Scotia, which Henry Wadsworth Longfellow memoralized in his epic *Evangeline* (Grand Pre). However, William Johnson did win a victory of sorts at Lake George, but failed to carry Crown Point.

Largely through his personal influence and intervention, William Johnson was able to get a body of some 300 Mohawk warriors to go along with him in the expedition he led against Crown Point. Among them was King Hendrick, Chief of the Mohawks. He was at Johnson's right hand in the planning of the campaign, and assisted him in its execution, in addition to being active in the actual fighting. On one occasion, Chief Hendrick warned Johnson about the folly of dividing his forces in the face of the enemy, and of sending out an inadequate force on a particular mission. "If they are to be killed," the old sachem said, "they are too many; if they are to fight, they are too few."[58] Nevertheless, Hendrick decided to go with the detachment, and in the ensuing skirmish the old warrior had his mount shot out from under him, and was killed when he tried to rise. The irony is that Hendrick's death came in the campaign against Crown Point, the fort that he had chided the English for not having let the Indians take in the last war before this one.

194

Braddock's defeat in the campaign against Fort
Duquesne was the most shameful one in the defeatful
year of 1755. It was brought about by an unhappy combination of skill on the part of the French and their
Indian allies and gross stupidity on the part of General Braddock. He was totally unaccustomed to the type
of warfare he was expected to wage in the forests of
America, and Franklin was probably right when he said,
"The general was, I think, a brave man, and might probably have made a good figure in some European war. But
he had too much self-confidence; too high an opinion
of the validity of regular troops; too mean a one of
both Americans and Indians."[59] In any case, Braddock
did everything wrong from the beginning to the end of
the campaign, and the result, in Washington's words,
was that "we have been beaten, most shamefully beaten,
by a handful of Men."[60] The only redeeming feature of
the campaign was the lesson General Braddock evidently
learned from the debacle of his plans. As he lay dying on the battlefield, he had nothing but the highest
praise for the despised Virginia "blues," and just before he died was heard to say of the French and their
Indian allies, "we shall better know how to deal with
them another time."[61]

Braddock's defeat had important reprecussions
among the Indian tribes of the Ohio Valley. Except for
the Iroquois, it convinced them that France was invincible in the west, and that the English sun was setting. This became all the more apparent to them as the
defeatful course of British and American arms continued right through 1755 and into 1756. Louis Joseph,
Marquis de Montcalm, became the commander-in-chief of
the French forces on January 25, 1756, and early in
August captured Fort Oswego, deep in Iroquois country.
This impressed the Five nations with the feebleness of
English power, and again raised the question of
whether it was in the Iroquois interest to continue
the English alliance. The following year, 1757, an
ambitious English plan to capture Louisbourg failed,
and the French tide continued to roll as they captured
Fort William Henry on August 9. French and Indian raiding parties penetrated central New York, and threatened Albany. This English outpost, founded by the
Dutch, for a time became one of the most important
cities in the world, for it was, as Francis Parkman
said, "the principal base of military operations on
the continent."[62] If the French had taken Albany, they
could have driven a wedge between New England and the
English colonies on the Chesapeake. They would also

have possessed themselves of the Mohawk Valley, the gateway to the west, and this would have been the end of the Iroquois alliance for the English. With the Hudson-Delaware region in French hands, the battle for North America would have been largely over. It was at this time that French power reached its peak in North America, and as one writer said, "never before was the prestige of French arms in North America so high --and never would it be so high again-- as it was in the fall of the year 1757."[63]

While England was undergoing one of the most defeatful years in her history, the disasters of 1757, colonial diplomacy was hard at work to regain some of the lost ground. To this end, a number of conferences were held with the Indians at sites in Pennsylvania, in Virginia, and in New York. This diplomacy was designated to strengthen the ties with the pro-English tribes, and to weaken the ties between New France and her Indian allies. The conference at Easton, Pennsylvania, in October 1758, was particularly important in this respect. There were 13 nations represented at Easton, and its primary purpose was to breath new life into the Iroquois-British alliance, but it also had a secondary objective, which turned out to be more important than the primary purpose, and this was to send "a message of peace to the tribes of the Ohio."[64] In other words, the subordinate objective of the Easton conference was to detach the Ohio Indians from their alliance with the French.

These colonial diplomatic efforts went hand in hand with important political developments in England, developments that were to put an entirely new face on the war in America. These political developments resulted in William Pitt's coming to power in England in 1758. As soon as he was in control, some fundamental changes were made in England's strategy, not only in Europe but in America as well. In Europe, Pitt opened a floodgate of money and supplies to Frederick the Great of Prussia so he could tie France down on the continent to prevent her from sending reinforcements to America. Then he made North America the main theater of war, and established an aggressive policy designed to root the French out of the New World. To this end, he pledged the full faith and credit of England's resources to pay for the costs of the war in America, and raked the deadwood out of England's military and naval establishments, so that younger and more energetic men could be put in command. The plan for 1758 was to take Forts Duquesne, Ticonderoga, and Louisbourg. If successful, this would turn the tables of the war in the New World, and put France in a position where she could be finished off with relative ease.

The part of the Easton conference that was aimed at the Indians of the Ohio was a matter of primary concern to the English commander who was charged with the reduction of Fort Duquesne. This was Brigadier General John Forbes. It was also a matter of concern to two of the regimental commanders under Forbes, Virginia's son George Washington and Henry Bouquet, a German-speaking Swiss with an excellent reputation as a soldier. The German-speaking was important because a large part of the men under Bouquet were the Germans of Pennsylvania.

General Forbes, after long deliberation, and against the advice of Washington, decided not to take Braddock's road across the mountains, but to build a new road across Pennsylvania. This was a wise decision. Braddock made the wrong one when he landed his troops in Virginia instead of Pennsylvania, and when he decided to take the long and circuitous route to Fort Duquesne. Forbes was determined not to repeat Braddock's mistakes. Another error of Braddock's that Forbes studiously avoided was the pell-mell approach to Duquesne. His troops inched their way over the mountains, and the plan was to hold back the attack until all his forces could be employed without being impeded with wagons or any other logistical burdens. Forbes was also careful to gain an understanding of Indian lore and politics, the better to avoid being surprised the way Braddock was. It was in consequence of this that the Easton conference was of such great importance.

The primary object of the conference at Easton, from Forbes' point of view, was to detach the Delawares and Shawanoes from their alliance with the French. They lived within easy reach of Fort Duquesne, and the French were relying on them. However, they were wavering in their loyalty at this time because the French had not been able to be as lavish as before in giving them the supplies to which they had become accustomed. The reasons for this were economic and military. French goods were always more expensive than the English and of lower quality, and now this was even more so because of the effects of the British

197

blockade.   Now also was the fact that a powerful British army was marching on Fort Duquesne. And to cap it all was the fact that the eastern Delawares had already made their peace with the English, and were urging their western brethren to follow their example. All this came out at Easton, plus the fact that the Five Nations, overlords of the Delawares, wanted them to break their ties with the French.

And to all this was added another factor of the greatest importance. General Forbes himself, as well as the governor and Council of Pennsylvania made a direct diplomatic appeal to the Indians of the Ohio to discontinue their alliance with France. The name of their envoy was Christian Frederick Post. He was a Moravian missionary who had lived among the Delawares, spoke their language, had taken as his wife one of their Indian women, and had their complete confidence. He made the journey to the Ohio because General Forbes believed it was absolutely necessary (considering Braddock's experience) to get the alliance (or at least the neutrality) of the Ohio Indians before attempting the conquest of Fort Duquesne. Moreover Post wea reasonably confident that he had enough influence with the Delawares to bring them around to this point of view. It turned out that he was right. When he arrived at Kushkushkee, his destination, he was cordially received, and, after some preliminary talks, was escorted to Fort Duquesne. There he was permitted to state his case, which had two parts, an invitation and a warning. The invitation was to renew the old chain of friendship with the English, and the warning was that if they did not, they would be crushed along with the French when the English army arrived at Fort Duquesne.[65] There is a certain irony in this message, for, with the benefit of hindsight, it is clear that Post was wrong in the advice he gave to the Ohio Indians about their interests and policy. As Francis Parkman said, if the Ohio Indians:

> had known their true interest, they
> would have made no peace with the Eng-
> lish, but would have united as one man
> to form a barrier of fire against
> their farther progress; for the West
> in English hands meant farms, villages,
> cities, the ruins of the forest, the
> extermination of the game, and the ex-
> pulsion of those who lived on it;
> while the West in French hands, meant

but scattered posts of war and trade, with the native tribes cherished as indispensable allies.[66]

In any case, Post delivered his message, and left Kushkushkee on September 8 to arrive at Fort Augusta on September 23. He then traveled to Raystown (Bedford) where he made his report to General Forbes, that the Ohio Indians were favorably inclined toward the English, and that they would very likely abandon their French alliance upon the arrival of the English army. At the Conference at Easton, Pennsylvania relinquished its claims to all lands west of the mountains in return for an Indian promise to abandon the French at Fort Duquesne.[67] This met with the approval of the representatives of the Six Nations at Easton, who considered the western Delawares their wards, and it also met with the approval of the Ohio Indians, also at Easton. Then it was also decided that a formal delegation to convey this message to the Ohio Indians should consist of representatives of the English, the Six Nations, and the other tribes at Easton. An immediate departure was made for the Ohio country. When this was accomplished, and a meeting was convened in the Ohio country, the representative from the Six Nations, Tojenontawly, a Cayuga Chief, laid down the law. He began by saying, "cousins, take notice of what I have to say," and then continued as though speaking from the throne:

we desire you would lay hold of the covenant we have made with our brethren, the English, and be strong. We likewise take the tomahawk out of your hands, that you received from the white people; use it no longer; sling the tomahawk away; it is the white people's; let them use it among themselves; it is theirs, and they are of one color; let them fight with one another, and do you be still and quiet in Kushkushing.[68]

To what extent the convention at Easton led to the stunning defeat of the French at Fort Duquesne is attested to by Colonel Bouquet who, referring to General Forbes, said:

the success of this expedition is entirely due to the General, who, by

199

bringing about the treaty with the Indians at Easton, struck the French a stunning blow, wisely delayed our advance to wait the effects of that treaty, secured all our posts and left nothing to chance, and resisted the urgent solicitation to take Braddock's road, which would have been our destruction. In all his measures he has shown the greatest prudence, firmness, and ability.[69]

An even more direct connection between Easton and the fall of Fort Duquesne is suggested by Anthony F.C. Wallace, who, in a biography of the Indian leader, King Teedyuscung, said:

the Easton settlement signalized the beginning of the end for the French in the Ohio. When, on November 20, 1758, Christian Frederick Post, escorted by Teedyuscung's son Captain Bull, brought the news of the Easton agreements to Kuskusky in the Ohio, the Delawares there raised the British flag. Five days later General Forbes occupied Fort Duquesne.[70]

If the fall of Fort Duquesne was the result of very effective Indian diplomacy, which it was, it was more of a diplomatic triumph than a military victory. Just the opposite was the case of the fall of the important post of Niagara the following year. Diplomacy did not figure in its capitulation at all. What did was a force of 1,000 Indians under the command of one of the most colorful leaders in the entire colonial period, the warrior-statesman Sir William Johnson, Lord of the Mohawks. He was second in command when the Niagara expedition started, but the death of John Prideaux moved him up to number one.

The French defenders of Niagara were outnumbered by the English besiegers, but were confident they could hold the fort until reinforcements arrived. These were expected momentarily because a large relief force under Charles Aubry and Francois de Lingery was known to be on the way. This force consisted of 1,100 Frenchmen and 300 Indians. On July 24 they walked into a trap set by Johnson at La Belle Famille, and suffered a major defeat. Niagara surrendered the next

200

day. Johnson regarded the battle with Aubry's reinforcements as a victory for the warriors of the Five
Nations. In some ways it was reminiscent of Braddock's
shameful defeat at the hands of the French-Indians,
the only difference being that this time it was the
American-Indians that won the victory over the white
men. James Thomas Flexner said of the Mohawk feat,

> the conquest of Niagara was the great-
> est English military victory so far
> achieved on the American mainland dur-
> ing the French and Indian War, and its
> effects were incalculable: It won the
> west. In their headlong flight, the
> survivors of Aubry's wilderness army
> burnt the French forts of Presqu'isle,
> Le Boeuf, and Venange before they
> holed in at Detroit, which was now as
> completely isolated from Central Cana-
> da as central Canada was from Louisi-
> ana. General Stanwix could build away
> at Fort Pitt without worrying about
> any danger. The French could not get
> at him, and the tribes were finally
> convinced that the English would win
> the war.[71]

The French and Indian War did not come to a formal
end until the Treaty of Paris was signed in 1763, but
as far as Americans were concerned, of course, the end
of the war came in 1759 with the fall of Quebec. In
the land battles that decided the fate of the American
west, which was what the war was all about, the Indians held the upper hand beginning with the French
victory over Braddock in 1755, and ending with the surrender of Fort Duquesne in 1758 and the fall of Niagara in 1759. This is also true from a negative point
of view. Had even the Iroquois, for example been on
the French side it would have been quite easy for the
French to have streamed down the waterways to drive a
wedge between New York and New England. This could
have been enough to tip the balance of the war. However, even though the Senecas and the Cayugas sympa-
thized with the French King, the Confederacy as a
whole held firm to the traditional alliance with the
English, or at worst to a benevolent neutrality. This
is what caused Benjamin Franklin to say at the time,
"I would only observe that the *Six Nations*, as a Body,
have kept Faith with the *English* ever since we knew
them, now near an Hundred Years; and that the governing Part of those People have had Notions of Honour,

whatever may be the Case with the Rum-debouched, Trader-corrupted, Vagabonds and Thieves on the Susque-hannah and Ohio, at present in Arms against us."[72]

The Iroquois policy of benevolent neutrality in the wars between France and England, a policy that allowed for occasional lapses in favor of the English, was a policy that stood the Five Nations in good stead as the 1700s moved on steadily toward the Revolution-ary War. Moreover, this turned out to be a better policy than those of some of the other Indian nations that allowed themselves to be used as cat's-paws by the French in a losing struggle, and it paid off in bringing a period of peace and civilized living for the Iroquois. After Pontiac's conspiracy sputtered out, with the formal end of the Seven Years' War, the pres-tige of the Five Nations was at a high peak, and there was even renewed talk of the Great Peace, only this time the Great Peace was to include all Indians, with the Iroquois, of course, at the head. Before anything could come of this, however, the most serious crisis ever to confront the Five Nations came to a head. This was the American Revolutionary War. The basic question was the stance of the Five Nations. Should they align themselves with their Great White Father across the sea? Or were their interests more closely identified with their brothers on this side of the shining Big-Sea-Water? Or finally, and in the last analysis, would their interest be served best by standing neutral, by letting the white men kill each other to their heart's content, while the Indians conserved their strength the better to defend the commonweal?

The League voted for neutrality in the white man's war, but the decision was not unanimous, and in any case was unenforcable. The Mohawk, Seneca, Cayuga, and Onondaga nations threw the weight of their power on the side of law and order, on the side of George III, whereas the Oneida and Tuscarora nations came down on the side of the Americans. The result was the undoing of the great Indian Confederation. As Dr. Underhill said, "this was the first time that members of the League had actually planned to fight on opposite sides, though there were occasions when they had failed to aid one another. The League was disrupted, the Great Peace ended; the council fires of the Six Nations were put out."[73]

The American Revolution was an unmitigated disas-ter for the Iroquois. Siding with the British (the

202

Oneidas and the Tuscarogas being the exceptions), it was the only important mistake the Five Nations made in the long history of the Confederation. However, this mistake was a fatal one. Not only did it pit brother against brother, and thus destroy the Great Peace that had lasted for over two centuries, but when the day of reckoning came the peace was made without the collaboration of the Iroquois, and to their disadvantage. However, during the war the Indians, quite inadvertently, made a major contribution to the colonial victory. This was when their capriciousness led to the defeat of Gentleman Johnny Burgoyne at Saratoga. Without Saratoga, there would have been no French alliance, and without the French alliance the Americans would not have won the war. So in a way the Indian allies of the British paved the way for the dissolution of an empire on which the sun never set.

Sir John Burgoyne was sent out to America in 1775, together with two other major generals, Sir Henry Clinton and William Rowe. Burgoyne was posted to Canada, and served under General Guy Carleton when the Canadian invasion force under Richard Montgomery and Benedict Arnold was repulsed on the morning of December 31, 1775. Carleton swung over to the offensive as soon as reinforcements arrived, and the American attempt to conquer Canada ended in total failure. Back in England at the opening of 1777, Burgoyne proposed that a large force be dispatched to Canada for an attack on New York straight down the Montreal-Albany Corridor. His plan contemplated another attack from Oswego through the Mohawk Valley. British forces from the Albany area would be available for support, if necessary. It was believed that this three-pronged attack would isolate New England, and possibly put an end to the rebellion.

Burgoyne was given command of the force from Canada when Carleton fell into disfavor, and by July 5, 1777, Ticonderoga, the first objective of the campaign, had been taken. But after that things began to fall apart. Not only had burgoyne begun to stretch his supply lines to Canada, but the advance from Oswego began to falter. This force, predominantly composed of Indian allies, was under the command of Barry St. Leger, and the Indians for a variety of reasons were beginning to melt away. He had Fort Stanwix at the carry to the Mohawk under siege, and a patriotic relief force under General Nicholas Herkimer had been ambushed at Oriskany, but the patriot forces were gaining in strength, and suddenly Gentleman Johnny found

203

himself facing possible encirclement. At this juncture the still loyal Benedict Arnold resorted to a stratagem that undermined the whole of Burgoyne's carefully laid plans. This was to infiltrate a semi-lunatic fanatic into St. Leger's encampment, one that the Mohawks considered a seer. His incantations played on the fears of the Indian allies to such an extent that they were convinced that St. Leger's whole force was doomed, and would soon be annihilated by the advancing patriot army under the popular general Horatio Gates. As a result, the Indians began to quietly steal away, and forced St. Leger into a retreat. The collapse of this front, and the failure of the British to support him from Albany, led to Gentleman Johnny's defeat.

The defeat of Burgoyne at Saratoga was the turning point of the Revolutionary War. The victory of the colonial forces was all France needed to come openly into the war against her old enemy, and open French aid, including the support of the naval forces of France, was all the colonial forces needed to win the war. The entry of France into the conflict gave England a war to fight, not a colonial uprising, and it is one of the ironies of history that the defection of the Indian allies of England played such an important part in determining the outcome of the decisive battle of the war, Saratoga. Had it not been for Saratoga there would not have been a Yorktown to celebrate.

American diplomacy with the Indian nations has a certain sadness about it, and it is clear in retrospect that it was a failure in the sense that it did not reconcile the conflicting interests between the red men and the white settlers. But was the extinction of the Indians inevitable? Nothing is absolutely inevitable, but since war between the English and the French advance guards of empire was accepted as inevitable, and since the Indians were the buffer nations on both sides, their extinction was probably inevitable. In spite of attempts to preserve them as allied nations or even to incorporate them by intermarriage, by education and assimilation into our own peoples, their ultimate extinction was difficult to avoid. In prerevolutionary days there were some efforts made, at least, to preserve the decencies in our official relations with the Indian nations. After the revolution there were none. During the whole of the period when we were still part of the British Empire, colonial diplomats attempted to deal with our Indian problems acdording to the usages of diplomacy, and were often successful. The objects of our early Indian diplomacy were the extension of English territory, the preservation of peace, and alliances with the Indians. All were diplomatic in their nature, and are so today, though no longer with the Indian nations.

FOOTNOTES--CHAPTER IV

[1]Francis Parkman, *The Old Regime In Canada* (New York: The Library of America, 1983), I, 1145.

[2]Moses Coit Tyler, *Patrick Henry* (Ithaca; Cornell University Press, 1962), 293-94.

[3]Francis Newton Thorpe, *The Federal and State Constitutions, Colonial Charters, and other Organic Laws* (Washington: Government Printing Office, 1909), V, 2775.

[4]Bernard Fay, *George Washington, Republican Aristocrat* (New York and Boston: Houghton Mifflin Company, 1931), 68.

[5]John Marshall, *A History of the Colonies* (Philadelphia: Abraham Small, 1824), 43.

[6]Benjamin Franklin, *The Writings of, Collected and Edited with a Life and Introduction by Albert Henry Smyth* (New York: The Macmillan Company, 1907), iv, 291-92.

[7]*Ibid.*, 294.

[8]*Ibid.*, 298.

[9]*Ibid.*, 40.

[10]Allan Nevins, *The American States during and after the Revolution 1775-1789* (New York: The Macmillan Company, 1924), 343-44.

[11]A. Leo Lemay, *The Frontiersman from Lout to Hero* (Reprinted from the Proceedings of the American Antiquarian Society, v. 28, part 2, October 1979), 187-88.

[12]Bernard Fay, *op. cit.*, 59-60.

[13]Benjamin Franklin, *op cit.*, I, 376.

[14]*Ibid.*, I, 375.

[15]Witham Marshe, *Journal of the Treaty held with the Six Nations by the Commissioners of Maryland, and other Provinces, at Lancaster, in Pennsylvania, June 1744* (Collections of the Massachusetts Historical Society for the year M,DCCC, New York: Johnson Reprint Corporation, 1968), 177.

[16]*Ibid.*, 183.

[17]*Ibid.*

[18]Francis Parkman, *Montcalm and Wolfe* (New York: The Library of America, 1983), 882.

[19]Witham Marshe, *op. cit.*, 190-91.

[20]*Ibid.*

[21]Francis Parkman, *op. cit.*, 882.

[22]Lawrence H. Gipson, *The British Empire before the American Revolution* (New York: Alfred A. Knopf, Inc., 1961), V, 79.

[23]Francis Parkman, *A Half-Century of Conflict* (New York: The Library of America, 1983), 712.

[24]Witham Marshe, *op. cit.*, 193.

[25]*Ibid.*

[26]*Ibid.*, 200.

[27]*Ibid.*

[28]*Ibid.*

[29]Benjamin Franklin, *op. cit.*, IV, 307.

[30]Henry F. DePuy, *A Bibliography of the English Colonial Treaties with the American Indians* (New York: Printed for the Lenox Club, 1917), i.

[31]Cadwallader Colden, *The History of the Five Nations* (New York: Allerton Book Co., 1922), 10-11.

[32]For another view of Parkman, see Francis P. Jennings, "Francis Parkman" (*William and Mary Quarterly*), July 1985), v. XLII, no. 3, and "A Vanishing Indian" (Penn. Mag. of Hist. and Bio., 87, 1963).

[33]Francis Parkman, *The Jesuits in North America* (New York: The Library of America, 1983), 367.

[34]*Ibid.*, 367-68.

[35]Ruth Murray Underhill, *Red Man's America* (Chicago: University of Chicago Press, 1971), 83.

[36]Cadwallader Colden, *op. cit.*, 5-6.

[37]Ruth Murray Underhill, *op. cit.*, 101-02.

[38]Lawrence Henry Gipson, *The British Empire before the American Revolution* (New York: Alfred A. knopf, 1961), V, 38.

[39]Ruth Murray Underhill, *op. cit.*, 102-03.

[40]Daniel K. Richter, "War and Culture: The Iroquois Experience" (*William and Mary Quarterly*, v. XL, No. 4, Oct. 1983), 539.

[41]*Ibid.*, 104.

[42]Cadwallader Colden, *op cit.*, xviii.

[43]Daniel K. Richter, *op cit.*, 551.

[44]Anthony F. C. Wallace, "Origins of Iroquois Neutrality: The Grand Settlement of 1701" (*Pennsylvania History*,

[45]Francis Parkman, *Count Frontenac and New France under Louis XIV* (New York: The Library of America, 1983), II, 321.

[46]Anthony F.C. Wallace, *op. cit.*, 223.

[47]Francis Parkman, *Montcalm and Wolfe*, *op. cit.*, 872.

[48]David Hawke, *The Colonial Experience* (New York: The Bobbs-Merrill Company, 1966), 384.

[49]Carl Russell Fish, *American Diplomacy* (New York: Henry Holt and Company, 1929), 17.

[50]Francis Parkman, *Montcalm and Wolfe*, *op. cit.*, II, 954.

[51]Lawrence Henry Gipson, *op cit.*, V, 111.

[52]James Thomas Flexner, *Lord of the Mohawks* (Boston: Little Brown and Company, 1979), 114-15.

[53]Journal of the Proceedings of the Congress held in Albany, in *1754 Collections Massachusetts Historical Society*, Boston, 1836 (Vol. V, Series iii), 26.

[54]*Ibid.*, 38.

[55]*Ibid.*, 42.

[56]*Ibid.*, 43.

[57]James Thomas Flexner, *op. cit.*, 120.

[58]Francis Parkman, *Montcalm and Wolfe*, *op. cit.*, II, 1052.

[59]*Ibid.*, II, 972-73.

[60]Oscar Theodore Barck and Hugh Talmage Lefler, *Colonial America* (New York: The Macmillan Company, 1958), 467.

[61]Francis Parkman, *Montcalm and Wolfe*, *op. cit.*, II, 999.

[62]*Ibid.*, 1064.

[63]Oscar Theodore Bark and Hugh Talmage Lefler, *op. cit.*, 469.

[64]Francis P. Jennings, "A Vanishing Indian: Francis Parkman Versus His Sources," *Pennsylvania Magazine of History and Biography*, 87 (1963), 317.

[65]Francis Parkman, *Montcalm and Wolfe*, *op. cit.*, 1296.

[66]*Ibid.*

[67]George T. Hunt, *The Wars of the Iroquois* (Madison, Wisc., 1940), 157ff.

[68]Francis P. Jennings, *op. cit.*, 322.

[69]Francis Parkman, *Montcalm and Wolfe*, *op. cit.*, 1306.

[70]Anthony F.C. Wallace, *King of the Delawares: Teeduscung* (Philadelphia: University of Pennsylvania Press, 1949), 207.

[71]James Thomas Flexner, *op. cit.*, 210.

[72]Benjamin Franklin, *op. cit.*, 306-07.

[73]Ruth M. Underhill, *op. cit.*, 106-07.

CHAPTER V

DIPLOMACY AND WAR

In the pursuit of their honorable profession, historians have always been inclined to pay a great deal of attention to the dictum of Lord Macaulay about what is important and unimportant in history. "What do we mean," he queried, "when we say that one past event is important and another insignificant? No past event has any intrinsic importance. The knowledge of it is valuable only as it leads us to form just calculations with respect to the future."[1] It is in this sense that the historian is a prophet looking backward but pointing forward. In doing so he fulfills the task Thucydides set out for him as a philosopher "teaching by examples." A man can have no higher goal than to achieve this lofty objective. He either succeeds brilliantly or fails miserably-- depending on the light he has been given to see the truth clearly.

At the college level, the study of World Politics, International Relations, or Foreign Policy was not offered as a separate discipline fifty years ago. Textbooks to support such courses began appearing only in the 1920s and the 1930s. At about the same time, a senior official in the State Department, J. Reuben Clark, published a Memorandum on the Monroe Doctrine that set the pattern for most historians to follow. At the outset, he posed a question, what were the facts of colonial history in the minds of the framers of the Monroe Doctrine? In answering the question, Clark covered the period in such a satisfactory way that it has been accepted ever since.

Clark reviewed the four principal wars between France and England in the colonial period, and said that these wars drained the colonies of their manpower, resources and money, and netted them nothing. He went on to say, "in the causes of none of these wars were the colonies directly involved; in the outcome of none of them were they immediately concerned. The wars had been fought, colonial life had been freely given,

large colonial funds had been expended, and great suf-
fering and hardship had been endured merely because
the mother countries in Europe were quarreling over
matters, the outcome of which was in no way related to
the colonies. The colonies were at war because they
were contiguous and the parent governments were fighting in Europe." Clark's conclusion was, "these were
great historical facts regarding colonial history
which must have been present in the minds of Monroe,
Adams, Calhoun, Jefferson, and Madison in their discussions and framing of the Monroe Doctrine. It is not
to be wondered at that they regarded European neighbors and the European system as dangerous to their
peace and safety."[2]

Clark's official memorandum, for all its 238 pages
and for all its heavy legal erudition and the bristl-
ing footnotes, is easy to read and to follow. Its con-
clusions appear to be plausible on the basis of the
facts presented, and this may explain why it has had
such a wide acceptance over such a long period of time,
more than half a century. He was obviously influenced
by the writings of Tom Paine, and his argument that
the colonies had been a "makeweight" in the scale of
British politics, and also by the Adams theory that
America had been a "football" among the Europeans all
during the colonial period. Just so Clark, in turn,
influenced later writers of diplomatic textbooks with
his pat ideas about the colonial background of our
foreign policies.

Accepting Clark's interpretation of the colonial
period it is easy to see why the Founding Fathers adopted some of the policies they did. The break with
the mother country is understandable in the light of
the wastage of human resources and lives in the senseless wars that netted us nothing; the rejection of war
as an instrument of foreign policy is also understandable; as is the policy of no entangling alliances;
plus the policy of anti-imperialism; and finally the
Monroe Doctrine, the policy of protecting America from
the "broils and wars" of Europe. The Doctrine states a
case of the United States versus Europe, not the
United States versus Latin America.

Professor Robert A. Divine used the colonial experience with foreign wars to explain why the hatred
of war is so deeply embedded in the American conscious-
ness that we are forever renouncing it, forging pacts

212

to outlaw war, and taking the lead in organizing machinery to make the world safe for democracy, or to save succeeding generations from the scourge of war. He said that the roots of this attitude "reach back to the arrival of the first adventurous Europeans in the New World. For whether they came in search of riches, religious liberty, or political freedom, they all sought isolation--isolation from poverty, from tyranny, from persecution, and most of all, isolation from war. But although the colonists longed for isolation from European conflicts, it was an immunity they could not achieve. As subjects of the British Empire they were automatically involved in its struggles for world supremacy. Four times, from 1689 to 1763, Britain went to war with France in Europe; four times the colonists marched off into dark Canadian forests to fight the French. Not until 1763, when England finally destroyed the power of France, did a promising peace settle upon the colonies."[3]

Thomas Bailey emphasized the same point, but on a broader scale. He said that the status of the colonists was one of second-class citizenship across-the-board, and that nowhere was this "better underscored than by the early international clashes. Whenever trade rivalries, dynastic embitions, or other schemings plunged England and Spain into war, Spaniards would massacre Englishmen along the southern frontier. Whenever France and England tangled, the war whoop of French-led Indians would split the night air along the northern frontier. The colonies were not supposed to reason why, they were but to do and die as the advance agents of empire."[4]

Professor Samuel Flagg Bemis, agreeing with Divine and Bailey that the colonies were merely pawns on the European chessboard, or stakes in the contest for the world balance of power, nevertheless had a point or two to make about the thesis as a whole. On the causes of the wars that the colonists were involved in despite themselves, he said they had so little comprehension of what they were all about that they changed names, thus the War of the League of Augsburg became King William's War (1689-1697), the War of the Spanish Succession became Queen Anne's War (1702-1713), the War of the Austrian Succession became King George's War (1744-1748), and the Seven Years' War became the French and Indian War (1756-1763). Finally, Bemis commented on how the colonists reacted to these wars. He said they "accepted their participation in these wars with undisturbed equanimity. Like the rise and fall of the tides, the movement of the heavenly bodies, or the apparent passage ot time itself, it seemed ineluctable. No one questioned this dispensation of fate."[5]

The colonial reaction that was depicted by Professors Bemis and Bailey is out of character for the American people as judged by subsequent events in the colonial period. Our colonial ancestors were not a supine or unquestioning lot. Quite the contrary. For a people willing to fight over a minor point of sovereignty, or because of a trivial tax on tea, the last thing one would expect would be "undisturbed equanimity" over the perpetration of a crime as horrendous as the four colonial wars are depicted to have been. In addition to this, when the Declaration of Independence was drawn up the authors in the opening paragraph said that a decent respect to the opinions of mankind required that they should declare the causes that led to the separation, and yet there is no mention of the crime of the four colonial wars even though 27 such causes were enumerated, including such inconsequential ones as quartering troops in private houses. If the four foreign wars were the crimes they were made out to be, is it not strange that they did not find a place among the 27 causes that impelled the separation? Of course it is, and the fact that they were not even mentioned is almost proof positive that such was not the case. This indicates that there is something wrong with the kind of history that has been offered the American people. The four great wars of the colonial period were not a crime in the colonial view, but a God-given opportunity to accomplish what they had always wanted to do, which was to expand and enlarge the rapidly increasing British Empire, of which they were a vital, if not the most important, part. Nor understanding this is one of the major shortfalls of our colonial history.

From the outset, the policy of empire was one on which there was substantial agreement between the mother country and the colonies, the only difference being that, by and large, the colonial leaders tended to be out in front of the mother country in their zeal for enlarging the empire at the expense of their rival claimants in America. The vision the original settlers brought with them was one of continental scope. They would not be satisfied with anything less than an English-speaking New World, and ideally this would include North and South America plus the connecting isthmus, as well as all the islands near the two continents in both oceans. We never forgot this vision of

ourselves as the western frontier of a British Empire
that was constantly expanding and which would dominate
the world eventually. On occasion, it was difficult
for us to hold ourselves in check when our own sovereign would give away something here of major importance in exchange for some petty advantage in Europe.
Franklin, in developing his imperial notions to Lord
Kames said, "I refrain, for I see you begin to think
my notions extravagant, and look upon them as the rav-
ings of a mad prophet."[6]

During the first half of the 17th Century all the
great and some of the not so great powers, New France,
New Netherlands, New Sweden, New Scotland, and New England, staked out claims to lands in the New World,
lands that were already claimed by Spain. The result
was total confusion over the conflicting and overlapping claims, and the only solution in each case seemed
to be the use of force, or the threat thereof. Among
all the potential zones of conflict there were three
flashpoints that were particularly dangerous. These
were St. Augustine in the south, New Amsterdam in the
center, and Acadia in the north. Of these three,
Acadia or Nova Scotia was probably the most important
as this was one where New England and New France confronted each other.

The province of Acadia had its beginning with John
Cabot's visit to Cape Breton Island in 1497, and got
its name Nova Scotia when James I of England (James VI
of Scotland) granted the whole peninsula to the Earl
of Stirling in 1621. Meanwhile the French had staked
out their claim to the land as a result of the voyage
of Giovanni de Verrazano, an Italian sailing for
France in 1524, and in 1604 the Sieur de Monts established a colony in Acadia. The name Acadia came from
an Indian word Acadie or Aquoddy, which simply means
place or region. The French themselves called their
settlement La Cadie or Acadie. The original boundaries,
if they can be called such, ran from about the lati-
tude of Montreal as far south as Philadelphia. Today,
Acadia is the maritime province of Canada called Nova
Scotia, and it includes Cape Breton Island, but not
Maine and New Brunswick, nor any parts of Pennyslvania
or the province of Quebec. However, during the colonial period the boundaries were so elastic that no one
knew for sure what they were. They were more or less
in the eye of the beholder as the territory switched
hands between the French and the English.

The strategic importance of Acadia during the colonial period was very great. It could almost be called the key to North America. Acadia was of vital importance to the New Englanders because of its proximity to the fisheries of the area, and also because of its importance as a base from which French privateers could prey on the commerce of the Boston merchants. Take away their commerce and the fisheries and our New England ancestors were dead in the water. For the French, Acadia was even more important. It commanded the St. Lawrence waterway at the mouth of the great river, and without the St. Lawrence in French hands Quebec and Montreal could not survive. Of course without them there could not have been any control of the Great Lakes region, and without that the grand strategy of France could collapse. This was to join hands behind the English by linking up the two extremities of the French empire, the one at Quebec and Montreal in the north, and the other at New Orleans in the South. The successful implementation of this strategy would have given France control of North America, limiting the English to a narrow strip along the coast. Thus it is not surprising that Acadia was called the key to the continent. In fact, if Halford J. Mackinder had been around at the time he might have expressed himself as follows:

Who rules Acadia commands the St. Lawrence waterway;

Who rules the St. Lawrence commands the gateway to the Great Lakes;

Who rules the Great Lakes commands the Mississippi, and

Who rules the Mississippi commands the Heartland of America.[7]

The conflict over Acadia began shortly after England and France planted their first settlements in the New World. The aggressor was England. One of her non-illustrious sons, Sir Samuel Argall, who was also one of the worst governors in the history of Virginia, took it upon himself to root the French out of Canada. Accordingly, he embarked for Acadia in 1613, and in the first expedition destroyed the Jesuit settlement on Mount Desert Island off the coast of Maine. Prisoners were brought back to Jamestown. The following

216

year he led another expedition to the same area, and succeeded in laying waste to Port Royal (Annapolis Royal), again carrying prisoners and booty to Jamestown. At the same time, and on the southward journey, Captain Argall looked in at the small Dutch settlement on the Hudson River. He issued an ultimatum to the governor, and did not leave until the English flag had been hoisted over the settlement. The Dutch agreed to submit to the King of England, and to the governor of Virginia under him. They also agreed to pay tribute. All the while, the mother countries were at peace with each other.

War broke out between England and France in 1626, and both countries reinforced their outposts in the New World. Under the leadership of the Cardinal de Richelieu, Louis XIII organized the Company of New France, and charged it with the mission of promoting the interest of France in the New World. The King also made available two ships of war, armed and equipped. For their part the English set on foot a mission to drive the French out of Acadia and Canada. The organizing force behind this mission was Gervase Kirke. He outfitted a force of three armed ships commanded by his three sons, David, Lewis, and Thomas and charged them, under letters of marque from the King, with the task of implementing the King's will. On their first expedition they seized a fleet of French vessesl near Newfoundland, and then proceeded to reduce the French stations in Nova Scotia, after which they returned to England. In 1629 the three brothers came back to the New World, and succeeded in forcing Samuel de Champlain to surrender Canada. Thus for the second time in 15 years English arms had conquered Acadia or Nova Scotia, the key to Canada, and for the first time ever Canada itself had been reduced.

This was a period of great travail for Charles I. He was beset with personal and constitutional problems that had nothing to do with the conquests of Acadia and Canada. Foremost among these was his personal feud with the Commons over money and privileges. The war with France was proceeding badly also, and with the disaster at La Rochelle in 1627 it became a lost cause. Passage of the Petition of Right in 1628 weakened his position with Parliament, and on March 10, 1629, he dissolved that body. This was the beginning of the period of personal rule, which lasted for 11 years or until 1640. Charles was so desperate for money at this time that he was living from hand to

217

mouth. On April 24, 1629, he entered into a preliminary treaty of peace with France. It was called the treaty of Susa.

There were so many problems arising out of the so-called treaty of Susa that it was eventually superseded by the definitive treaty of St. Germain-en-Laye. According to the terms of this treaty Charles gave up practically everything he had gained in North America. The treaty provided for the restoration to France of "la Nouvelle France, la Cadie, et Canada," as well as "la Port Royal, Fort de Quebec, et Cap Breton."[8] Charles's motive in restoring to France her empire in North America has often been questioned. However, the reason is not complicated. Charles's kingdom was practically bankrupt, and his throne was on the line in the war he was waging against Parliament. In addition, it was well known that Richelieu was making extensive and expensive preparations to recover France's possessions in America. If they could not be held against a determined French attack, why not do the gracious thing, and surrender them lock, stock and barrel? Also, there was the face-saving legalism put forward by the French diplomats, that the conquest of Canada had been made during the interval between Susa and St. Germain, making the conquest invalid since it had taken place in time of peace.

Even so, however, the matter of money still figured in the transaction. Charles did nothing without taking into consideration the matter of money, and this was of necessity, not of choice. In this case it was the matter of his marriage to the sister of Louis XIII of France, Henrietta Maria, and the promised dowry. It had not been paid in full, and he accordingly instructed the English ambassador to the French court to hold out for the money before signing the definitive treaty of peace. However, the ambassador was also instructed that upon receipt of "the balance due, and not before, he is to give up to the French both Quebec and Port Royal" captured by Kirke. Parkman's conclusion was that it was thus "for a sum equal to about two hundred and forty thousand dollars that Charles entailed on Great Britain and her colonies a century of bloody wars. The Kirkes and their associates, who had made the conquest at their own cost, under the royal authority, were never reimbursed, though David Kirke received the honor of knighthood, which cost the King nothing."[9]

218

The treaty of St. Germain was viewed with alarm by serious men on this side of the Atlantic. The day the treaty was signed, March 9, 1632, was considered a day of shame. Thomas Hutchinson, the last American-born royal governor of Massachusetts, said it was just blind good luck that "the frenchified court of King Charles the first"[10] did not give up Massachusetts as well as Acadia in the treaty, because the French could make out no better title to Acadia then to Massachusetts. In that case, he said, "the Dutch, the next year, would have quietly possessed themselves of Connecticut river, unless the French, instead of the English, had prevented them. Whether the people of either nation would have persevered is uncertain. If they had done it, the late contest for the dominion of North America (the Seven Years' War, 1756-63) would have borne a very different proportion to that of the rest of Europe from what it does at present."[11]

Governor Hutchinson's concern about the lack of empire-consciousness on the part of Charles I was a recurring irritant in the relations between the mother country and the colonies. The colonial vision was much clearer than that of many little Englanders in the mother country, and the colonists were just as exasperated as Hutchinson was to see the sovereigns of England deal away important parts of the New World for a pittance in the Old, in this case a paltry sum of money.

The treaty of St. Germain was no sooner signed than France began to assert its sovereignty in the area of Acadia. Claude de Razilly arrived at Port Royal with a strong reinforcement of settlers. One of the holdovers from the old regime was Charles de la Tour. His ambition was to make himself master of Acadia, and while he accepted the authority of Razilly, as soon as he died, which was within three years of his arrival, de la Tour set himself up as his successor. He was challenged by Charles de Menou d'Aunay, who claimed the authority by virtue of having been second in command to Razilly. A civil war resulted, and both sides tried to enlist the support of the Bay Colony. For the Massachusetts, the trick was to be on the winning side in the duel between Le Tour and D'Aunay. Fishing rights and trade were in the balance.

In 1641, La Tour made the first overture by sending an emissary, described as a "protestant of Rochel,"[12] to Boston seeking military aid against

D'Aunay. He also held out the prospects of a free trade treaty, which he knew would be attractive to the Boston merchants. However, the Massachusetts men were cautious. They were not satisfied with the "credentials" of the envoy, and "the governor and council declined any treaty."[13] This did not discourage La Tour. He tried again the following year with another mission to the Bay Colony, and while they still would not treat with him on a formal basis, relaxed enough to allow the merchants to send some of their goods to the River St. John to trade with La Tour. The merchants encountered D'Aunay on their return trip, and La Tour's rival sought to put the fear of God in them. He showed them "a printed copy of an arret he had obtained from France against La Tour, and threatened, that if any vessels came to La Tour he would make prize of them."[14]

On June 12, 1643, La Tour himself came to Boston. This time he brought a sizeable force with him, and it was duly noted that the master and crew were "protestants of Rochel." La Tour called on the Governor, and showed him the official papers wherein he was referred to as the "King's Lieutenant in Acadie."[15] He also renewed his request for a military alliance. Just as the President today might summon a special session of Congress to meet a grave national emergency, so the Governor of Massachusetts called together the magistrates and deputies to make a decision on this vital matter. After considerable discussion, a decision was arrived at, that,

> they could not, consistent with the
> articles they had just agreed to with
> the other governments, grant aid without
> any advice; but they did not think
> it necessary to hinder any, who were
> willing to be hired, from aiding him,
> which he took very thankfully; but
> some being displeased with these concessions,
> the governor called a second
> meeting, where, upon a more full debate,
> the first opinion was adhered
> to.[16]

The reference to "the articles they had just agreed to" was to the treaty-union that went under the style of the New England Confederation, which included beside Massachusetts the colonies of Plymouth, Connecticut, and New Haven. The dissenters in Massachusetts

Bay based their case on the virtues of a policy of strict neutrality in the war then in Progress in Acadia. They could not see any wisdom in exposing "their trade to the ravages of D'Aulney, and perhaps the whole colony to the resentment of the French King, who would not be imposed upon by the distinction of permitting and commanding force to assist La Tour." In addition, the conservative dissenters simply did not like La Tour. They said he "was a papist attended by priests, friars, &c. and that they were in the case of Jehoshaphat who joined with Ahab on idolater, which act was expressly condemned in scriptures."[17]

La Tour's primary military object was to collect enough military force to enable him to raise a blockade that D'Aunay had thrown across the mouth of the river St. John, which is where La Tour had his main military base, after he had removed himself from the base at Cape Sable. The force he raised, with the tacit consent of the Bay Colony, consisted of four armed vessels with adequate crews to handle them under combat conditions. The understanding he had with the magistrates of the Bay Colony was that they would sail without any formal "commissions," and that they would not fight except in self-defense, but it was also understood that if there were any plunder and spoils, they would be divided in accordance with the ordinary rules in such cases.

The rules applied, as it turned out. La Tour's task force, augmented by the volunteers from Massachusetts, broke the blockade put up by D'Aunay, and La Tour's vessels pursued the fleeing ships of D'Aunay back to Fort Royal, where the blockade-breakers had a field day with the furs and other assets of the defeated foe. But this was not the end of D'Aunay. Going back to France, he picked up reinforcements, and returned to Acadia with a new force, plus a royal warrant for the arrest of La Tour as a rebel and a traitor. However, D'Aunay was also ordered to make his peace with the men of the Bay Colony, and not to hold them responsible for the breach of "international law"[18] of which they had been guilty in giving unofficial aid to La Tour. Accordingly, D'Aunay opened up negotiations with Massachusetts as soon as he returned to the New World. The upshot was a treaty of peace signed at Boston on October 8, 1644. A codicil to the treaty was the stipulation that, while it was to go into effect immediately, its "full ratification" could not take place until it had been approved at the "next

221

meeting of the commissioners of the united colonies of New England."[19]

An interesting feature of this treaty negotiation, as Dr. James Brown Scott pointed out, is that "the negotiations were concluded -- quite contrary to European precedent -- within the space of three days. For our Massachusetts ancestors were a frugal lot, and they even complained about the expense incurred in a diplomatic transaction of but three days."[20] Another interesting point is that the treaty negotiations were carried on entirely in Latin, the traditional diplomatic language of Europe. A copy of the original, in Latin, is available in the Hutchinson Papers (Publications of the Prince Society, 1865; Albany, 1865, p. 164). Ratification by the New England Confederation, when that was obtained, was also in the diplomatic language of Europe. The English translation of the original Latin is a footnote on page 165 of the Prince Society edition of the Hutchinson Papers. Even though at this date the French language was making inroads on Latin as the accepted diplomatic tongue of Europe, and though it would have been equally good form to have drawn the treaty and its ratification in French, the colonists were determined that there should be no question of the formal diplomatic character of the agreement. Therefore, Latin, the old, classic and accepted diplomatic tongue was chosen.

The treaty of D'Aunay established a "firm peace" between the contracting parties. However, it was also a trade convention, guaranteeing not only free trade between D'Aunay and New England, but stating the right of New England to trade with others "whether French or others wheresoever they dwell," and finally, it was an arbitration agreement like William Jennings Bryan's famous "cooling-off" treaties of 1913, stipulating that "neither part shall attempt any thing against the other in any hostile manner, until the wrong be first declared and complained of, and due satisfaction not given."[21]

The treaty itself, it will be recalled, was signed on October 8, 1644, and in the last paragraph it was stipulated "that the full ratification and conclusion of this agreement be referred to the next meeting of the commissioners of the united colonies of New-England, for the continuation or abrogation, and in the mean time to remain firm and inviolate."[22] The full ratification was not effected until September 2, 1645,

222

and D'Aunay was apparently peeved at the delay, for in the same year he intercepted a Massachusetts vessel carrying supplies to La Tour. This was contrary to the Commerce provisions of the treaty, and Massachusetts lodged a formal complaint. D'Aunay replied "in very high and lofty language, and threatened them with the effects of his majesty's displeasure."[23] This was something, it is significant to observe, that was at no time mentioned by the New Englanders. A paragraph from the Massachusetts reply is of much interest as showing the attitude taken by the colony,

and whereas he oft threatened us with the king of France his power, etc., we answered that we did acknowledge him to be a mighty prince, but we conceived withal he would continue to be just, and would not break out against us, without hearing our answer, or if he should, yet New England had a God, who was able to save us and did not use to forsake his servants.[24]

They did not reply that the King of England was also a mighty prince, apparently because they did not think he entered into the matter.

A good opportunity to reconcile these outstanding obstacles to a firm peace seemed to offer itself in the ceremony of exchanging ratifications. The commissioners of the New England Confederation selected an envoy with great care, gave him full powers, and instructed him to obtain a ratification of the treaty from the hand of D'Aunay. This proved to be very difficult. D'Aunay received the envoy courteously, but refused to treat with him seriously, and refused to give his full ratification of the treaty. He also declared that "he would sit still until spring expecting their answer." He even scolded the Massachusetts, saying "that he perceived their drift was to gain time, whereas if their messengers had been furnished with power to have treated with him and concluded about their differences he doubted not all might have been composed, for he stood more upon his honor than his interest."[25]

The Massachusetts Governor and General Court then, on May 22, 1646, decided to go the last mile with D'Aunay to meet all his objections about "full powers," and informed him that the Deputy Governor of the Colony would head the next mission with other high

223

personages (just as today the Secretary of State might be selected), and that therefore he could put his mind at rest about "full powers." An extended correspondence then ensued to make preparations for the conference, which the Massachusetts people said should take place sometime in the month of September. They also suggested that D'Aunay should decide on the specific time and the place. This was opposed by some of the Massachusetts men who argued that it was,

> too great a condescension, and they would have had him come to the English settlement at Pemaquid; but his commission of lieutenant-general for the King of France was thought by others to carry so much dignity with it, that it would be no dishonour to the colony to go to his own house; but it seems he was too good a husband to put himself to the expence of entertaining the messengers, and wrote in answer that he perceived they were now in earnest, and desired peace, as he did for his part, and that he thought himself highly honoured by their vote to send so many of their principal men to him; but desired he might spare them the labour, and he would send two or three of his to Boston, in August following (1646) to hear and determine, &c.[26]

D'Aunay's embassy arrived in Boston on schedule. There was no demonstration on the day of their arrival, as it was Sunday. The envoys were conducted quietly to their lodgings, and after service, an armed guard escorted them with much dignity to the Mayor's residence, where they were suitably entertained. The following day, Hutchinson records,

> they began upon business, and every day dined in public, and were conducted morning and evening to and from the place of treaty with great ceremony. Great injuries were alleged on both sides, and after several days spent, an amnesty was agreed upon.

Governor Hutchinson concluded by saying that both sides were well satisfied by the conference, "the treaty renewed, and all matters amicably settled."[27]

224

In the meantime, D'Aunay's motive in not coming to Boston himself, and in choosing Boston as the site of the conference, became clear. He wanted to keep the Massachusetts men busy with treaty-making while he proceeded to destroy his enemy, La Tour. This he did by storming the fort with all the forces at his command, and succeeded in driving La Tour out. He then confiscated a fortune in furs and sterling -- which belonged in large part to the un-neutral merchants of Massachusetts who had backed La Tour so heavily. La Tour himself escaped to Newfoundland, where he vainly sought to enlist the support of Sir David Kirke, who had been made governor of that important post after his exploits in Nova Scotia and Canada just prior to the Munich-like treaty of St. Germain in 1632. Disappointed in this, La Tour returned to Boston where he talked some of the merchants into sending good money after bad, by backing him in a trading venture in the Bay of Fundy. The merchants lost their money for the second time, and did not hear from La Tour again until, after D'Aunay's death, the defeated La Tour returned, and married D'Aunay's widow, thereby repossessing himself of the whole of Nova Scotia. Which all goes to show how hard it is to keep a good man down.

American diplomacy with our rival European claimants to empire in the New World was not confined to the delicate business of deciding between D'Aunay and La Tour, and to finding a way out when it was discovered that we had backed the wrong horse; there was also the question of the Dutch and the Swedes, to say nothing of the vulnerable southern flank, where the debatable land was between the English and the Spanish. Thus, moving southward in our survey, we find that the Swedes had attempted a colony in what is now Delaware, and the Dutch, in the form of a trading company, a form so successful in English colonization, had thrust in a formidable enclave at the mouth of the Hudson River between the colonies of New England and the English colonies in the Chesapeake Bay area. The Dutch challenge was to the most vulnerable sector of the English position on the continent. If successful, the Dutch would be able to challenge the English for the dominant position in North America. In other words, the Dutch wedge was like a dagger aimed at the vital center of the English position.

The Swedes were at first successful against the Dutch, capturing their outpost on the Delaware River,

but the Dutch retook the fort, and also forced the surrender of the few remaining Swedes. With the English,
it was another matter. When the Dutch built their Fort
Good Hope on the Connecticut River, Massachusetts and
Plymouth objected, and then pushed their settlements
of Windsor and Saybrook to virtually isolate Fort Good
Hope. Peter Stuyvesant sent a Dutch ship to deal with
the English, but finding them too strong, gave up the
effort to dislodge them by force. The English continued with their peaceful aggression, and soon there
were four "river towns" in the area united in a Confederation. Also the New Englanders planted several towns
on both shores of Long Island. Stuyvesant did the only
thing he could do under the circumstances, which was
to resort to diplomacy, not war, in his dealings with
the English. This led to the Treaty of Hartford in
1650.

In accordance with the terms of the Treaty of Hartford, the full text of which is in Hutchinson's history, the "bounds and lymyts, both upon the island and
maine," were agreed upon. The bounds of Long Island
were determined by giving the English the easterly
part and the Dutch the westerly part of a line drawn
from Oyster Bay south to the sea. On the Connecticut
River, except for a small area near Hartford, both
sides of the river were "to be and remaine to the English." However, the colonists were not so lucky with
respect to the Hudson River line. There it was provided that the English were not to settle "within tenn
miles of Hudson's river."[28]

The Dutch were not happy with the Hartford settlement. When Peter Stuyvesant returned to New Netherland
he was criticized for having been overreached in the
treaty negotiations. "All the arbitrators were English and friends of the English," wrote Van der Donck,
"and in the affair they pulled the wool over the Director's eyes."[29] This was being unfair to Peter Stuyvesant. The Dutch were weak in the New World, hardly
up to a war against Connecticut and New Haven, and
hopelessly outmatched if Massachusetts and Plymouth
joined the struggle. Considering the circumstances,
therefore, the Director did very well at Hartford. Getting the English to recognize a Dutch sphere of influence over the Hudson was a major accomplishment. The
Hudson leads to the Mohawk Valley, and that was the
key to the west. By obtaining this for a small part of
Long Island he was getting almost as big a bargain as
Peter Minuit did when he purchased Manhattan Island
for $24 in trinkets.

226

The Treaty of Hortford brought a degree of tranquility to the relations between New Netherland and New England. A brisk trade developed in Dutch bottoms in and out of New Amsterdam, which was fast becoming the most important trading center in the New World, just as Amsterdam was fast becoming the entrepot of Europe. This was to the great advantage of the colonists, particularly to the merchants of Boston, but at the same time it was to the disadvantage of the merchants of England, who resolved to outlaw the Dutch trade with the English colonies by the simple device of requiring that all such trade should be carried in English bottoms. Understandably, the Dutch were furious, and when the British added insult to injury by arbitrary visit and search procedures on the high seas, the Dutch retaliated by declaring war on England in 1652.

The Navigation Act of 1651, which brought on the first Anglo-Dutch War, was as unpopular in New England as it was in New Amsterdam. Strict enforcement of it would ruin the Boston merchants, and even jeopardize the solvency of the colony, faced as it was with a crushing balance of payments problem in the trade for British manufactures. Peter Stuyvesant was not unaware of this, and accordingly he advanced a proposal, theoretically to the commissioners of the New England Confederation, but actually to the merchants of Boston, that "the English and Dutch colonies maintain a policy of neutrality in the war between their Nations in Europe."[30]

His proposal made sense. This Anglo-Dutch War, which began in 1652 and ended in 1654, was essentially a contest for supremacy in the world of trade, and since it would be decided on the high seas anyway, the question rose as to why the war should be allowed to disturb the tranquility of the colonies in the New World, particularly when that tranquility was profitable to both sides? The arguments were so powerful for neutrality in the New World that Stuyvesant's request in 1653 was readily granted. This was not the first nor would it be the last time when the New World asserted its neutrality in the wars that were devastating the Old. Contrariwise, the New World had its own wars to protect vital interests, and it was not uncommon for them to take place when the mother countries were at peace with each other. Max Savelle explained the reasons for this when he said, "the geographic situation of the English and Durch colonies not only took them outside the stream of European conflict, in this

227

case, but had actually created interests for them which made for the maintenance of peace. Nor was this an isolated case." He then proceeded to cite the Anglo-French treaty of Whitehall in 1686, stipulating, "Article XVII of this treaty provides that hostilities between the French and English colonies in America shall not be made a cause of war between the mother countries, and Article XVIII provides that war between England and France shall not be a cause of war in America."[31]

In this case, the First Dutch War, the English colonies considered themselves at liberty to make their own decisions on the war, whether they were involved or not, and the Massachusetts General Court so informed Oliver Cromwell.[32] But there was more to it than that. This was the trade question. The merchants of the Bay Colony were bound and determined that nothing should interfere with their profitable trade with the Dutch, and they were even willing to risk the displeasure of the London Parliament over this vital issue. In these hard times, the Massachusetts men traded for a living, and it was not until much later that it could be said that they lived for trade. On the other hand, the colonies of Connecticut and New Haven worried less about trade, and more about the Dutch menace to their territorial existence. In other words, Connecticut and New Haven were the fire-eaters in the dispute with the Dutch, and open war (not neutrality) was their preference, provided, of course, that they could count on strong support from the powerful Bay Colony. As usual in colonial diplomacy, trade and alliance with the Indians inflamed the dispute.

In fact, in 1653 the Indian question came to the fore in the diplomacy of the period, and raised a very serious question about the policy of neutrality, whether it could even be afforded in the Anglo-Dutch war? This happened when a rumor began to circulate among the commissioners of the New England Confederation that the Dutch governor was privately inciting the Indians to a general uprising against the English. A special meeting of the Confederation was called, as the President today might call a special session of Congress, and the matter up for discussion was whether they should not act before it was too late, in other words, an immediate declaration of war, as urged by Connecticut and New Haven? Meanwhile, the commissioners sent agents to the Dutch governor to hear his side of the case. While they were gone, the quotas were set for each colony in the event of war. They were as follows: Massachusetts 333, Plymouth 60, Connecticut 65, and New Haven 42.[33]

When the agents returned from their session with the Dutch governor, they were divided in opinion as to whether the rumors were well founded enough to justify them in resorting to a preemptive war. Massachusetts resolved to lay the issue before its General Court, and that body put it up to their elders. The elders appointed counsel to present both sides of the case, and after a full hearing handed down the following judgment:

> that the proofs and presumptions of
> the execrable plot, tending to destruc-
> tion of so many of the dear saints of
> God, imputed to the Dutch governor and
> the fiscal, were of such weight as to
> induce them to believe the reality of
> it; yet they were not so fully conclu-
> sive, as to clear up a present proceed-
> ing to war before the world, and to
> bear up their hearts with that fulness
> of persuasion, which was meet, in com-
> mending the case to God in prayer and
> to the people in exhortations, and
> that it would be safest for the colo-
> nies to forbear the use of the sword;
> but advised to be in a posture of de-
> fence and readiness for action, until
> the mind of God should be more clearly
> known, either for a settled peace or
> more manifest grounds of war.[34]

A month later, on May 26, 1653, Connecticut came up with more details concerning the preparations for war on the part of the Indians, and the outlook was so alarming that a full meeting of the New England Commissioners except one were convinced that war was imminent, and that action was required under the collective security provisions of the New England Confederation. The lone dissenter was one of the two commissioners from Massachusetts, the other being in favor of war. According to the Articles, the lone dissenter from Massachusetts should have made no difference, because Article 6 of the Confederation clearly provided that any six of the eight commissioners (two from each colony) had the power to invoke the military provisions, that is to "determine all affairs of our war or

229

peace, leagues, aids, charges, and numbers of men for war."[35] But when the one dissenter came from Massachusetts it made a difference, a big difference in this case because the General Court of Massachusetts intervened with a resolution "that no determination of the commissioners though they should all agree, should bind the general court to join in an offensive war which should appear to such general court to be unjust."[36]

The only thing that justified this high-handed action on the part of Massachusetts was the importance it attached to the trade with the Dutch and with the Indians, and the only reason it got away with it, at least at the outset, was because of its power position. The weaker colonies in the Confederation threatened its dissolution, but since they could not stand alone, they could not follow through on the threat. Their weakness was one of the reasons for the confederacy in the first place, and because of it they decided to appeal their case to Oliver Cromwell, the Lord Protector of England. They did this through their Agents, calling upon them to intercede with Cromwell in order to make Massachusetts abide by the terms of the New England Confederation, and if possible to send them some aid in the war against the Dutch and their Indian allies.

The request came at a very propitious time as far as Cromwell was concerned, because it was near the end of the European phase of the Anglo-Dutch war, and just before the beginning of the conflict with Spain. Thus the Lord Protector dispatched a small squadron of four ships with 200 soldiers to the New World, and put them under the command of Major Robert Sedgwick and Captain John Leverett, both men of high standing in the colonies. The Bay Colony was enjoined by Cromwell, together with Connecticut, New Haven, and Plymouth, to give prompt and hearty cooperation to the undertaking. Massachusetts hesitated no longer. While she still refused to take an active part in the campaign, she allowed 300 volunteers to enlist, Connecticut raised 200 men, New Haven 133, and Plymouth promised 50 men, but failed to get them ready. The interesting thing is that Connecticut raised nearly five times as many men as would have been her quota according to the figures worked out in the previous meeting of the commissioners, and New Haven raised three times her quota. Another interesting thing is that this Old World intervention in the affairs of the New was entirely at the behest of the New. It was certainly not a case of the New World becoming reluctantly involved in the affairs of the Old, or as Thomas A. Bailey and other distinguished diplomatic historians would have us believe, a case of the American colonies being pushed around like pawns on the European chessboard. This was a case of the New World actively seeking the aid of the Old in order to pursue the policy of empire in America. Finally, this disposes of the notion that the early settlers, above everything else, were seeking in their new homes, "isolation-- isolation from poverty, from tyranny, from persecution, and most of all, isolation from war."[37] The early Americans were like later Americans in their attitudes toward most things, including poverty, tyranny, persecution, and above all war.

As for the war against the Dutch in New Netherland, when Sedgwick's fleet was preparing to sail out of Boston's harbor in July, 1654, an English ship came sailing in with the news that an Anglo-Dutch treaty of peace had been signed at Westminster on April 15, 1654. Cromwell had never been inspired about the war with Protestant Holland because it always seemed to him that the real enemy was Catholic Spain. However, the termination of the war with the Dutch in April did pose a problem for the Lord Protector, for it raised the question of what to do with the task force in North America? The Massachusetts men solved the problem by pointing northward to another enemy and bitter rival in the New World, Catholic France. Here was an opportunity to right the wrong of St. Germain. Accordingly, with or without orders directly from Cromwell, Sedgwick sailed northward, even though the mother countries were at peace with each other. He drove the French out of their forward base at Penobscot, and reduced the whole of Acadia. This boosted the morale of the merchants of Massachusetts who were happy to see their somewhat illegal trade with the Dutch restored, and the General Court of Massachusetts took pleasure in seeing their forces employed in the right place and against the right enemy. This turn of events also gave New Netherland a new lease on life, a lease that was to run for the next 10 years.

The lease ran out in 1664, when Charles II decided to place his brother, the Duke of York (later King James II), on a vast track of land in the New World. The boundaries of this grant were princely. Regardless of any other grants, the boundaries of this one included all of New Netherland, Long Island, and most of

231

New England. But first, New Netherland had to be conquered. The military task was not expected to be difficult. The task force Charles II sent to do the job
consisted of four ships under the command of Colonel
Richard Nicolls, who had already been appointed governor of the province he was about to seize. The four
frigates were armed with 120 guns, and carried not
less than 1,000 troops. To oppose them, Stuyvesant
had no ships of any consequence, and not more than 150
trained soldiers. He had warned his government as
early as 1663 that he would not be able to keep his
sinking ship afloat if he was not given substantial
reinforcements. In other words, effective resistance
was out of the question.

All this was the case even if the "Fifth Column"
in New Netherland was not taken into consideration.
As it was, the number of English settlers in New
Netherland was nearly half the total population as
early as 1650, and had grown larger. In other words,
Stuyvesant had on his hands a Trojan horse in New
Netherland, not unlike the one the Loyalists had to
deal with in Madrid during the Spanish Revolution. The
English in New Netherland also represented the kind of
threat to Stuyvesant that Quisling posed to Norway in
1940. It was clear to the Director that he not only
faced overwhelming military force, but his rear was
also in jeopardy from the English Fifth Column. There
was even an additional factor. When the English came,
they did so in stealth. The attack on New Netherland
came like the Japanese attack on Pearl Harbor, entirely without warning, and without benefit of a declaration of war. The only saving grace when the fleet arrived was that instead of opening fire on the Dutch
position Colonial Nicolls offered the Dutch very gener-
our terms of surrender. In his delightful history of
the American colonies, John Marshall relates what happened then:

> upon the appearance of Colonel Nichols
> before New Amsterdam, Stuyvesant, the
> governor, was disposed to defend the
> place; but the inhabitants, feeling no
> inclination for the contest, took part
> with their invaders; and Stuyvesant
> was compelled to sign a capitulation,
> by which he surrendered the town to
> the English, stipulating for the inhab-
> itants their property, and the rights
> of free denizens. New Amsterdam took

the name of New York, and the island
of Manhattans that of York Island.[38]

The conquest of New Netherland does not always get
the place it deserves in the annals of the Republic.
Much is made of the purchase of Louisiana in 1803, and
of the tremendous impact it had on the history of the
United States, how it doubled the original endowment,
provided limitless room for expansion, and eliminated
France, Spain, and England from the contest over the
Mississippi, but not as much attention is usually
given to the effects of the conquest of New Netherland
in 1664. What is its place in the chain of historic
causation?

John Fiske had a ready answer to this question. He
recognized at once the strategic importance of New
York in the scheme of things, and what its acquisition
meant to the course of empire in America, as well as
to the course of union in 1787. Writing in 1899, the
famous historian said,

> the acquisition of New Netherland by
> the English was an event scarcely sec-
> ond in magnitude to the conquest of
> Canada in later days. The position of
> Nicolls in the seventeenth century an-
> swers to that of Wolfe in the eigh-
> teenth. The earlier conquest was the
> first great link in the chain of ev-
> ents that brought about the latter,
> for it brought the British frontier in-
> to direct and important contact with
> the French frontier, all the way from
> the headwaters of the Hudson River to
> those of the Ohio. It gave to the Eng-
> lish the command of the commercial and
> military centre of the Atlantic coast
> of North America; and by bringing New
> England into closer relations with Vir-
> ginia and Maryland, it prefigured and
> made possible a general union of At-
> lantic states.[39]

Halford J. Mackinder would have said the same thing
about the geopolitical importance of the conquest of
New York in 1664, and of how its acquisition led directly to the conquest of Canada in 1759, as well as to
the more perfect union in 1787.

With the expulsion of the Dutch from the center position on the Atlantic coast in 1664, and the establishment of South Carolina on the southern flank in the 1670s, England had an unbroken line from Florida to Canada, and it was a line that could be nourished and defended from the sea approaches to the continent. We had no fear of our European rivals on the sea, but on land we had a healthy respect for them, and here in the wilderness we feared them, not only because of themselves, but also because of their Indian allies, who could and were being used against us. But the English line, while impressive on maps, was not a solid one. It was open at both ends. In the north, Acadia was ceded back to France by the treaty of Breda in 1667, and in the south, up to the treaty of Madrid in 1670, Spain had not even recognized the validity of Virginia, much less that of Carolina. In other words, the only validity the English line had was what could be derived from its appearance on English maps, and these were subject to change without notice.

About twenty-five years after the conquest of New York, and 19 years after Carolina was thrown forward as a shield for Virginia, the first of the four great European conflicts over North America began. On this side of the water it was called King William's War, and on the other side it was known as the War of the League of Augsburg. It began, not in Europe in 1689, but in America some years earlier, when the Indian allies of the antagonists battled each other in the wilderness. These conflicts were the same as those when the principals were engaged, or nearly so. The relationships between the Indian nations and their European patrons were much the same as that which exists today between the satellites and the superpowers. Legally the satellites are independent and responsible for what they do, but actually their independence is curtailed, and the orbit they move in is that of the appropriate superpower.

The wilderness of America was made to order for proxy wars, and the war-like aborigines were perfect client states, perfect in the sense that they liked to fight, and perfect also in the sense that they were always in hock to their patrons because they alone controlled the fire-arms and ammunition. What it amounted to was that the Indians were the tools of the patron states in the New World, and victory would go to the side that made the best use of its tools. Thus King William's War can be said to have begun in 1680 when the Indian allies of the English invaded the west to

234

crush the Indian allies of the French.   In any case,
King William's War of 1689 was not an American echo of
a war that began in Europe and spread to America.
Quite the reverse.

Five years before King William's War broke out in
Europe Governor Thomas Dongan of New York made arrangements for a strategy conference with the Iroquois at
Albany.   The primary purposes of the meeting were to
cement the alliance with the Indian allies, and to
prod them into attacking the French.   With Machiavellian artistry, the new York governor double-crossed
the governor of New France by showing the Indians a
letter explicitly stating that the French were going
to attack the Iroquois. The purpose of the letter was
to request the English not to supply the Iroquois with
firearms.   It served quite another purpose when Dongan
used the letter to incite the Indians against the
French, and this is what he did because shortly thereafter the Iroquois, emboldened by the promise of support from the English,   struck deeply into French territory, penetrating westward as far as Michilimackinac,
Michigan, and returning with a fortune in beaver skins.
The French governor was discouraged and disheartened.
"If we have a war," he wrote to his King, "nothing can
save the country but a miracle of God."[40]

Louis XIV did not want to trust the fate of New
France to a miracle of God, and accordingly recalled
the discouraged and disheartened governor in favor of
an old war-horse, the Comte de Frontenac.   However, he
kept him on a short string, making it clear that he
would have to make do with the forces France had in
the New World, that no reinforcements would be forthcoming.   This was a decision the French King made reluctantly, but he had no choice, as the new alignment
of European powers forced him to conserve his strength
on the continent.   Prior to this time England and
France had been in alliance against Holland; and now
it was England and Holland against France.   This made
Frontenac's task almost impossible. Canada was impov-
erished and depleted, almost brought to ruin by the
Iroquois alone, and without any reinforcements Frontenac was supposed to turn them around, while at the
same time he took on all the English colonies, rich,
strong and populous.

In the performance of this impossible task, the
first thing Frontenac did was to cancel a plan Louis
had approved for an attack on New York down the Albany-
Montreal corridor.   It could not be executed with the

235

resources at hand, and since Louis could not afford to send any additional forces, Frontenac felt free to cancel the whole thing, king or no king. Instead, the old warrior turned to a scheme of his own, small-scaled to be sure, but highly sophisticated, and involving diplomatic as well as military skills. His immediate target was his old enemy, the Iroquois, and one of his first acts on returning to New France was to open up a dialogue with them. However, while this was going on, the Iroquois succeeded in working out a triple alliance involving themselves, the tribes of the Great Lakes, and the English at Albany. The moment Frontenac got word of this he knew that he would have to block it because its successful culmination would mean the end of New France, since the fur trade would be diverted to Albany. Therefore he directed all his energies to the task of breaking up this life-threatening alliance. In order to do this, Frontenac boldly weakened his small force on the St. Lawrence, and turned his diplomatic guns on the nine tribes in the Great Lakes region. He demanded that they renounce the triple alliance, and said he would destroy them if they did not obey. "I am strong enough," Frontenac boasted, "to kill the English, destroy the Iroquois, and whip you, if you fail in your duty to me. The Iroquois have killed and captured you in time of peace. Do to them as they have done to you, do to the English as they would like to do to you, but hold fast to your true father, who will never abandon you."[41]

Frontenac's arrogance and bluff was quite successful, and the tribes of the Great Lakes promised not to ratify their treaty with the Iroquois. Thus the triple alliance died aborning, but the great French leader knew only too well how quickly the Indians could change their minds. He also knew that force was the only thing they respected, and that he must act quickly to convince them of the absolute superiority of French arms in North America. What he needed, in other words, were a few quick victories, and these are what he set out to get. New York and Massachusetts were ideal targets at this time because both colonies were weakened by internal revolutions, civil wars. Jacob Leisler was in de facto possession of New York, except for Albany, and in Massachusetts all was chaos and confusion as a result of the uprising of the people against Sir Edmund Andros and his ill-fated Dominion of New England.

Frontenac's first blow in the campaign to restore the image of France in the New World was aimed at New York, and the specific target was Albany. The base was Montreal, and the force consisted of more than 200 men, of which about half were Indians. After a forced march of 17 days through the worst kind of terrain and weather, Schenectady, an alternative target, was attached. By noon of February 9, 1690, the Dutch town was in flames, and New York's farthest outpost existed no longer. Frontenac was getting his act together. "You cannot believe, Monseigneur," Frontenac wrote, "the joy that this slight success has caused, and how much it contributes to raise the people from their dejection and terror."[42]

Schenectady was only the first blow. Two others were planned and executed with the same lightning skill and daring. One was at Salmon Falls on the Maine-Newhampshire border, and the other at Fort Royal on the site of modern Portland. However, it was part of the genius of Frontenac not to make war on more than one colony at a time. Fully conscious of the separate interest of each individual English colony, the last thing he wanted to do was to give them any provocation for united action. To a certain extent, Frontenac followed this policy in all his warfare and relations with the Indian nations, particularly in connection with the great confederacy of the Five Nations. However, in this case the policy seemed to backfire to a certain extent at least. After the Schnectady massacre, Jacob Leisler of New York called a conference of all the American colonies to assemble in New York on May 1, 1690, to take into consideration a joint plan of action against the French in Canada. Though none of the southern colonies took any part in it, not feeling themselves threatened, the meeting was attended by envoys from New York, Massachusetts, Plymouth, Connecticut, and Maryland, and they drew up an elaborate plan for invading Canada, each colony pledging a certain number of soldiers, with a disproportionate number coming from New York, for a total of 855, to which the Iroquois promised 1,800.[43] The idea of soliciting aid from the mother country was also discussed.

The Schnectady massacre backfired in another way. The Indians of New York rallied to the colonial cause, and the Mohawks proposed a combined attack on Canada, one by land up the Albany-Montreal corridor, and a simultaneous attack by sea from Boston Harbor. Their orator said, "brethren, our covenant with you is a silver chain that cannot rust or break. We are of the race of the bear; and the bear does not yield, so long as there is a drop of blood in his body. Let us all be bears. We will go together with an army to ruin the country of the French. Therefore, send in all hast to New England. Let them be ready with ships and great guns to attack by water, while we attack by land."[44]

The Massachusetts men got the message, and moved first. Their target was Acadia, the key to Canada. The colony had been sorely put upon by the French commerce-raiders operating out of Port Royal, and it was also being used as a supply base for hostile Indians. Accordingly, a force was organized in Massachusetts against the French in Acadia. It consisted of seven small vessels manned by 208 sailors, and upwards of 400 militiamen. The commander was Sir William Phips, a rough-hewn New England sailor and adventurer who had been knighted because of some of his exploits in the recovery of a sunken Spanish treasure ship. He put to sea toward the end of April 1690, and reached Port Royal on May 11. Landing his men, he encountered no effective opposition, and took possession of the fort without a fight. His men then pillaged the area to their heart's content, and on May 30 he returned to Boston in triumph with a number of prisoners and enough booty to defray all the costs of the expedition.

The Boston merchants were elated over Phips's success in the operation against Acadia, and wanted more of the same. Quebec was the next logical target, and Phips found Boston alive with preparations to back him in an expedition against that stronghold. For such a project it was deemed prudent to enlist the support of the mother country, and as Governor Hutchinson said, a small vessel was "sent to England express, the beginning of April, with a representation of the exposed state of the colony, and the necessity of the reduction of Canada, and praying for a supply of arms and ammunition, and a number of the King's frigates to attack the French by sea, whilst the colony forces should march by land and perform their parts."[45]

The mother country did not heed the plea from its Massachusetts kinsmen. All her resources were engrossed in the European war, plus the difficulties she was encountering in Ireland, and there was nothing left over that could be spared for the conflict in America. Not only did the mother country not heed the plea from America, but inadvertently she impaired the patriots in Massachusetts by not telling them at once

238

that no aid would be forthcoming. The Massachusetts
men simply went ahead on their own, and when the
muster revealed that more men were needed, a forced
draft was initiated, so that in some small towns over
two-thirds of the eligible men found themselves in the
service, depriving the townships of the energy necessary to even keep the rural economy going. Nevertheless, no stone was left unturned to ensure the fall of
Quebec. Finally all was ready by the middle of July.
The force consisted of some 30 to 40 vessels, one of
which carried 44 guns, and over 2,000 men. It was the
largest force that had ever been assembled in America.
Phips sat with the force from the middle of July to
August 9 waiting to hear from England. By this time
he could wait no longer--the best of the season was already behind him-- and so he set sail for the St. Lawrence and Quebec. He did not arrive before Quebec
until October 5, and then it was almost too late for
an operation such as this to succeed. The Canadian
winter was a powerful weapon in the hands of the defenders. And its onset was very near.

Meanwhile, the supporting operation from Albany,
the land invasion, had run into difficulties. The independent spirit that had practically wrecked the New
England Confederation raised its head again, and
plagued the colonists as they tried to work out the details of the attack on Montreal. As a joint operation
there were many interests to reconcile, and there were
differences of opinion on everything connected with it.
These included the number of men each colony should
provide, who should be responsible for the supply side
of the operation, and all the command problems. In
addition, there were other difficulties. The Indian
allies of the English were now wavering in their support, having acquired a new respect for Frontenac, and
failed to put in their appearance on schedule. They
also failed to provide the canoes to transport the
troops across the lakes. This is when the colonial
leaders decided they had had enough. The campaign simply collapsed at the lower end of Lake Champlain, and
everyone returned home. Frontenac was delighted with
the debacle, news of which reached him quickly through
his Indian sources, and he promptly uncovered Montreal
to concentrate the whole of his forces at Quebec.

The collapse of the plan to attack Montreal at the
same time Quebec was assaulted was the ruin of both
plans, and the salvation of Canada. This is almost always the case when the success of the whole depends

239

upon the execution of all its parts. Phips contributed to the debacle by making mistakes of his own before and after his arrival before Quebec. The worst of these was to fritter away time when it was of the essence. He lay at anchor for three weeks off Tadoussac when he was within three days' sail of Quebec, and spent the time holding senseless councils of war and gathering intelligence, most of which proved to be wrong. From one source he obtained information that Quebec was defenseless, that its cannon were dismounted, and that it had less than 200 men to defend it. This pleased him for he could anticipate another victory such as the one he had at Port Royal, where there was almost no organized resistance. Trying for the same thing, as soon as he reached the Basin of Quebec, Phips put out a boat with an envoy to Frontenac demanding unconditional surrender within one hour. Frontenac gave his answer in less than an hour. It was the traditional one, "I will answer your general only by the mouths of cannon."[46] Phips's response to this was to begin holding another series of meetings called councils of war. In the midst of one of these, a great noise was heard from the rock. A French prisoner of war was queried as to what it meant, and his reply was, "Ma foi, Messieurs, you have lost the game. It is the governor of Montreal with the people from the country above. There is nothing for you now but to pack and go home."[47]

Phips foolishly ignored the intelligence he got from the prisoner of war, and landed the bulk of his forces in the vain hope that he could carry Quebec by direct assault. It was an act of desperation, and ended in total failure. The game was up, and Phips took his badly mauled forces back to Boston, from whence he came. Parkman's analysis of the defeat was the unkindest cut of all. He said that Phips, for all his bad luck and serious mistakes, could have carried the day after all if his timing had not been so bad. "Nearly all the adult males of Canada were gathered at Quebec," Parkman said, "and there was imminent danger of starvation. Cattle from the neighboring parishes had been hastily driven into the town; but there was little other provision, and before Phips retreated the pinch of famine had begun. Had he come a week earlier or stayed a week later, the French themselves believed that Quebec would have fallen, in the one case for want of men, and in the other for want of food."[48]

When Phips returned from his inglorious attempt to conquer Canada, he immediately set about trying to get the Bay Colony to back him in another attempt. He was booed out of court. The Massachusetts men had counted on Phips's success, not his failure, and they had also banked on the booty from Quebec to pay for all the expenses of the war, perhaps leaving them with a tidy profit. Now, there was not only no booty, but there was not even enough money in the treasury to pay the soldiers. So the idea of backing Phips in another go at Quebec was out of the question. Now, instead of dreaming their dreams of empire, the frugal men of Massachusetts had to figure out a way of keeping their colony from going bankrupt.

Phips's failure before Quebec was a great victory for Frontenac, and also a turning point in the war. The French gained the momentum that the English lost from this defeat, and the rest of the war was a succession of victories for Frontenac. First off, the French moved against the English traders in the Hudson Bay region, and drove them from some of their positions along the Severn. Port Royal was retaken in 1691, to the great joy of the French inhabitants who were thrilled at being able to throw off the yoke of the "Bostonnais." Subsequently, all of Newfoundland was overrun. In 1696, Frontenac's forces destroyed Fort William Henry at Pemaquid, Maine, which had been built at great expense by the New Englanders in 1692. The tide of French power in North America was nearing a flood state.

Frontenac's parade of victories was impressive, but not conclusive. The Iroquois, backed by their English patrons, still stood in his path, and prevented him from winning the final victory. Accordingly, in 1696 Frontenac, at age 76, set out to crush the one outstanding obstacle to the spread of French power in North America. He won a victory of sort, but it fell far short of what he had hoped. while he was meditating his next move in this complicated game of empire news arrived that his King had betrayed him by signing the peace of Ryswick whereby everything reverted to the *status quo ante bellum*, that is the return of all captured territory. This was dated September 30, 1697, and Frontenac received the official announcement in July 1698. Four months later, on November 28, he died. Had he lived, it is not outside the range of possibility that French instead of English would have survived as the official language in North America. Parkman was more restrained in his evaluation of the man and

241

his accomplishments. "Greatness," he said, "must be denied him; but a more remarkable figure, in its bold and salient individuality and sharply marked light and shadow, is nowhere seen in American history."[49]

The most notable thing about King William's War is that it started here, not in Europe, and was vigoroursly prosecuted here, primarily by the Massachusetts, but not to the exclusion of New York and some of the neighboring colonies. It was not a question of our being drawn into a European war, and forced to fight over matters that meant nothing to us. Quite the contrary. We were determined to conquer this land ourselves, and in King William's War this meant rooting the French out of Port Royal, Montreal, and Quebec. If we could not involve King William in our war, we would fight it ourselves without any help from the mother country. Our failures in this war were military and diplomatic; diplomatic in the sense that we never succeeded in drawing King William fully into this war with all his kingly weapons and manpower, and military in the sense that Frontenac was always one step ahead of us with his strategy and tactics. The lessons we learned in King William's War were the very opposite of those set forth in our textbooks. We did not learn that imperialism was a vice, and isolationism a virtue. We did not learn that colonial wars had no intrinsic importance because they were only echos of European rivalries that were of no concern to us. And we did not learn that all wars should be condemned, renounced, and outlawed because they were immoral. What we did learn was that it was going to be hard for us to drive the French out of Canada, and that, sorrowfully, we could not always count on our mother country to put our ambitions in America ahead of her interests in Europe. In other words, the great lesson of King William's War, as far as we were concerned, was one of self-reliance, if our imperial interests were to be served.

Our principal complaint coming out of King William's War was that the mother country was not aggressive enough in pursuing the imperial design in North America. Our vision was the one set forth in the original charters, the "Sea to Sea" vision extended to include all the islands on the "Coast of both Seas."[50] Manifest Destiny and the Monroe Doctrine were both planted in the soil of the New World during the colonial period, and by the time of King William's War it was apparent that both had taken deep root. It is not those ideas that are new and un-American, but our

242

modern perversion of them as we rewrite the history of our country to make it fit the mold that is fashionable today.

Queen Anne's War (1702-1713) was an extension of King William's War, the only important difference being that France was now allied with Spain. This meant that England had two formidable foes to contend with in the New World, France and Spain, and that meant that to the northern and western fronts a third would be added, the southern front. However, we were prepared for it. As far back as 1629 Charles I had granted a great tract of land in the south to Sir Robert Heath for the express purpose "of enlarging the Christian religion as our Empoire."[51] This grant and the subsequent charters for Carolina made it clear that the colony was designed to serve as a shield for Virginia. More than that. It was also planned that it would be a forward base from which Spain could be attacked in the Floridas and France on the lower reaches of the Mississippi. In many ways, the southern was the most dangerous border in America. And there is where the fighting started in Queen Anne's War.

Spain took the initiative in Queen Anne's War. Before word reached the English colonies that war had been declared in May, Spanish and Indian forces invaded South Carolina claiming it as a part of Florida. The settlers had been forewarned of the attack by some friendly Indians, and easily repulsed it. South Carolina was the debatable land in this part of the world. The charter of 1665 had extended the southern boundary two degrees so that it would include St. Augustine.[52]

The defeat of the invasion forces was a tonic to the settlers of South Carolina, and their governor immediately convened the Assembly for the purpose of organizing a counter-stroke against St. Augustine. The colonists had mixed feelings about the governor's proposal. Marshall said that "temperate men were opposed to this enterprise; but the assurance of the governor, that Florida would be an easy conquest, and that immense treasure would be the reward of their valour, were too seductive to be resisted. A great majority of the assembly declared in favour of the expedition, and voted the sum of two thousand pounds sterling for its prosecution. Six hundred militia were embodied for the service, and an equal number of Indians engaged as ausiliaries."[53]

St. Augustine was defended by San Marcos, an immense stone fortress completed by the Spanish in 1687 to block the southward drift of the English colonists. Thus the plan of attack was a two-pronged affair with the governor and the main body of troops attacking by sea, and a smaller force making the assault by land. The smaller force arrived first, and had an easy time of it, because all the defenders retired to San Marcos, which was prepared for a long siege. Giving up on the fort, the colonists contented themselves with plundering the town while they awaited the arrival of the fleet. When the fleet arrived it laid siege to the great stone fort, and this was all it could do since it did not have the heavy artillery to pound it into submission. While waiting for the blockade to starve out the defenders, the South Carolinians were surprised by the appearance of two Spanish vessels of war. This clinched it. The siege was lifted immediately, and the English colonists beat a hasty retreat both by land and sea. Thus the Carolinians learned the hard way that imperialism did not always result in a harvest of plenty, and that it was not going to be easy to singe the beard of the King of Spain.

The Spanish counter-attack was long in coming, but come it did. It was launched in August, 1706, and the target was Charleston. The Carolinians got early warning of the attack, and were ready for it. The Spanish underestimated the defensive capabilities of the colony, and the attack was a failure from the beginning. Beachheads were never established, and the invasion fleet was routed by the defensive fire-power of the port. Afterwards, a French man-of-war sailed into the port completely unaware of the fact that it was not in the hands of the Spaniards. The victorious Charlestonians cut off his retreat, and took off some 200 prisoners. For the rest of the war the southern front was of diminished significance. The really important clash of empire was taking place on the northern frontier.

Along the northern frontier, the whole weight of the war fell on New England. The reason for this goes back to the Grand Settlement of 1701. This consisted of two treaties, one at Montreal and the other at Albany, whereby the Iroquois Confederacy established a policy of armed neutrality between the French and the English.[54] The idea was that the powerful Indian Confederacy would stand neutral in the conflict between England and France. Of the importance of this policy

244

in the struggle for the New World, a contemporary French historian said it was strange "that four or five thousand should make a whole new world tremble. New England is but too happy to gain their good graces; New France is often wasted by their wars, and our allies dread them over an extent of more than fifteen hundred leagues."[55]

The Grand Settlement of 1701 dictated French strategy at the beginning of Queen Anne's War, and it also dictated the strategy of the English, at least as far as New York was concerned. Trade was the key. And it was not the ordinary kind of trade. The Dutch merchants of Albany were starved for trade in King William's War, and were just in the process of developing a very lucrative trade with the French on the St. Lawrence. The last thing they wanted to happen was to have it interrupted by a new war. Furs from the Great Lakes region came down to the St. Lawrence, and were exchanged for English trade goods, including firearms and ammunition, brought up from Albany. This undercover trade was profitable to both parties, to the French on the St. Lawrence, and to the Dutch merchants in Albany. "Therefore," Professor Douglas Edward Leach said, "New York, relying upon the pledge made by New France not to invade the Iroquois country if the Five Nations remained neutral, saw no good reason why it should become involved in this war to the jeopardy of its own frontier and the disruption of the valuable fur trade. With the onset of Queen Anne's War, then, New England was left to battle the French and their Indians virtually alone."[56]

One of the ugly aspects of the Albany trade was the fact that it enabled the French-Indians to buy the guns they used to kill New Englanders, and another was that some of the plunder ravaged from settlers in New England had a way of turning up in the markets of Albany. It is not any wonder that there was much bad blood between New York and New England at this time. Typical of the way the French kept the New England border stirred up were the raiding parties that massacred the exposed settlements from Wells on the Maine coast to Northampton in Massachusetts, including the bloody outrage at Deerfield in 1704.

For five years the governor of New York played the game, and kept the peace in the midst of war. New England had to fight the war unaided, despite the fact that she begged for help not only from New York, but also, and also unsuccessfully, from Pennsylvania and Virginia. The Quakers stalled the bid in Pennsylvania, and Virginia was looking southward. Therefore, for the first half of Queen Anne's War, it was a war between New England and New France, with Massachusetts and Maine bearing the brunt of it.

For Massachusetts, the war held out great promise in the sense that there was a world out there to win, including Acadia and beyond that Canada, and if she could not count on her sister colonies to supply her with much in the way of support, she could always rely on her own resources. In addition, there was always the possibility of getting aid from the mother country. Moreover, there was the crime of Deerfiled to avenge. In 1704, Colonel Benjamin Church, a Plymouth man who had made a name for himself in King Philip's War, was summoned to lead a force of some 700 New Englanders and Indians in an invasion of Acadia. The purpose of the mission was to let the French and Indians know that the Massachusetts men would not tolerate another Deerfield. Accordingly, he laid waste to a number of undefended posts in Acadia, and transmitted a message to the governor of Acadia asking him to inform "the governor of Canada, that if he did not prevent his French and Indians from committing such barbarities upon poor helpless women and children, as the people of Deerfield had suffered the last year, he would return with a thousand Indians and let them loose upon the frontiers of Canada to commit the like barbarities there."[57]

Among the terrorized settlements to which Church and his men laid waste were Minas and Beaubassin, two principal sources of supply for the French-Indians. However, no attempt was made to reduce Port Royal, the main French stronghold in the area. The rumor was rife that Governor Joseph Dudley of Massachusetts had forbidden an attack on Port Royal because he was personally interested in the lucrative trade between that place and Boston. This was probably without foundation. However, a rich trade between Boston and Port Royal existed just as it did between Albany and Montreal, and it is a fact that Governor Dudley was not the impetus behind Church's mission of revenge, which was undertaken in response to public demand.[58]

The interest in Acadia manifested itself for a second time in Queen Anne's War in 1707 when Governor Dudley laid before the General Court a proposal for

246

organizing an expedition against Port Royal. To no one's surprise, the response was enthusiastic, and a bill was passed that the necessary shipping should be impressed. The bill also called for raising a thousand soldiers from volunteers or by impressment. Colonel John March was named the commander-in-chief. Volunteers filled the ranks from the rural militia, and the expedition set sail on May 13. Arriving in early June, the invasion was a complete failure largely due to the incompetence of Colonel March. In fact, when the soldiers returned to Boston the children ran after Colonel March in the streets crying "wooden sword."[59] However, there was enough blame to go around, and a general court martial was ordered for all the leaders of the expedition. The only reason it did not take place was because of the number of charges involved. There were not enough officers left to try those being charged. This was the most discreditable of all the attempts to conquer Acadia.

Following the English debacle at Port Royal, the French proceeded to consolidate their position in Newfoundland by reducing St. Johns in 1708, after having conquered Bonavista three years before. It was time for the English to come to their senses about the northern frontier, that is for the home government to make up its mind about following the lead of Massachusetts and the New England colonies or resigning itself to the loss of the northern and western parts of the continent, possibly the whole of North America. It was also at this time that Samuel Vetch made his appearance in colonial history.

Vetch was a Scotsman of good family who had had some military training and experience, and had come to New York at an early age, when he had the good fortune of marrying into the distinguished family of Robert Livingston, one of the leading men in the colony. Vetch then prospered in the Canadian trade, and made several trips to Canada. By the time of Queen Anne's War, he was living in Boston, and had become a good friend of the governor, Joseph Dudley. It was then that Vetch began to gravitate toward a life in the public service. In this connection he participated in several diplomatic missions to Canada concerning the exchange of prisoners and other matters. He did not neglect his own personal business while on these trips, and was once convicted and fined for personal participation in the clandestine trade between the two countries.

Vetch was more than a man of business, and a diplomat. He also fancied himself an expert on military intelligence, and demonstrated this by making a detailed survey of the French defenses in the whole of New France. This survey paid particular attention to Port Royal, Quebec, and Montreal, including the St. Lawrence waterway. He once boasted that he knew more about the St. Lawrence "than the Canadians themselves." In other words, Vetch was a sort of one-man Central Intelligence Agency with an up-to-date portfolio on New France.

He was in the right place at the right time. The General Court of Massachusetts resolved to make a determined effort to get the mother country involved in the colonial struggle, and Vetch was the logical man to represent the colony to the Queen. To support himself in this endeavor, the colonial diplomat prepared a situation paper that he called, "Canada Survey'd."[60] This was a long report, containing more than 5,000 words, and was divided about half and half between military and economic findings. As a soldier, he did not leave out a single detail on the fortifications of each position, number of troops stationed there, and the strengths and weaknesses of each position. And as a businessman, Vetch was very specific about the value of Canada's trade and resources, how much it cost the English to defend themselves against the French in Canada, what it would cost to root them out, and whether it would be good business to undertake the project. The conclusion he came to was that this was a God-given opportunity to strike a blow for the empire. He said that "the half of one year's loss we sustain in trade"[61] was more than enough to pay all the expenses involved in conquering Canada, and that there was a world to win. He pointed out that two advantages of the conquest were that it would no longer be necessary to garrison the Canadian frontier in time of war, and that we would not have to continue bribing the Indians for their peace or cooperation. Vetch then repeated himself, "the half, I say, of one year's loss we sustain would, if rightly aplyed, wholly dispossess them of the Continent and Newfoundland, and by so doing render H.M sole and peaceable possessor of all the North Continent of America, large enough to form four kingdoms as bigg as Great Brittain."[62]

Colonel Caleb Heathcote, an articulate New York farmer, expressed the same thought roughly at the same time when he said the real purpose of the widely scattered raids by the French Indians was to nibble us to

248

death, "to angle us away, province by province, till at last all will be gon." Like Vetch, Heathcote said there was only one way out, "it is impossible that we & the French can both inhabit this Continent in peace but that one nation must at last give way to the other, so 'tis very ncesssary that without sleeping away our time, all precautions imaginable should be taken to prevent its falling to our lotts to remove."[63] Benjamin Franklin and William Pitt used the same arguments half a century later to justify England's strategy in the Seven Years' War.

Samuel Vetch's strategy paper was dated July 27, 1708, and the arguments he presented appealed to the Queen. Thus when he returned to America the colonial diplomat did so with the Queen's promise to send a fleet and five regiments of royal troops to America. She also gave her approval to Vetch's plan of a joint operation against Canada, with the fleet and royal troops attacking Quebec from the base at Boston, and with the colonial soldiers attacking Montreal from the base at Albany. In addition, Vetch had the Queen's promise that when Canada was conquered he would be the royal governor. A more important post could hardly be imagined because when Vetch used the word Canada it included the entire Mississippi valley, the whole of France's empire in America. The date set for the arrival of the British fleet in America was the middle of May, 1709.

Sir Francis Nicholson was designated as the commanding officer of the land forces against Montreal. He was one of an elite group of professional royal governors, and in his American career presided at different times over New York, Maryland, South Carolina, and Virginia. His choice was also an important one, for there were many others who sought the same honor, and the appointment went to him because he was the only one upon which the governors could agree. The colonial troops that made up his command were raised without difficulty, and in the case of New York this was remarkable because, in accepting the plan of conquest, New York had to abandon the policy of neutrality in the war, a policy that had governed her conduct ever since the war started. Colonel Nicholson immediately began the march to Wood Creek, where his orders were to wait until the fleet arrived at Boston harbor, after which he could proceed to Montreal, while the fleet and royal troops would proceed to Quebec by way of the St. Lawrence waterway.

Meanwhile, at Boston 1,200 men had been raised, and were encamped ready to embark on a moment's notice. This was the middle of May, 1709, the date that had been set for the arrival of the British fleet. But it did not. And as the days grew into weeks, and the weeks into months, the troops became dispirited, and the leaders anxious. "Pray God hasten the fleet,"[64] Vetch implored, and Governor Dudley wrote in the same vein. But it was to no avail. The fleet was not even on the way, having been diverted to Portugal to meet an emergency in the European war. The news reached Governor Dudley on October 11, and by this time it was too late to undertake an operation against Quebec, fleet or no fleet. It was also too late for Colonel Nicholson to proceed against Montreal. By this time his army at Wood Creek had been decimated by an epidemic, and he had turned back, foreclosing any possibility of an operation against Canada in 1709.

Following the debacle of 1709, the frugal men of Massachusetts began to take stock of the money they had lost thus far in the futile attempts to possess themselves of Acadia, much less Canada. They reckoned that a considerable sum had been spent (22,000 pounds) on Church's expedition in 1704, and double that amount in 1707 when March had failed, and now in 1709 another costly failure had been added. The question was where was it all going to end? At a conference of the colonial governors in Rhode Island it was decided that the Queen's help should be solicited again for another attempt against Acadia. Colonel Nicholson was already on the point of sailing for England, and the governors begged him to carry their plea to the Queen. He readily agreed, and the Queen was again receptive to the proposals brought from America. Thus when Nicholson returned it was with a commission to command an expedition against Port Royal in 1710 with Vetch as second in command.

The promised naval aid arrived in July 1710, and the Massachusetts legislature proceeded to round up the transport vessels, and raise 900 men for service. Connecticut, Rhode Island, and New Hampshire sent their quotas, and by September 24 the force sailed into the harbor at Port Royal. There was no organized opposition to the landing, and within a week the fort was within English hands. There it remained. Three times before (Argall in 1616, Sedgwick in 1654, and Phips in 1690) Port Royal had been taken, but each time it was restored to France by treaty. The conquest was final this time, and in honor of the Queen, Nicholson changed the name to Annapolis Royal. Four hundred British marines and a goodly number of colonial soldiers were all that was needed to settle the long controversy over one of the most troublesome borders in America. For the Massachusetts men, the only remaining debatable land was Canada itself.

When Colonel Nicholson repaired to England after the reduction of Port Royal he again raised the issue of Canada. The conquest of Canada was the objective that had been sought at the meeting of the colonial governors after the British fleet failed to show up in 1709. It was still their objective. In his pleadings with the English authorities on the subject, Nicholson was helped by the fact that the war in Europe had taken a favorable turn for the British, and thus the forces were available for a major effort in America. As a result, the Queen bowed to the colonial appeal again, and promised to send a large force to America, and to do so at once. Accordingly, when Nicholson arrived in Boston in June, he did so with orders from the Queen to the colonial governors to put themselves in readiness for a major effort against Canada. This meant quotas and provisions. Sixteen days later, the fleet arrived. The time for action had come, and this Marshall said accorded "perfectly with the wishes of the people as well as of the governors." He continued by saying, "every practicable exertion was made; and difficulties were overcome which, on other occasions, might have been deemed insurmountable. To supply the money which the English treasury could not then advance, the general court of Massachusetts issued bills of credit to the amount of forty thousand pounds; and the example was followed by Connecticut, New York, and New Jersey. Provisions were obtained by impressment."[65]

Queen Anne sent a very large force to the New World, equal in size to that which reduced Quebec in a later war when the defenses were much stronger. The Naval command was given to Admiral Sir Hovenden Walker, and command of the troops devolved on Brigadire John Hill, both of whom turned out to be incompetents of the worst sort. The governors had a meeting at New London, and there the plans were laid for a two-pronged attack, by sea against Quebec, and by land against Montreal. It was also agreed that Sir Francis Nicholson would again be in command of the move against Montreal by way of the Hudson and Lake Champlain. Admiral Walker's force consisted of 5,500 British regulars, 600 marines, and 1,500 colonial troops, in all about 12,000 men counting the sailors. Vetch was in command of the colonial troops.

All being in readiness, the fleet set sail from Boston on July 30. It consisted of some 70 ships, including nine ships-of-war, and 71 other vessels such as transports, hospital ships, and the like. Everything went well with the flotilla until after it had entered the St. Lawrence River, but on August 23, when they were some distance above the large island of Anticosta, all hell broke loose. The weather was foul, and eight transports were wrecked, causing the loss of up to 1,000 troops. Bad as this was, the fleet could have absorbed the loss, and continued on to Quebec, particularly since none of the men-of-war suffered any damage, but Walker lost his head, and ordered a hasty retreat. His excuse was that he did not have a river pilot he could trust, and flatly rejected Vetch's offer to pilot the fleet to Quebec. The irony of it, as Marshall noted, was that in its retreat the fleet had to spend "eight days beating down the river against an easterly wind which, in two, would have carried it to Quebec."[66] Of this performance, Parkman said, "so discreditable a backing out from a great enterprise will hardly be found elsewhere in English annals."[67]

Meanwhile, Colonel Nicholson with about 2,300 troops was encamped at Wood Creek preparing for the passage of Lake Champlain. When the news reached him of Walker's cowardly retreat, he flew into a great rage, and according to Parkman, "tore off his wig, threw it on the ground, and stamped upon it, crying out 'Roguery! Treachery!' When his fit was over, he did all that was now left for him to do, --burned the wooden forts he had built, marched back to Albany, and disbanded his army, after leaving one hundred and fifty men to protect the frontier against scalping parties."[68]

This was the last important event in Queen Anne's War. Peace came with the Treaty of Utrecht in 1713. As far as we were concerned, the important features of the treaty were that Acadia (without defining its boundaries) and Newfoundland became English possessions; the Iroquois (without being consulted) became English subjects; English sovereignty over Hudson Bay was recognized; and France was allowed to retain Cape Breton Island, as well as certain fishing privileges off the coast of Newfoundland. About the only other thing that can be said about Queen Anne's War is that it followed the pattern of King William's War in that it started in America, was fought here for American causes, and was not an echo of a European war. Also, and again like King William's War, the colonists did everything in their power to get the mother country actively involved in the colonial quarrel, not vice versa. Finally, it is simply fatuous to say, think, or believe that Queen Anne's War was one that was forced on the colonists, one in which we were in no wise interested, and one that we fought merely because the mother country was battling in Europe. That is a distortion of history.

To move on from Queen Anne's War (1702-13) to King George's War (1744-48), it started the same way, on the southern front, and moved to the north, but ended in a very different way. Queen Anne's War ended in a blaze of shame with Admiral Walker's defeat on the St. Lawrence, but King George's War came to an end in a blaze of glory when a rag-tag army of colonial civilians conquered what may have been the strongest fortress in North America, Louisbourg on Cape Breton Island, the French Gibraltar and key to Canada. The English were not surprised by the outbreak of war on the southern front, nor were they unprepared for it. Just as Carolina had been thrown forward as a shield for Virginia in 1663, so Georgia was thrown forward as a shield for Carolina in 1732. One hundred years before that a visionary Scotsman, Sir Robert Montgomery, had obtained a grant of land between the Savannah and Altamaha Rivers, and it was there that he planned to establish a colony called the Margravate of Azilia. A Margravate is a fighting border state presided over by a Margrave. Azilia is a fanciful name for Asylum. The Georgia part of South Carolina was founded that way. It was also intended to be a forward military base. This is why James Edward Oglethorpe was chosen to be one of the leaders and trustees of the Georgia colony. He was a proven military man, as well as a politician, and he was also an empire builder. Calling on all three capabilities, and anticipating a conflict with Spain and France, he constructed two forts, one on the Savannah at Augusta, and another on an island in the Altahama called Frederica. The former was to serve as a bulwark against the French in Louisiana, and the latter as a bulwark against the Spanish in Florida. Spain reinforced her garrison in East Florida, and remonstrated promptly and vigorously against the fort

253

at Frederica. She demanded that it be demolished at
once, since it was built on land that belonged to the
King of Spain. Oglethorpe ignored the remonstrance,
and paid no attention to the angry demand. To back him
up, the British ordered a regiment into Georgia, and
gave Oglethorpe the command of all the troops in both
Georgia and the Carolinas. All this was in a time of
perfect peace between Spain and England.

While the war between England and Spain was still
in its covert stage, before June 1739, a slave uprising took place in Carolina. This was just as much the
result of Spanish intrigue as the deadly Yamassee War
in 1715. The surprising thing is that, for all her
efforts, Spain was not more successful in exploiting
the slave weakness of the southern colonies. One of
the reasons slavery came as late as it did in Georgia,
was because the trustees did not want to introduce a
system that could be exploited by an enemy. Spain
spared no efforts to organize the blacks in Carolina
against their masters. She formed an underground rail-
way system for slaves to gain their freedom by escap-
ing to St. Augustine, and once there the blacks were
put into a military training camp officered by themselves. The Spanish-Indians acted as recruiting agents
for the blacks, and also as couriers to supply them
with small arms and ammunition. The need for this was
obviated in the 1739 uprising in South Carolina because the slaves were successful in forcing a ware-
house containing the colony's store of firearms.[69]
They seized all the arms they could carry, and began
their march to freedom, killing and looting until they
were satiated, which was when the freedom march came
to an end. Unfortunately for the slaves, the day they
had picked for the uprising was Sunday, and this meant
that the whites were all assembled in church well
armed, as required by law, and it also meant that pursuit would be swift and in great strength. The leaders
of the uprising were executed on the spot, and a
severe code of laws was adopted against another such
uprising.[70] Meanwhile, Oglethorpe continued his preparations for the impending war.

The incident that finally brought the conflict between Spain and England to a head took place in the
Caribbean off the coast of Florida. Illegal trading in
this area was an honorable profession in those days,
and one of the smugglers, Captain Robert Jenkins, was
engaged in his trade when he was intercepted by one of
the ever-watchful *guarda-costa* vessesl of the Spanish.

254

In the ensuing fight Jenkins lost an ear, and this touched off an uproar in England. The English merchants and shippers had a large stake in the contraband trade in the Caribbean, and made the issue of Jenkins's ear a matter that involved the nation's honor. The ruling prime minister, Robert Walpole, was unable to calm down the public clamor, and as a result England declared war on Spain in June 1739. The battlecry was not "Remember the Maine," but "Remember the Ear."

Almost immediately upon the declaration of war, Admiral Edward Vernon was ordered to take the offensive in the Caribbean. It was no secret that commerce with the New World was Spain's life-line, and thus this was the logical target for England to attack. Within the target system one of the major objectives was Porto Bello on the Isthmus of Panama. It was such because it was one of the main transshipment points for the Spanish Pacific domains. The only rub was that it was believed to be impregnable. Vernon struck the blow on November 2, 1739, and succeeded in capturing the town. Immediately, the admiral became a household word in England, and as the hero of Porto Bello his name began to be associated with the other greats in the island's history, Sir Francis Drake and his kinsman, Sir John Hawkins.

Not to be outdone by Admiral Vernon, General Oglethorpe began his move on St. Augustine in January 1740. Like Vernon, Oglethorpe was under orders to act offensively against the Spanish settlements, and in planning the expedition against Florida he requested the assistance of South Carolina. "That colony," Marshall records, "ardently desiring the expulsion of neighbors alike feared and hated, entered zealously into the views of the general, and agreed to furnish the men and money he requested."[71] The arrangement was for the Carolina forces to join up with those under Oglethorpe at the mouth of the St. John's River on the coast of Florida. But there was a delay, and Oglethorpe was impatient. He crossed over into Florida without waiting for the reinforcements from Virginia and the two Carolinas, and began the trek to St. Augustine. However, he had some second thoughts about his reinforcements, and turned back to the original place of rendezvous. This was probably a mistake. The Spanish reinforced St. Augustine while Oglethorpe dallied, and when he finally got there it was only to discover

255

that it was too late. Discouraged, he eventually concluded that he would have to admit defeat, and with-
drew his forces to Frederica. Lieutenant-Governor
William Bull of South Carolina was furious, and took
his anger out on General Oglethorpe. They exchanged
insults, and set the stage of a tragedy of non-cooperation in the future.

Meanwhile, the imperialists in London were champ-
ing at the bit, and ordered Admiral Vernon to repeat
his triumph at Porto Bello by striking a blow against
Cartagena, the treasure city of the Spanish Main. To
no avail did the admiral protest that he could not succeed in this venture. A fleet of over 100 ships,
manned with nearly 30,000 men, was put at his disposal,
and he was ordered to proceed. But first, however, he
was told to put in at Jamaica where 3,600 colonial soldiers waited to join the colors. These troops came
from all the 13 colonies, and it was the first time
anything like this had happened in America. Benjamin
Franklin used this example to good advantage in his
famous testimony before the House of Commons in 1766.
The question was whether the colonies would support
Great Britain if she were engaged in a war in Europe,
and Franklin's answer was the case of Cartagena. He
pointed to the 3,600 colonial troops, and said, "it is
true, Carthagena is in America, but as remote from the
Northern Colonies, as if it had been in Europe. They
make no distinction of wars, as to their duty of assisting in them."[72]

The Cartagena attack was opened on March 9, 1741,
and the campaign was abandoned on April 11. It was a
defeat almost without a redeeming feature. Only 600
Americans survived the catastrophe, and fully two-
thirds of the invasion force succumbed to disease and
enemy bullets. One who survived, however, was Lawrence
Washington, older brother of our own George. He was a
Virginia volunteer, and obviously remembered the English admiral with affection for he called his estate
on the Potomac the name it still bears, Mount Vernon.

Following the fizzle at Cartagena, and before
that the failure of Oglethorpe at St. Augustine, it
was only natural that the Spanish would counter-attack,
and this is exactly what they did in the spring of
1742. Some of Oglethorpe's Indian allies got wind of
the Spanish intentions, and brought the word to Oglethorpe. He immediately appealed to South Carolina for
aid, as he hea every right to do, and was just as immediately turned down. This was a sovereign decision,

and there was nothing Oglethorpe could do about it.
The Carolinians, with the full approval of their governor, flocked to Charleston for protection instead of
marching to the camp of Oglethorpe. One experience
with that general was enough for them, and as a result
Oglethorpe was thrown on his own very meager resources
to repel the Spanish attack. The non-cooperation on
the part of South Carolina put in jeopardy the whole
southeastern flank of the empire, and but for a stroke
of luck on Oglethorpe's part the Spanish might have
carried Georgia and possibly South Carolina as well.

On May 25, 1742, a major Spanish fleet set sail
from Havana to recover the lost colony of Georgia, and
to reassert Spanish authority over as much of the
coast as possible. It was the largest force the Spaniards had ever assembled in this part of the world,
consisting of 36 vessels carrying some 2,000 soldiers
from Havana, plus an additional 1,000 brought aboard
at St. Augustine. Among the latter group was a regiment of blacks destined to lead an uprising of the
40,000 slaves in South Carolina. The fleet arrived at
St. Simons Island on July 4, and Oglethorpe was forced
to remove his force of about 700 to the safety of
Frederica. This is when the bad luck that seems to
have been Oglethorpe's constant companion took a holi-
day.

The odds were about four to one against Oglethorpe
at this juncture, and the only advantage he had was being on the defensive in rugged country that he knew
like the back of his hand. The result was the Battle
of Bloody Marsh on July 7, 1742. This was another wood-
land encounter very much like the ambush on the Monon-
gahela that cost General Edward Braddock his life on
July 9, 1755. The only difference is that this time
the Spaniards were the victims. When the slaughter was
over some 400 Spaniards lay dead, and 100 were captured. Unlike Braddock's defeat, this was not enough
to break the back of the Spanish invasion. It was the
aftermath of the Battle of Bloody Marsh that did that,
an aftermath that involved many bizarre things such as
deserters, spies, double agents, planted intelligence,
psychological warfare, and the appearance of a small
British fleet that confused everybody, not only the
Spanish, but Oglethorpe as well. All this, however,
was of the first order of importance. Margaret Davis
Cate put it in proper perspective when, in an excellent article on the Battle of Bloody Marsh, she said,

during the invasion, the fate of the
English trembled in the balance. Had
Oglethorpe been less resourceful in
overcoming obstacles or less resolute
in his determination to hold these
lands for England, or had Monteano and
the other Spanish leaders been more
united in their purposes and more aggressive gressive in their campaign to destroy
Georgia and the other American colonies, the outcome might easily have
been a Spanish victory.[73]

The Monteano that Dr. Cate referred to in the ex-
cerpt was General Don Manuel de Monteano, commander-in-
chief of the Spanish forces. While he was pursuing
Oglethorpe in his withdrawal to Frederica, one of the
English prisoners he had taken managed to escape, and
brought some intelligence to Oglethorpe that put a new
face on things. This was that all was not well in the
Spanish camp. Oglethorpe was informed that the men
were in low spirits, and that to preserve harmony they
had been divided into three forces, the Cubans in one
camp, the St. Augustine forces in another, and the
"Italick Regiment" in a third. Whereupon Oglethorpe
decided he would launch an attack on the divided
forces, and proceeded to do so at once. Taking about
500 of his best men, he embarked on a forced march to
the enemy camp, and arrived just before dawn. However, just before the attack order was given, one of
his own men, a Frenchman, fired his gun to give warning, and then darted into the enemy lines. Having thus
lost the element of surprise, Oglethorpe did the only
thing he could do, which was to beat a hasty retreat
to Frederica.

The question that confronted Oglethorpe was what
to do now. The deserter did exactly what Oglethorpe
knew he would do, advised the Spanish general of the
weakness of Frederica, and urged him to launch an attack now. He stressed the now of the attack by pointing out that Oglethorpe's men were tired after the
long march through woods and morasses, and would not
be capable of any hard fighting. He also presented detailed plans of the fortress, and showed the general
how he could curcumvent the approach obstacles. In
addition, the deserter told the general that, while
the fort was undermanned at the present time, it would
not be so for long, as Oglethorpe had sent out appeals
in all directions, to Boston, Carolina, Virginia, and
Philadelphia, for both ships and men.

While all this was going on in the Spanish camp, Oglethorpe was busy with plans of his own. Deciding that the only way he could save himself was to discredit the French deserter, Oglethorpe finally hit upon a plan to accomplish this. As he told the story,

> the next day I prefailed with a Prisoner and gave him a sum of money to carry a letter privately and deliver it to that French Man who deserted. This letter was wrote in French as if from a friend of his telling him he had received the money that he should strive to make the Spaniards believe the English were weak. That he should undertake to pilot up their Boats and Galleys & then bring them under the Woods where he knew the Hidden Batterys were, that if he could bring that about he should have double the reward he had already received. That the French Deserters should have all that had that had been promised to them.[74]

Oglethorpe's ruse worked perfectly. The Spanish prisoner did not deliver the incriminating letter to the Frenchman, but took it straight to his commanding officer, as Oglethorpe knew he would. Now, Don Manuel was in a quandary, not knowing whether to believe the French deserter or the former Spanish prisoner. What did either or both have to gain in this sordid game of intelligence and counter intelligence? The basic question, of course, was whether he should attack the English fort or withdraw. The one thing he did not want to do was to walk into another trap such as that which led to the Battle of the Bloody Marsh. Could it be that Oglethorpe wanted him to attack Frederica so that all the Spanish ships and soldiers would be tied down here while Admiral Vernon, for example, launched an attack on Havana or St. Augustine? Or worse still, had Oglethorpe already been reinforced, and desired the attack in order to get the Spanish forces in the crossfire of the guns of Frederica and English or colonial warships?

Don Manuel deliberated on these questions in one council-of-war after another, just as Phips had deliberated before Quebec, and while he was wasting his time in this manner, the Spanish lookouts sighted four

259

English warships on the horizon. The general deliberated no longer. Prudence got the better of valor, and the decision was made to run away and fight another day. The odd thing is that Oglethorpe was just as surprised to see the small English fleet, consisting of one man-of-war, two sloops-of-war, and a galley from South Carolina, as Monteano was. The message he read in the presence of the fleet was rescue at long last, and he immediately dispatched an aide-de-camp to the ships with a letter to the commander telling him of the strength and disposition of the Spanish ships. He also proposed a plan for a coordinated attack. However, to the consternation of the aide, and the dismay of Oglethorpe, the British fleet not only failed to come any closer to shore, but calmly sailed over the horizon out of sight. Later, Oglethorpe learned that the fleet had been sent there on a reconnaissance mission, and had been under strict orders not to engage in combat, but to return to Charleston if they sighted the Spanish fleet. However, this was the last time the Spanish made any kind of serious attempt to recover the lost colony of Georgia in the course of this war. It was not Oglethorpe's last fling. He made another attempt at St. Augustine in 1743, and failed again, to be finally court-martialed (but acquitted). These repeated failures on the part of the English and Spanish discouraged both belligerents, and when France entered the war on Spain's side in March 1744, the War of Jenkins's Ear became King George's War.

The outbreak of war between England and France in 1744 ended 31 years of peace between the two countries. The transition from peace to war was marked by a sudden incursion from French Cape Breton to English Nova Scotia. The French governor of that strategic island received news of the outbreak of war on May 13, and it was not until June 2 that the news was proclaimed at Boston. Taking advantage of this, the French governor was able to surprise the small settlement of Canseau, and put it to the torch. Canseau was at the tip of the Acadian peninsula right where it abutted on Cape Breton Island. Advancing to the capital, Annapolis, the French with their Indian allies stood before it in August. However by this time the English stronghold had been reinforced from Massachusetts, and the French did not feel they were strong enough to carry it by assault. Accordingly, they suddenly lifted the siege, and decamped toward the end of September. This was something of a strategic victory for the English because Acadia was Canada's lost colony in the same sense that Georgia was Spain's lost colony.

The Massachusetts governor, William Shirley, was not satisfied with coming to the rescue of the forlorn English colony at Annapolis, and thus preventing the French from reasserting their sovereignty over Acadia, and proceeded to think some unthinkable thoughts about the possible reduction of the great French fortress of Louisbourg on Cape Bretan Island. The French had begun to fortify this place shortly after the treaty of Utrecht in 1713, and by this time it was one of the strongest fortresses in the world, hardly surpassed by even Gibraltar or Quebec. It guarded the approaches to the St. Lawrence, and gave the French an excellent base from which they could attack Boston or threaten any other English city on the Atlantic Coast. It was madness to think of assaulting it, but this was what was in Shirley's mind, and to nourish his thoughts the governor busied himself with negotiating the release of some English prisoners-of-war taken by the French in their surprise attack on Canseau. The French had taken these men to Louisbourg, and it was from there that Shirley secured their release in an exchange program. The released men pictured the fort at Louisbourg as being in bad shape with the supplies low and the men dispirited. They also said the guns pointed in the wrong direction, out to sea, and the fortress "would not be capable of long resisting if attacked by land."[75] Of course, this is the reason Singapore fell to the Japanese in 1942--all her guns were pointing in the wrong direction, and when the Japanese came from behind, the great fortress was finished.

The explanation the men gave for the condition of Louisbourg was that the supply ships that had arrived at Cape Breton this year had arrived too late to penetrate the ice in the harbor, and consequently had proceeded to the West Indies where the supplies were always in demand, but it had left Louisbourg very short on everything. The men also said that the governor of Cape Breton had gone to France to get reinforcements, and that the French plan, once the fort had been reprovisioned and brought up to full strength, was to take the offensive against the English on a broad front, not only in Nova Scotia, but against Maine and Massachusetts as well, possibly including an attack on New York down the Montreal-Albany corridor.

These reports were alarming and exciting at the same time. They pointed to an opportunity, possibly a

261

fleeting opportunity, to reduce the great fortress by a bold stroke, and to the great danger that otherwise might result. Shirley discovered that he was not alone in thinking that this might be a very propitious time to launch an attack on Louisbourg. In conversations with some of the leading merchants -- the Wendells, Pepperrells, and Waldos -- some of whom had supported his appointment as governor, Shirley found that they were out in front of him on the proposition, and one of them, William Vaughan, way out in front. Vaughan advised the governor that a successful attack against Louisbourg could be carried out with as few as 1,500 raw New England militia. It was his bandwagon that Shirley got on when he decided to dedicate himself to this project, and once decided he threw himself into it with all the energy he had.

First off, Shirley commissioned one of the re- leased prisoners-of-war, an officer, to carry several letters to the Admiralty Lords in London advising them of the project, and earnestly requesting naval support. The officer chosen was one who had first-hand knowl- edge of Louisbourg, of Cape Breton, and of Nova Scotia. At the same time, Shirley communicated directly with Commodore Peter Warren on station in the West Indies, asking him to support the operation, and to do so on the authority of a colonial governor. This being ac- complished, Shirley addressed himself to the legisla- ture, but only after taking the unprecedented step of swearing all the members to secrecy.

It was apparent at once that the legislature was divided. The division was not between the bold and the meek, not between the imperialists and the non-imper- ialists, but between the conservative and the ultra- conservatives. At bottom, was the question of money. All our New England ancestors were a frugal lot, and some were more so than others. They all hated and feared their French neighbors, and all wanted to be rid of them, so they could live in peace (and profit) with their fisheries and commerce, without fear of privateers (that were not their own), and without fear of the devastating border raids of the French and their Indian allies (such as Deerfield). But the ques- tion in their minds was one of money. Could they af- ford to go it alone (or nearly so) against mighty France holed up in the strongest fort in the New World with the possible exception of Quebec? Did not common sense (which these Massachusetts men had in full mea- sure) dictate that the "mad scheme" of their popular governor be put off until the full support of the

mother country could be guaranteed? After all, the defense of Nova Scotia and the reduction of Louisbourg
were problems of empire, not the exclusive responsibility of Massachusetts. In other words, this was at
best conjointly a British and a new England interest,
not one for Massachusetts alone. Besides, it was es-
timated that the cost would be 50,000 pounds (a low
estimate).

In order to resolve the issue, the General Court
referred the whole subject to a committee of both
houses for further study. The arguments pro and con
sere considered at length, and in a surprisingly short
time (by today's standards) a decision was reached.
The cons came out on top, and the decision was that
"the expedition was thought to great, too hazardous,
and too expensive."[76] But this was not the end of it.
Whether by accident or design, word leaked out that
the subject had been considered in the legislature and
that the governor's plan had been rejected. There was
a groundswell of public opinion in favor of the plan,
and numerous petitions were circulated praying for a
reconsideration of the matter in order to give more
weight to public opinion. This was done, and by a
majority of one the resolution in favor of the enterprise was passed. Now all that remained was to collect
the shipping, raise the supplies, enlist the men, appoint the leaders, and wait for word on the naval support.

All this took time, but Shirley did not waste a
moment of it. He was greatly facilitated in his task
by the fact that the men of Massachusetts closed ranks
once the decision was made to go ahead with the plan,
and as Parkman said, "now doubt and hesitation vanished. All alike set themselves to push on the
work."[77] The preachers got out their Bibles, and the
newspapers did their part to pump the people up for
the great crusade. All was energy, ardor, and confidence. The ministers led prayers without ceasing to
support this pious expedition against the Catholic
anti-Christ in Canada, and the Boston *Evening Post* dug
into the classics to find "that the conflict between
England and France was remarkably similar to the ancient war between Rome and Carthage and that this expedition against Louisbourg was of particular historical importance as the beginning of another epic struggle; he, like Catos of old, encouraged the people to
cry out 'Delenda est Carthago'."[78] (Carthage must be
Destroyed).

The one big thing that was missing in all the exciting work Shirley was doing was the matter of naval support. True, Shirley had two irons in the fire, his application to the Admiralty in London, and the personal appeal he had made to Warren in the West Indies, but he had received no assurance from either. The date set for the departure of the expedition was March 24, 1745, and as it approached, everything was in readiness with the men aboard the fully loaded transports, but still no word had been received about the naval support. Suddenly, just one day before departure, an express boat from the West Indies brought the unwelcome intelligence that no aid could be expected from Warren without orders from the Admiralty. Shirley did not disclose this shocking news to anyone other than William Pepperrell, the designated commander-in-chief of the invasion. They decided it was now too late to cancel the operation; the die was cast. Unbeknownst to Shirley, his first appeal to the Admiralty the previous year, before the legislature had even consented to the operation, had been approved, and Warren now had the orders he needed to support the operation. These had reached him two or three days after he had sent the message to Shirley that he could not come to his assistance. Thus all was well again even though there was no way for Shirley and Pepperrell to know it when the fleet sailed. Anticipating the worst, that there would be no naval support, Shirley sent a message to the Admiralty on March 24, the date of the departure, saying that "accidents apart, four thousand New England men would land on Cape Breton in April, and that, even should they fail to capture Louisbourg, he would answer for it that they would lay the town in ruins, retake Canseau, do other great service to His Majesty, and then come safe home."[79]

Shirley was true to his word. On April 5, the transports reached the harbor of Canseau, 50 miles from Louisbourg, and on the 23rd Warren showed up with the first elements of the naval fleet to support the project. At daybreak on April 30 the landings began, and continued through the next day, until at its end 4,000 men were on shore. The critical period in the invasion, as was the case at Normandy two centuries later, was in the first 48 hours, during which the beachheads were established. But then the dirty work began. The heavy cannon had to be offloaded, and dragged for a distance of two miles through a morass. There were constant skirmishes with the French defenders, and colonial losses were heavy. Finally, the cannon were in place, and the battle for Louisbourg began. During the battle, some three thousand cannon balls were poured into the great fortress. The French put up a good fight for 49 days. The straw that broke the camel's back, however, was the capture of the *Vigilant* off Louisbourg by the naval force under Peter Warren. The *Vigilant* had on board a heavy reinforcement of French troops, and large quantities of the badly needed food and military supplies. This loss took the heart out of the defenders, and on June 17, 1745, the impregnable fortress of Louisbourg fell to the ragtag and bobtail of the Bay Colony.

The people of New England were electrified by the great victory of Louisbourg. Their appetite was also whetted for the grand prize, Canada, which seemed to be there for the taking, now that Louisbourg had fallen. Shirley had said that the conquest of Louisbourg would open the way "for an easy Reduction of that Country,"[80] and it was obvious that the time had come. The clergy added its powerful voice to the clamor. The Reverend Charles Chauncy said that he did not know "of a conquest since the days of Joshua and the Judges wherein the finger of God is more visible."[81] The Reverend Thomas Prince of Old South Church agreed. He said that the fortress of Louisbourg was the Dunkirk of North America, and in some respects of even greater importance, so "that for above these *Twenty Years*, it has seem'd to me, 'twere worth the while to engage in a *War* with *France*, if 'twere for nothing else but to recover this most important *Island* to the *British Empire*. Tho' a War was dreadful, the Necessity and Hazard seem'd every Year to encrease: The longer 'twas deferr'd, the more powerful and dangerous they grew, and the less our Hope of their being ever reduced."[82]

This is why Shirley was such a great leader of his people, why he was such a popular hero. His vision of empire did not put him out in front of the people of New England at the time. He and the merchants and the powerful religious groups reflected the mood of the people. It was one of conquest, of empire, and of manifest destiny. As one careful scholar of the period pictures it,

> Shirley saw unusual opportunities now
> for the capture of more French terri-
> tory -- perhaps all of Canada might be
> won for the effort of a campaign

against Quebec. He advocated a war of conquest that would open the continent to colonization as far west as the Mississippi, that would gain Britain a monopoly of the fur trade, enlarge her fishing industry, and increase her market for manufactured products. His was a vision of empire that foreshadowed William Pitt's of a decade later, when Pitt sent British legions into the very heart of Canada."[83]

With the people of New England in this mood, Shirley, on April 4, 1745, two months before the fall of Louisbourg, sent a message to London saying "that should the expedition succeed, all New England would be on fire to attack Canada, and the other colonies would take part with them, if ordered to do so by the ministry."[84] Some months later, after Louisbourg was taken, Shirley urged the policy "of striking while the iron was hot, and invading Canada at once."[85] The Duke of Newcastle, on March 14, 1746, sent a circular letter to all the Provincial Governors from New England to North Carolina. In it, he directed that should an invasion be ordered, they should call upon their assemblies for as many men as they would grant, and "that Warren would again command the North American squadron and that he had been instructed to consult with Shirley."[86] The idea was to raise 8,200 troops, 3,500 from Massachusetts, 500 from New Hampshire, 300 from Rhode Island, 1,000 from Connecticut, 1,600 from New York, 500 from New Jersey, 300 from Maryland, 100 from Virginia, and 400 from Pennsylvania.[87]

The operational plan was the familiar one, an advance to Montreal from Albany, and a main-force attack on Quebec by way of the St. Lawrence. It is said that the fleet sailed from England to implement this plan seven times, and seven times was turned back because of unfavorable wind conditions.[88] In any case, when the end of August came without the fleet arriving, Shirley wrote to Newcastle that it was now too late to undertake the project. Instead, he proposed an attack on Crown Point, a strong French fort on Lake Champlain that had been erected to guard the southern approach to Montreal and Quebec. The project was no sooner approved, and 1,500 Massachusetts men put in motion to join the New York troops, then it exploded like a thunder-clap. News came in that a large French fleet and army had arrived with plans to not only reconquer

Cape Breton and Nova Scotia, "but the total devasta-
tion of the sea coast, if not the conquest of New
England."[89]

This wrecked the attack on Crown Point, and put
all the emphasis on defense. In Massachusetts, 8,000
men were put under arms, and Connecticut promised
6,000 more as soon as the French fleet appeared. Governor Hutchinson said, "England was not more alarmed
with the Spanish armada in 1588, than Boston and the
other North American sea ports were with the arrival
of this fleet in their neighborhood."[90] However, there
was no occasion for alarm. Pestilence and storms had
come to the aid of the self-righteous New Englanders,
and the French fleet was in total disarray when it
arrived in the New World. At the outset it was one of
the strongest French fleets ever to put to sea, com-
prising nearly half of the total French navy, and
counting nearly 65 ships in all. At the end of the
outward cruise, two commanders-in-chief had been lost,
at least one of them a suicide, and there were not
enough ships left to constitute an organized fleet.
The individual ship captains were ordered to make
their way back to France any way they could, each on
his own. However, the French were so mortified that
their great American fortress had been snatched from
them by a despised militia that another fleet was assembled, not equal to the first but neverthelsee formidable, and put to sea on May 10, 1747. This fleet
had the misfortune to encounter a superior British
fleet on May 14. The result was a total defeat for the
French, and the end of their chances to recapture
Louisbourg in King George's War. A hero of the battle
was one of England's newest admirals, Peter Warren.

British reaction to the fall of Louisbourg was
mixed. There was much rejoicing and jubilation on the
part of the public. Guns were fired in honor of the
victory, and great celebrations were held with music
and fireworks. The popular acclaim that greeted the
victory was like the spontaneous outburst of a nation
in celebration of a great event. On the other hand,
for those in the government who wanted to bring about
a peace between England and France, the conquest of
Louisbourg was not a blessing, but an embarrassment.
It was clear to them that France would never consent
to a peace without the restoration of Louisbourg, and
it was also becoming obvious that a British government
that gave up Louisbourg in a peace treaty might not be
able to stand, at least as long as public opinion remained the way it was on the subject. The British had
had nothing much to cheer about thus far in the war,

267

and the public was almost as thrilled about Louisbourg
as the patriots in America who had brought off the
miracle. On the other hand, France was humiliated by
the loss to the point where peace was unthinkable without a restoration. This was the dilemma that faced the
peace party in England.[91]

The division in England was not only between those
who desired peace, peace at almost any price considering the way the war was going, and those who wanted to
continue the fight until a more favorable time for
peace, but also between the little-Englanders who
favored fighting the war on the continent, and the imperialists who would make the war mainly a maritime
one, downgrading the struggle on the continent to a
sort of holding action. William Pitt was an outsider
in the government, but his views were well known, and
they were that England's future was on the seas, and
that it was there that she should establish her supremacy, not on the continent of Europe masquerading as
a land power. He found a powerful ally in the person
of the Duke of Bedford who, as First Lord of the Admiralty, took personal credit for the great victory at
Louisbourg.[92] This alliance kept the idea of a Canadian invasion open all during the period from 1746 to
October 1748, when the treaty of Aix-la-Chapelle put
an end to the idea. Meanwhile, however, English policy
was indecisive about further conquests in America, and
even as late as 1748 Shirely was being encouraged to
organize expeditions against Canada while the ministry
was slipping into the peace without Louisbourg, a peace
that was without honor, in the colonial view.

The treaty of Aiz-la-Chapelle was another of
England's boring status quo treaties. In this case,
the agreement was to restore all the territory captured during the war, and this included Louisbourg.
Colonial reaction was one of shocked disbelief. It was
1632 all over again, an echo of the treaty of St. Germain, which had ceded Acadia back to France after its
conquest by Argall. The anti-treaty argument in 1632
was also the same, that the French had no better claim
to Acadia than they had to Massachusetts, and that if
the former was valid so might be the latter. The *Independent Advertiser* of Boston, a paper that was out-
spoken in its anger at the terms of Aix-la-Chapelle,
said, "who can tell what will be the Consequence of
this Peace in Times to come? Perhaps this goodly Land
itself-- Even *this* our beloved Country, may share the
same Fate with this its Conquest --may be the Purchase

of a future Pease."[93] Schutz's conclusion seems justified,

> for many people the return of Louis-
> bourg was an insult to their Protestant
> faith, a contempt for the victory that
> God had given them on Cape Breton is-
> land, a submission to the satanic
> French. In language that recalls the
> biblical inheritance of New England
> but is also infused with the spirit of
> trade and imperial expansion, local
> poets tried to capture the depths of
> exasperation that had settled upon New
> England. Darkness, they said, had
> come upon the land. Joy was turned to
> sorrow; sacrifices of lives and spirit
> were made profane by the signature of
> a diplomat's hand.[94]

In the colonial view, King George's War was simply
another imperial conflict that had not only led nowhere, but which had actually backfired when the
mother country failed to support colonial arms, and
then proceeded to repudiate the victory that colonial
arms had won. The net result was a failure everywhere,
against Crown Point in the west, against Louisbourg on
Cape Breton, and against St. Augustine in the south.
The London government was accused of making imperial
policy without regard to the right course of empire,
and of allowing itself to be shamefully swindled at
the conference table. It was not enough to reimburse
the colonies, even with the princely sum of 235,000
pounds that went mainly to Massachusetts. What was
needed was a government with imperial vision, a government that could see the great continent as it was, not
just the thin shoreline. In short, what was lacking
in London was what the colonies had in abundance-- men
with empires in their brains.

King George's War was a total misfit from the
point of view of the pattern of the colonial wars that
has been handed down to us as the backdrop for our
diplomatic history. John Adams would not recognize it
as being a good example of America's being used as a
football between contending nations, and Thomas Paine
would find it hard to view it in connection with his
theory of the colonies being used as a make-weight in
the scale of British politics. Quite the opposite.
The colonists took the lead in the prosecution of the
war against the Spanish in Florida, and furnished

3,600 colonial troops to support Admiral Edward Vernon's attempt to conquer Cartagena in modern Colombi . The colonists were equally as active and aggressive in the north as they were in the south. Governor William Shirley of Massachusttts rushed reinforcements to Nova Scotia, and it was the only thing that saved that strategic outpost from falling to the French. The same thing is true of the reduction of Louisbourg. With the exception of the last minute support provided by elements of the royal navy, this was a colonial enterprise in its entirety, from the early planning to its final execution.

Thus the ideas that have come to us from our diplomatic textbooks are all wrong, that colonial Americans were peaceniks who came to America because they all sought above everything else isolation from war (Divine); that they were not supposed to reason why in the bad old European conflicts (Bailey); and that even though they were involved in these senseless wars, despite themselves, they accepted their fate with undisturbed equanimity, and no one questioned the great sufferings and hardships they had to endure in the senseless wars that cost them so much, and netted them nothing. (Bemis)

The last of the four great wars in our colonial history was called the Seven Years' War in Europe and the French and Indian War in America. The fact that King George's War had ended with a status-quo treaty, Aix-la-Chapelle, meant another war was inevitable. It came in less than a decade, and this time it was decisive in determining which of the two great powers would be dominant in America. England wanted to keep it that way, a limited war for limited objectives, a war designed to determine whether England or France would be dominant in North America. It was for this reason that when she decided to intervene with British regulars she did so on a limited scale, and without a declaration of war. France followed suit. As soon as it was learned that a couple of regiments, numbering about 1,400 regulars under General Edward Braddock, were being shipped to Virginia, a force of 3,000 men was started for Canada under the command of Baron Ludwig Dieskau, a German officer in the French Service.

One of General Braddock's first acts on arriving in America was to convene a military staff conference at the camp at Alexandria, Virginia, on April 14, 1755. It was apparent at this meeting that the colonial leaders had ideas of their own about how to deal with the French in America, and that they were considerably advanced over those that were current in England. For example, it was Braddock's understanding that he had been sent to America to push the French back to the positions they had occupied in 1748, and thus to put an end to their encroachments on lands claimed by the English. But it was soon apparent that the colonial leaders would not be satisfied with this, and that what they had in mind was the expulsion of the French from North America. Governor Shirley is a good example of this. He had been one of the peace commissioners in Paris during August of 1750, when they had tried to make some sense out of the territorial boundary disputes left unsettled at the peace conference, and when that failed, he returned to America convinced that another war with France was inevitable. In the spring of 1754 he had built several forts in northern Maine, and predicted that these "thunder clouds" would do more to preserve the peace "than a thousand treaties."[95] Now that warfare had broken out in the Ohio Valley --with the young George Washington involved, first as an "assassin" of the French "diplomat," Coulon de Jumoville, and later as the losing commander when Fort Necessity was surrendered to the French on July 4, 1754--Shirley was mobilizing men and planning expeditions against French strongholds in Acadia and at Crown Point. He said that destruction of the latter would put it in our power "to march an army in a few days to the gates of the city of Montreal itself and pour our troops into the very heart of their country."[96] This was the kind of thinking Braddock encountered at the staff conference in Virginia, and it was his job to reconcile that with his own mission.

The general did what came naturally, which was to say yes to all the plans of Shirley and the other colonial leaders, and at the same time to go ahead with his own plans. It was difficult to do otherwise because Shirley had mobilized 7,000 men, and was eager, as indeed all the men were, to get on with the job of rooting the French out of Canada. As for his own mission and plans, Braddock had a force that was more than adequate for the job, and it had just been augmented by 450 colonial militia under the command of Lieutenant-Colonel George Washington. So Braddock made all the necessary decisions to launch a series of attacks on a broad front. In addition to the main-force offensive against Fort Duquesne, which he would lead, there would be an attack against Fort Niagara led by

271

Governor Shirley, who would also be his deputy and second in command; an attack on Crown Point led by the Indian trader and expert, William Johnson; and an offensive against the French strongpoints in Nova Scotia led by Colonels Robert Monckton (a regular) and John Winslow (a colonial). All the while, Admiral Edward Boscawen would blockade the St. Lawrence to prevent the French from bringing reinforcements to any of the threatened areas.

Of the four separate forces involved in this coordinated attack on the advance salients of the French in North America, the first to move was the main-force under General Braddock. His target was Fort Duquesne at the forks of the Ohio, where Pittsburgh now stands, and which at the time was on land claimed by Canada on behalf of the French king, and both Virginia and Pennsylvania on behalf of the English king. Braddock's jumping off place was at Fort Cumberland on Wills Creek, which he reached on May 10, 1755, but his forward progress was at a snail's pace because of the heavy terrain, and what happened to him is well known. He was surprised by a small force of French and Indians, mostly the latter, when he was only 10 miles from his objective, and cut to pieces. This was on July 9, 1955. When the killing was over, Braddock himself was drawing his last breath, and 900 of his 2,500 men were dead or wounded, with the rest in disorderly rout, thus exposing all the frontier settlements to the ravages of Indian warfare. It was not only a defeat, but a very humiliating one, the land-power equivalent to the sea-power fiasco under Admiral Hovenden Walker in Queen Anne's War.

The invasion of Nova Scotia to root the French out of their outposts there, including Beausejour, the strongest fortified place on the peninsula, got underway at about the same time General Braddock jumped off for Fort Duquesne. When he was at Wills Creek on May 10, 1755, the fleet bound for Nova Scotia was just getting ready to sail from Boston. Shirley had been planning this expedition for a year, and had already received a clearance from London. John Winslow, a company commander in the abortive Cartagena invasion of 1741, was the principal organizer of the expedition, having recruited 2,000 volunteers to serve under his command. The landing was unopposed, in sharp contrast to Braddock's reception at Fort Duquesne, and after very slight resistance the Fort was given up to the English. The other French outposts were overrun just

272

as quickly, and the whole of old Acadia or modern Nova Scotia was now in English hands. What followed was the deportation and relocation of at least 5,000 Acadians, many being sent to Louisiana and South Carolina, and the destruction of some quaint villages in Nova Scotia, including Grand Pre, an event that Longfellow let no one ever forget.

In January 1755, while the Campaign in Nova Scotia was in the planning stage, Shirley had sounded out the Ministry on another of his favorite projects, the reduction of the strong French fort at Crown Point. Confident that it would be approved, he moved right ahead with his own legislature, and on February 13 laid the project before the Assembly. It was approved immediately, and to show that they meant business the legislature voted the money for the pay and maintenance of her men, provided only that the adjacent colonies would contribute in due proportion. This was done just as speedily. Connecticut raised 1,200 men, 500 from New Hampshire, 400 from Rhode Island, and 800 from New York. The Massachusetts contingent was 4,500, or one in eight of her adult males. In other words, out of a total population of roughly 220,000, Massachusetts put 4,500 under arms. While this is not a high percentage, considering the ratios reached when wars became total in character, it must have seemed high at the time. Nearly a century before, during King Philip's War (1675-76), Massachusetts had suffered the loss of a tenth of all her males of military age. In proportion to population, the losses in this war were greater than any other in our history.

The Massachusetts men were a hardy lot, and they knew from first-hand experience the human costs of war. Nevertheless, they did not blink at the governor's request for volunteers, and were of one mind with him as to the necessity of it. And the men themselves, the ones who would have to face the enemy on the battlefield, felt the same way. As Parkman said, "forty-five hundred of her men, or one in eight of her adult males, volunteered to fight the French, and enlisted for the various expeditions, some in the pay of the province, and some in that of the King."[97]

Shirley was very circumspect in making the decision as to who should command the expedition against Crown Point. He needed the support of the other New England colonies and, above all, that of New York and

her Iroquois allies. Thus he did not name a Massachusetts man to command the expedition, but instead
picked William Johnson, a son of New York who was at
the same time the number one choice of the Indians, an
adopted Mohawk. This was a popular choice with everyone except Johnson. He had just been given a royal
commission to the job he had always wanted, to be the
King's representative to all the northern Indians,
Indian Superintendent. Accordingly, he asked to be
relieved of his military assignment the better to concentrate on Indian affairs, which he believed (quite
rightly) were more important than anything else. His
request was denied, however, and he had to shoulder
both responsibilities.

The next question was one of strategy, and here
again Johnson was a dissenter. Braddock's orders when
he came to America were to liberate the Ohio, which
meant that he must take Fort Duquesne. Johnson challenged this. "Instead of traversing deadly mountains
and deadlier thickets in a march on Fort Duquesne," he
said,

> the main British force should float
> comfortably to Niagara, 'leaving a few
> men towards the Ohio to keep the
> French on expectation of a visit there,'
> If the French lost control of the Nia-
> gara River, their communications would
> be cut not only with the further Great
> Lakes and the posts on them dependent,
> but also with the Ohio Valley: they
> would be forced to abandon not only
> Duquesne but all their northwestern
> posts.[98]

Braddock's rejoinder to this was to say that it
was not open to discussion since he was committed to
the operation against Fort Duquesne. However, he could
appreciate the logic of the Niagara strategy, and
ordered Shirley to take the lead on that attempt,
using the two royal Massachusetts regiments (his and
Pepperrell's) as the nucleus of his forces. The idea
was that Shirley would advance up the Mohawk Valley to
Oswego, the embarkation point for the ascent on
Niagara, and Johnson would march northward toward
Crown Point, either by way of Lake George or Wood
Creek.

274

This pitted Shirley against Johnson in the sense that the former had control over the colonial troops by virtue of his orders from the king, and the latter had control over the Indians, again pursuant to orders from the crown. The overlapping of authority did not bode well for harmony between the two colonial leaders, and discord soon became the order of the day. Shirley exercised his authority by diverting the New Jersey regiment from Johnson's Crown Point operation to his against Niagara, and Johnson retaliated by blocking Shirley's efforts to recruit Indian allies. In the midst of all this confusion and back-biting France won a major victory when the French fleet slipped by Admiral Edward Boscawen, and landed Baron Dieskau and his 3,000 regulars safely at Louisbourg and Quebec. This upset the balance of power in the area, and gave France the wherewithal to counter the English thrusts at Crown Point and Niagara.

Baron Dieskau's initial orders, upon arriving in Canada, were to undertake an operation against Oswego. They were changed, however, as a result of some intelligence that fell into his hands indicating that Crown Point was to be the object of an English attack. This vital information was gleaned from some papers found on the battlefield after Braddock's defeat. In July, Johnson's force of about 3,000 provincial soldiers was gathered in Albany. All was confusion bordering on chaos, however, because the whole movement depended on the cooperation of five colonial governments. On August 21 four Mohawk scouts returned from Canada with the report that 8,000 men, including Dieskau's regulars, were coming to defend Crown Point. By the 26th, 2,000 of Johnson's men were on the March for Lake George, having decided not to take the route by way of Wood Creek. The crunch came on September 8 when Dieskau fell, and William Johnson won a great victory at the Battle of Lake George. This atoned somewhat for Braddock's defeat in July, and gave the colonists something to cheer about. In their eyes, the French Braddock was the German baron Dieskau, and the American hero was William Johnson. The king also cheered by knighting the colonial hero, and Parliament voted him a gift of 5,000 pounds. None of this, however, could compensate for the fact that Johnson was content to rest on his laurels, and no power on earth could move him to take the offensive against Crown Point, which had been his target from the beginning. As a result, the defeated and retreating enemy was allowed to hold and even reinforce Ticonderoga and Crown Point. Later in the same war James Abercromby lost 2,000 men, half of them colonials, in a vain attempt to reduce Fort Ticonderoga.

At the same time Johnson was winning his hollow victory at Lake George, Shirley was pushing up the Mohawk Valley to Oswego for the assault on Niagara. The strategy of this campaign was sound -- Niagara was the linchpin that kept the wheel of French empire on the axle-- but the strength was not there to take it. When he got to Oswego at the end of August the French force at Fort Frontenac, 50 miles across the lake, was about 1,500, roughly the equivalent to Shirley's force. The same thing was true of Niagara. If Shirley had been foolish enough to leave for an assault on Niagara, without first reducing Fort Frontenac, he would have laid himself open for a summary court-martial. By taking Oswego while Shirley was at Niagara, the French would have turned the Niagara victory (assuming there was one) into a crushing defeat. Even so, Shirley had several serious discussions with his commanders about doing just this until he reluctantly decided it was out of the question. Boscawen's blunder with the French fleet had check-mated Shirley, and Johnson's refusal to push on to Crown Point had added to his woes. At the end of October, Shirley gave up the ghost, and returned to Albany, leaving 700 men to defend Oswego.

Shirley's failure to get beyond Oswego ended the active campaigns for 1755, and set the stage for 1756. It had been a defeatful year on the whole, with the only real victory being in Nova Scotia. Great exertions had been made by the northern colonies, and the mother country had given them good support, but there was nothing to show for it. The west was still up for grabs, with the French winning, and the colonies were not one iota closer to a dominion of Canada than they had been at the beginning of the year. What was needed was a strong hand at the helm of the ship of state, a hand that could consolidate the energies and make them apply as a single force against the desired objectives. A step in this direction was taken, or so it seemed, when Governor Shirley, on his return to Albany, found himself in possession of a commission appointing him commander-in-chief of the King's forces in North America.

With the King's authority in his knapsack, Shirley immediately called a conference of all the governors, and plans were made for an enlarged offensive in 1756, one that would include attacks against Duquesne, Niagara, and Crown Point. It was also agreed that larger forces should be raised, 10,000 for the expedition against Crown Point, 6,000 for that against Niagara, and 3,000 for the mission against Fort Duquesne. No sooner were these arrangements made than Governor Shirley found he was powerless to implement them. He fell a victim to an underhanded campaign of vilification, and was ordered home in disgrace, relieved not only of his position as commander-in-chief, but also of his position as governor of Massachusetts.

Shirley's fall came in March of 1756. Two months later, on May 18, England declared war on France, and on June 9 France declared war on England. Prior to this there had been a reshuffle of alliances in Europe. This saw England allied with Prussia, and Austria with France, instead of the old alignment of England and Austria against France and Prussia. The new alignment was such a momentous thing in Europe that it was called a diplomatic revolution, but it was considered hardly worthy of notice on this side of the water. What mattered here was the extent to which the colonies could get the mother country to aid them in the accomplishment of their objective, which was to win the war against their rival claimants to empire in America, particularly France. Nothing else really mattered.

The recall of Shirley was a vote of no-confidence in the war plans of 1756, and the colonial troops began to grow impatient and restless at the delays and apparent indecision on the part of the leaders in the colonies and in England. When Shirley's recall orders arrived in June, there was already much dissatisfaction apparent in the troops assembled for the three expeditions. In fact, the main-force operation against Ticonderoga-Crown Point was about to break up because the commanding general, John Winslow, delcared himself unable to proceed without reinforcements. Shirley's orders were to turn over his command to General James Abercromby, who in turn would be relieved by John Cambell, Lord Loudoun. It was at this critical time in his life that the news reached Shirley that the new French commander, Louis Joseph, Marquis de Montcalm, had turned the tables on him by taking the English outpost, Fort Oswego, on August 14, 1756. With this disaster, the grandiose plan for the year 1956 collapsed like a deck of cards. Perhaps the best that could be hoped for in 1756 was to escape defeat themselves. Duquesne, Niagara, Crown Point, could all be forgotten.

The French king had at last found a man to command the troops in Canada. Montcalm had seized the initiative, and put the English on the defensive.

Loudoun's contribution to policy in America was to go on the defensive everywhere, particularly after the fall of Oswego, which he blamed on Shirley. His next contribution was to subordinate the colonial role in the war to that of mere auxiliaries. This meant that colonial troops would be commanded, wherever possible, by regulars in the future, and that the decision-making process would operate without any colonial bumpkins of the Shirley type. Accordingly, when the plans were laid for 1757, Loudoun was completely satisfied by only a very nominal levy on the colonial legislatures (only 4,000 men from the four New England governments), and they were to be used as guards and garrisons for the frontiers, while the main thrust would be made at Louisbourg by the Royal Navy in conjunction with regular regiments. Loudoun was not even satisfied with this douwngrading of colonial troops, and insisted, for example, that "the 1,800 men, raised by Massachusetts, should be under one field officer only. Thus the provincials came under the command of the colonels in the regular service."[99]

The force that Lord Loudoun set out with for the attack on Louisbourg consisted of a main body of about 6,000 regulars, all he could lay his hands on, embarked on a number of transports that would be convoyed to Halifax under the protection of several elements of the Royal Navy. The whole fleet consisted of about 90 sail, and it set out for Halifax on June 30, 1757. The plan was for it to be joined there by another fleet under Admiral Francis Holbourne, which was to consist of 15 ships of the line, plus supporting craft, and about 5,000 troops on transports. The British fleet put to sea on May 5, and arrived in Halifax on July 9. The stage was thus set for the main act of 1757, the conquest of Louisbourg, but this time a proper conquest, not one of irregular provincials, but one led by Lord Loudoun with proper British forces, soldiers and seamen alike. It would be a fitting way to inaugurate the advent of the new leadership in America.

Unfortunately, everything did not work out the way Lord Loudoun had hoped and expected. He was outguessed on both sides of the Atlantic, not only by the Canadian authorities, but also by the French Court.

This process began as soon as the new Year rolled around, and the French began assembling a large reinforcement for the Canadian forces. It was given impetus by the fact that a French spy in London informed the French Court that a great armament was being fitted out in England for America. This was the one that Lord Loudoun was counting on to implement the plan against Louisbourg. While this armament was forming, the French dispatched three strong French squadrons to Louisbourg, with a contingent of 2,400 soldiers for Quebec. The French squadrons reached Louisbourg a full month before Holbourne's fleet arrived at Halifax. Lord Loudoun's chances against Louisbourg were probably killed by this development.

As it was, some elements of the French fleet were seen off the coast of Cape Breton Island while Lord Loudoun was in New York waiting for word that Admiral Holbourne had set out for Halifax. Not receiving any word, Loudoun set out for Halifax anyway, trusting to luck that Holbourne would meet him there, and that he would not encounter any elements of the French fleet during the ten day period when he and his transports were between New York and Halifax -- June 20-30. His luck held, and on July 9, the English admiral arrived with his ships of war and loaded troop transports. He found Lord Loudoun in high spirits, happily drilling his soldiers, and planting a small garden to improve the diet of the troops. Everything was now in readiness for the grand assault on Louisbourg. Or so it seemed.

Appearances were deceiving, deceiving because Loudoun had failed to take into consideration what was happening in the French camp on this side of the water. At first, Montcalm had his hands tied because he did not know what the English plans were for 1757, and did not want to make a move that would play into their hands. Shirley's idea of strategy was well known, of course, Crown Point, Duquesne, and Niagara, but what was Loudoun's plan? Was Louisbourg the centerpiece for 1757, and if so would Loudoun be foolish enough to starve and weaken the frontier outposts in order to feed the Louisbourg expedition? Apparently this is exactly what Loudoun planned to do, and as soon as that became common knowledge, Montclam made his move. This was to attack in the Albany-Montreal corridor, and to do so while the garrisons were weakened for the Louisbourg assault. The result was the expedition against Fort William Henry, and its fall on August 9. The only thing that marred the victory was the hideous massacre that followed, when Montcalm lost control of his Indian allies.

Meanwhile, where was Lord Loudoun, and how did he react to the ruin of his plans for 1757? After greeting Admiral Holbourne upon his arrival at Halifax on July 9, Lord Loudoun continued to amuse himself drilling his well-drilled soldiers, and working his vegetable garden. Finally, realizing that the season for battle was late, he embarked the troops on their transports, and planned to move against Louisbourg on August 1. However, another delay ensued, and this one was probably fortunate in that it gave him an excuse to go back to New York, and call off the entire campaign. What happened was the appearance of an English vessel from Newfoundland that had just captured a French ship out of Louisbourg, on board which letters revealing the current strength of the French were found. The captured letters revealed the fact "that all three of the French squadrons were united in the harbor of Louisbourg, to the number of twenty-two ships of the line, besides several frigates, and that the garrison had been increased to a total force of seven thousand men, ensconced in the strongest fortress of the continent."[100]

These sober facts convinced Lord Loudoun that success against the Louisbourg was now hopeless, and he at once abandoned the entire campaign, taking his transports and their convoy back to New York. Admiral Holbourne, however, steered in the opposite direction to cruise off Louisbourg on the off-chance that the French fleet would come out to give battle. However, the French admiral was not that foolhardy, and stayed in the protected harbor of the fortress. The following month a September gale did his work for him. At its end, Admiral Holbourne did not have a single ship left that was fit for immediate action. The whole Atlantic coast lay exposed to the powerful French fleet at Louisbourg. "The French fleet," Governor Hutchinson said, "had an opportunity, the whole month of October, of laying waste the sea-ports of New England; and the people of Boston were not free from fears, until news arrived of its having sailed for Europe."[101]

The sloop from Newfoundland that gave Lord Loudoun the order-of-battle intelligence on Louisbourg came into the harbor of Halifax on August 4, and the last day of the month the lordly general came into the harbor of New York with his transports and convoy. He first learned of the tragedy of Fort William Henry when he

280

was at sea off the coast of Nova Scotia. The news came
to him by express boat from Boston. He was not alarmed,
and there is no evidence that he felt any guilt at having brought the tragedy on himself by drawing off the
British forces from the frontier where they were
needed, in order to undertake the wild goose chase to
Louisbourg. Instead of this, Loudoun took everything
in stride, as befitting his dignity, and airily informed all who would listen that they need have no
fears, that the French would not attack Fort Edward,
and that Albany and New York were not in danger.
Nevertheless, he sent his troops up the Hudson, and
mumbled something about an attack on Ticonderoga. This
would have made sense before the fall of Fort William
Henry, but hardly after it? The only thing that made
sense at this time was a strong defense of what was
left of the English position in the Montreal-Albany
corridor, while making every effort to restore the English position at Oswego. Instead of doing any of
these things, however, Lord Loudoun kicked up a very
lively quarrel with Massachusetts over the issue of
quartering troops in private houses, and threatened to
use force if the colony did not submit to his orders.
In other words, given his way, to his one enemy,
France, he would have added another, Massachusetts.

At this time, all eyes turned to the campaigns of
1758, and it was well they did so, for the campaigns
of 1757 had been disastrous for British arms, not only
in America, but on every other continent as well. On
the other hand, France was at the pinnacle of its
power in America at the end of 1757, the highest it
would ever reach, and correspondingly, the fortunes of
the British were at their lowest ebb. The great John
Marshall painted the picture accurately when he said,

> the affairs of great Britain in North
> America wore a more gloomy aspect, at
> the close of the campaign of 1757,
> than at any former period. By the ac-
> quisition of Fort William Henry, the
> French had obtained complete possess-
> ion of the Lakes Champlain, and George.
> By the destruction of Oswego, they had
> acquired the dominion of those lakes
> which connect the St. Lawrence with
> the waters of the Mississippi, and
> unite Canada to Louisians. By means
> of fort Du Quesne, they maintained

281

their ascendency over the Indians, and held undisturbed possession of the country west of the Allegheny mountains; while the English settlers were driven to the blue ridge. The great object of the war in that quarter was gained, and France held the country for which hostilities had been commenced.[102]

Lord Loudoun's days as the commander-in-chief of His Majesty's forces in North America were nearing an end. So were the defeatful years of England's history. The nation was about to have a rebirth of energy and purpose. Waiting in the wings to rescue England from the nadier of her despair was one of the towering figures of England's history, William Pitt, Earl of Chatham. He was also known as the Great Commoner, but was not a commoner in any but the political sense. He came from a rich and influential family, but being a younger son was not entitled to hereditary privileges, and had to make his own mark in life. The England of his day loved and respected him, and would follow him to the ends of the earth, to which he nearly led them. He was like Winston Churchill in many ways. Both men came on the scene when England had her back to the wall, and both saved her, snatching victory from the jaws of defeat only by dedicating the nation to "blood, sweat, and tears." And the odd thing is that victory in each case was brought about by the use of allies to pull England's chestnuts out of the fire, to use the hackneyed phrase. In the case of Churchill it was the United States that tipped the scales against the Axis, and in Pitt's day the reliance on Frederick the Great was so important that Pitt himself boasted that "he would conquer America in Germany."[103] Finally, both great men ended the same way. As soon as they had done their work for England, she kicked them out--in a democratic way, of course. And did it in each case just before the great war they had won came to an end.

As soon as Pitt became the principal Secretary of State for the prosecution of the war in 1757, he carried out a thorough house-cleaning of England's decrepit defense establishment, and removed as much of the deadwood as possible. Among the new men he brought up were James Wolfe, William Howe, and Jeffrey Amherst. The idea was to find able young military and naval commanders, put them in positions of responsibility, and back them to the hilt. Also, the old Navy and War

Offices were streamlined for greater efficiency, and a new system was installed whereby Pitt could communicate directly with officers in the field. A new urgency was introduced into operations, and each commander in the field began to feel a personal connection between himself and the great Pitt. Morale soared. The flag began to mean something. It meant victory, no matter what the odds, and in spite of any obstacles. Napoleon knew how to impart this feeling to the men on the battlefields, and so did the Great Commoner.

For Pitt, the next order of business was to forget about the hit-or-miss strategy that had prevailed thus far, and to lay out a plan of action that would produce the desired results. The plan of action that evolved was one of world-wide scope. The Royal Navy would be used to exploit the sea power of England on the seven seas; the American colonists would be supported to the hilt in order to clear North America, including the adjacent islands, of the enemies of England; and Frederick the great would be given a blank check to guard against the extension of European power, particularly French, to any part of the New World. The response to the new strategy was a miracle of sorts, a good example of which was in the American colonies, particularly Massachusetts.

One of Lord Loudoun's last official acts, after the defeatful and disgraceful year of 1757, was to meet with the governors of New York and the New England colonies to determine upon a plan of measures for the forthcoming year. From Massachusetts, it was stipulated that a force of 2,200 men would be required, and the hint was that these men would be used for a new assault on Louisbourg. "The proposal," Governor Hutchinson said, "laboured in the assembly. Six days were spent without any vote. Certain queries were then laid before the general to which answers were desired. How long are the men to continue in service? What officers are they to be under? Where is the command to be? How are they to be paid, armed, and vitualled? What is their destination? What will be the whole force, when they shall have joined it?"[104]

While Lord Loudoun was considering these impertinent questions, an express came from New York bearing the news that he had been relieved of his post as commander-in-chief in North America, and that James Abercromby was his successor. The people of New England, and of Massachusetts in particular, were overjoyed to be rid of the lordly general, the butt of

Louisbourg, and the bane of the colonies. The same express brought another message from William Pitt reccommending that the Assembly raise as many men as possible for military operations in the immediate future, presumably against the French in Canada. Hutchinson said the House made no queries, but came instantly to a resolve "to raise seven thousand men by enlistment for the intended expedition against Canada."[105] He also said, "this was the greatest exertion ever made by the province. From the proposals made by Lord Loudoun, they expected nothing more than another attempt upon Louisbourg. Now, they had in view the country westward, considered the reduction of Ticonderoga and Crown Point to be certain, and that the possession of all Canada would soon follow."[106] This is a good example of the way Americans reacted to the appeal of the Great Commoner, as opposed to their negative response to the little-Englanders and pettifoggers in the London government.

Pitt's plan for 1758 called for a general offensive comprised of three separate campaigns. The specific targets were Louisbourg, assigned to Jeffrey Amherst, Ticonderoga and Crown Point, given to James Abercromby, and Fort Duquesne, the responsibility of John Forbes. The first to get underway was the campaign against Louisbourg, the French Gibraltar in North America. It was only fitting that this should be so, for of the three targets for 1758, Louisbourg was the only one that directly involved the navy. In other words, the forts at Ticonderoga, Crown Point, and Duquesne, could be taken by ground forces alone, but this was not the case with Louisbourg on Cape Breton Island. Thus it was that the troops embarked at Halifax on May 24, and arrived before Louisbourg on June 2. After more than seven weeks of hard fighting, and a gallant stand by the French defenders, the great fortress was forced to capitulate on July 26. There was great joy in England and throughout the colonies too long accustomed to disappointments and defeat. Amidst the victory celebrations, however, there was one sour note. In Boston, where a stately bonfire had been built on the top of Fort Hill in honor of the occasion, certain jealous patriots objected to celebrating "a victory won by British regulars, and not by New England men."[107]

Louisbourg was the great victory in 1758. The pity is that the follow-through was bad. Only one English soldier in high position seemed to be aware of the strategic demands of the moment. This was Brigadier James Wolfe, who had commanded the troops that captured Louisbourg. To him, Louisbourg was only the beginning, not the end, of the campaign on the St. Lawrence. As Parkman said of Wolfe, "he was only half pleased with what had been done. The capture of Louisbourg, he thought, should be but the prelude of greater conquests; and he had hoped that the fleet and army would sail up the St. Lawrence and attack Quebec."[108] However, this was not to be. His commanding general Jeffrey Amherst, agreed that, other things being equal, Quebec should be the next objective, and that the shortest and most logical approach was up the St. Lawrence. On the other hand, everything was not equal. Right or wrong, plans had been laid for a main-force operation in the Albany-Montreal corridor against Ticonderoga and Crown Point, with another land operation against Fort Duquesne at the forks of the Ohio. Thus General Amherst said he felt the only thing he could do under the circumstances was to go with five or six regiments to the aid of General Abercromby at Lake George. Wolfe threatened to resign his commission and quit the army over the issue, but instead was persuaded to return to England for the rest and relaxation he needed before assuming further command responsibilities.

General Abercromby was something of a misfit among the officers who survived the house-cleaning that took place when Pitt came to office. Pitt would have been glad to have seen him go, but because of other considerations that he could not disregard he allowed him to remain. To compensate for his presence, however, Pitt appointed Brigadier Lord Howe to be his second in command. James Wolfe described Howe as being "the noblest Englishman that has appeared in my time, and the best soldier in the Britich army."[109] Pitt obviously meant that Howe, not Abercromby, would be in actual command of the army. The command was a very important one because the army encamped at the head of Lake George in June of 1758 was the largest one that had ever been assembled in North America. It consisted of more than 9,000 provincial soldiers, and 6,000 British regulars. The mission of the army was to pick up where William Johnson had left off in 1755, and destroy the French forts at Ticonderoga and Crown Point, as a prelude to an invasion of Canada by way of the Albany-Montreal corridor. Unfortunately, Lord Howe was killed in a skirmish that preceded the main battle, and the onus of real command fell on the incompetent Abercromby. The result was one of the most costly and disgraceful defeats in colonial warfare.

Abercromby's opposite number in the wilderness battle was Montcalm, and it was not one of his shining moments either. He chose to defend Ticonderoga by throwing up a wall of fallen trees with intertwisted boughs that could not be penetrated by any kind of a frontal charge. His communications could have been cut in the rear, and he had only enough supplies to last for eight days; or Ambercromby could have brought up his cannon, and made a wreck of the wooden wall. Montcalm's only hope was that Abercromby would make a fool of himself, which he did. Instead of marching to the rear of Montcalm's wooden wall, instead of bringing up his cannon to blast it away, Abercromby, influenced by a rumor that reinforcements were coming up for Montcalm, threw his men blindly at the impenetrable wall of fallen trees. Their charges were gallant, and there were six of them on that dreadful July 8, but they were also of no avail, and by day's end Abercromby had lost 2,000 men, killed and wounded. Montcalm's losses were less than 400. But the worst was yet to come. Abercromby still had a vastly superior force, but acted like he was in danger of annihilation, and beat a hasty retrest to the head of Lake George as though the devil were after him. Officers and men began to refer to him as an old woman, Mrs. Nabbycrombie, and it is no wonder that he was removed from command, being replaced by General Amherst.

Fortunately, Abercromby's ailment was not contagious. Colonel John Bradstreet, not one of the New England Bradstreets, persuaded Abercromby to let him proceed to Fort Frontenac with 3,000 provincial soliders, and on August 22 he pushed out on Lake Ontario for the French fort. This was the fort that gave Montcalm the means of controlling the lake, and it was also the one that had baffled Shirley in his attempt against Niagara in 1755. The fort was not prepared for the surprise attack, and Bradstreet took it with ease, the surrender coming on the morning of August 27. This was a substantial success because it seriously weakened the French position in two important sectors, Niagara and Duquesne. It was followed by an even greater victory, that of John Forbes at Duquesne. When the French Indians detached themselves at the approach of Forbes' army, the French general realized that resistance was hopeless, and on November 24 put the torch to the great French fortress. It was still smoldering when General Forbes arrived the next day. This terminated the active campaigning for the year 1758.

Pitt's plan for 1759 was to launch three separate operations, and to do this simultaneously on three widely separated fronts, against Niagara in the west, against Montreal in the center, and against Quebec in the east. The idea was to spread France thin, and to prevent one sector from being able to support another. The only unifying principle was that of converging lines. If everything went well, the English forces would eventually join up for the knockout blow at Montreal, or more likely Quebec. This was pre-Napoleonic strategy, of course. It did not emphasize what became the first law of military strategy, concentration of force, and instead elevated diversion and diffusion to the status of principles. The more modern method would have been to concentrate upon a single objective, and to avoid like the plague diversions against subordinate targets, other than what was absolutely necessary to disguise the real objective. The fallacy of the pre-Napoleonic strategy became apparent as Pitt's 1759 plans unfolded.

The Niagara offensive was entrusted to John Prideux with William Johnson as second in command. The force made available to him was considerable, over 6,000 men, of which one-half were provincials, plus 1,000 Indians, chiefly the responsibility of Johnson. The French garrison was only a skeleton force, not over 500 men. The idea was that after taking Niagara Prideaux would proceed to Lake Ontario and the St. Lawrence to Montreal where he would reinforce Amherst, or if that were not necessary, would go on to Quebec, and join forces with Wolfe. Unfortunately, Prideaux was himself killed in the fighting before Niagara, and on July 16 the command devolved on Johnson. The challenge he had to face was posed by the fact that a large relief force was on its way to lift the siege of Fort Niagara. This was a combined force of over 2,000 French and Indians. Johnson, in a brilliant maneuver, trapped and annihilated the relief force. This was on July 25, and the next day the white flag was run up over Fort Niagara. This phase of the three-pronged attack, therefore, was a complete success. How important it was is another question. Certainly, if a stalemate had developed on the other two fronts, in the vital center and on the Quebec side, and if the war had ended that way, the Niagara victory would have been very important, as it was the key link in a chain of forts guarding France's inland empire. In other words, with Montreal and Quebec alive, and in French hands, Niagara was very important, but otherwise probably not.

287

The Amherst of 1759 was not the Amherst of 1758, and the difference could well have been the presence of Wolfe in the former year, and his absence in the latter. All during the fight for Louisbourg, Amherst had Wolfe at his side to make the daring decisions, and keep the attack moving. Such was not the case in 1759. There was no one there to prod him along, and his movements were marked by his usual policy of caution and excessive deliberation. It was a great pity because speed and action, not deliberation, were what were required to get his job done. And the job was of critical importance. The colonies had pretty much staked their all on the success of the 1759 campaigns, of which Amherst's was the kingpin. Massachusetts raised 7,000 men for the year's service, Connecticut 5,000, New Hampshire and Rhode Island 1,000, New York 2,600, New Jersey 1,000, Pennsylvania 2,700, Virginia 2,000, and South Carolina 1,200. This was a grand total of 22,500, and when to this is added the 22,000 British regulars, the total force was over 44,000 troops for the overthrow of French power in America. The only thing missing was a spark of genius at the operational level, a commander-in-chief that could knit the parts together so that this mighty force could strike the blow as coming from one man.

Amherst was just not equal to the task. While he was not devoid of common sense the way Lord Loudoun and James Abercromby were, he was nevertheless a set-piece general who could not see the forest for the trees, and who never seems to have heard of the idea of striking while the iron was hot. The result was that the army he commanded (13,000 men) advanced at a snail's pace beyond the Hudson River in the direction of Ticonderoga. This played right into the hands of the French, whose strategy was to tie down and delay the advance as long as possible, knowing that their efforts would be crowned with success if Amherst could not reach the upper end of Lake Champlain until the onset of winter. Thus, beginning with Fort Ticonderoga, the French tactics were not to fight, but to hold their positions until the last minute, then blow them up upon retreating. Amherst would then pause, and rebuild the fort, before proceeding to the next objective, when what he should have been doing was fighting in order to compel the French to weaken the force at Quebec in order to delay his advance. But he never seemed to catch on to what was happening, and as a result by the time he reached the upper end of the lake, the season was too far advanced for him to proceed,

288

and he did what the French wanted him to do, which was to back-track to Crown Point, and go into winter quarters. He kept his men busy, and himself happy, by adding additions to the fort at Crown Point.

Wolfe at Quebec was left on his own. Governor Hutchinson was kind to Amherst. He ventured the opinion that "if a great part of the French force had not been withdrawn from Quebec to attend the motions of general Amherst, the attempt made by general Wolfe must have failed."[110] The general verdict of history, however, has been different. Amherst has been much criticized for his failure to move faster, and even the Niagara operation has been adjudged to have been a mistake. Parkman speculated that if Amherst had been more vigorous in his pursuit of the fleeing French, and if he had not directed Prideaux against Niagara, but instead had ordered him to descend "the St. Lawrence toward Montreal, the prospect was good that the two armies would have united at that place, and ended the campaign by the reduction of all Canada. In this case Niagara and all the western posts would have fallen without a blow.[111]

Wolfe was not idle before Quebec. He moved up the St. Lawrence in June, 1759, with 9,000 men, and over the next two months deployed his soldiers in many directions, making it difficult for Montcalm to determine the point from which the major attack would come. Meanwhile (July 26) Johnson was reducing Fort Niagara, and Amherst was cautiously advancing up the Albany-Montreal corridor, occupying Fort Ticonderoga on July 26, the same day that Niagara fell, and Crown Point on August 1. By this time, Wolfe was nursing his wounds after the disaster at the heights of Montmorenci, and attempting to figure out another way to force Montcalm to come out and fight. It was all to no avail. The French commander stuck with his original strategy, knowing full well that all he had to do to win was to wait until the advent of winter forced Wolfe to lift the siege. Of course, Wolfe knew this too, and was about convinced that his mission was impossible when fate intervened to give him a chance. This was the discovery of an undefended path up the cliff adjoining the upper part of the city of Quebec. He knew that his troops could scale the heights, and that this would put them in a position where Montcalm would be forced to fight. It was that or face starvation because from this position Wolfe could cut off all his supplies. Thus it was that on September 13, 1759, on the Plains of Abraham, one of the decisive battles of the world was fought. Both sides fought valiantly, and the English won. Both Montcalm and Wolfe died in the battle, a battle that cost France her empire in North America, and sealed the fate of the New World. A year later Montreal fell, and nearly four years later peace broke out among the European belligerents, but as far as we were concerned the war ended with Wolfe's Great triumph on the Plains of Abraham on September 13.

To the consterantion of the colonists, it was suddenly discovered that the great issue which had been decided on the Plains of Abraham had not been decided there at all, and the status of Canada was an open question, depending on the terms of the treaty of peace. In other words, Canada was still up for grabs, and the New England men were fully aware of the fact that there was ample precedent for a treaty of peace surrendering conquests that had been won the hard way on the field of battle. Whether this would be the case again, and again with respect to Canada, was the subject of a very lively dispute in a paper war that began in 1760. The first pamphlet to hit the bookstalls was entitled "A Letter addressed to Two Great Men, on the Prospect of Peace, and on the Terms necessary to be insisted upon in the Negotiation," and it was followed by at least 36 others, not including second or third editions and reissues.[112] The question was whether England should take Canada or Guadeloupe in the treaty of peace with France. The arguments in favor of the sugar island were weighty, and even the great Pitt found himself in a quandary. When he finally came down on the side of Canada, it was whispered in London that he did so because he was "under the thumb of the group of West Indian planters in the House of Commons, for whom the conquest of Guadeloupe meant a new and dangerous competitor."[113] The most skillful and effective proponent of the American and colonial point of view was Benjamin Franklin, and his contribution to the war of words was made in what was known as *The Canada Pamphlet*, which was published under the title *"The Interests of Great Britain considered with regard to her Colonies and the Acquisition of Canada and Guadeloupe. To which are added, Observations concerning the Increase of Mankind, peopling of Countries,* etc."[114]

The Canada Pamphlet was really two separate studies. The added one, entitled "Observations concerning the Increase of Mankind, Peopling Countries, etc.," was a think-piece Franklin prepared in 1751, ten years before the public debate over Canada and Guadeloupe. The purpose of this study was to examine the concept of mercantilism from the point of view of the relations between the mother country and the mainland colonies. Was mercantilism the key to the future grandeur and security of the British Empire? In a word, was Jean Colbert right about self-sufficiency and a favorable balance of trade? Franklin's findings were surprising. Unlike Thomas Malthus 50 years later, Franklin was optimistic about the future in America. Matthus's argument was that since population increased by a geometrical ratio and the means of subsistence by an arithmetical ratio, poverty and distress were unavoidable unless relieved by famine, war, and disease. Franklin rejected this prognosis for the new World, and argued that since there was ample room for man to increase and multiply here he would do so, and it would make both the colonies and the mother country stronger and more powerful.

Thus, Franklin pointed out, there were not "upwards of one million English souls in North America (though 'tis thought scarce 80,000 have been brought over sea), and yet perhaps there is not one fewer in Britain, but rather many more, on account of the employment the colonies afforded to manufacturers at home. This million, doubling suppose but once in twenty-five years, will in another century be more than the people of England, and the greater number of Englishmen will be on this side of the water." Franklin drew the obvious conclusion, "what an accession of power to the British Empire by sea as well as land! What an increase of trade and navigation! What numbers of ships and seamen! This was the vision Franklin wanted to communicate to England. It was a world vision, an imperial vision, one that he thought (and sincerely believed) could be made possible and could be nurtured by colonial will and strength. It was not the unglamorous vision of an accountant worrying about the balance of payments in a mercantilistic economy. It was an American vision.

In bringing this argument up at the time of the dispute over Canada and Guadaloupe, Franklin sought to point out the difference between commercial and territorial imperialism and to emphasize that colonies should be governed with a view to their revenue and man power, not exclusively with a view toward self-sufficiency and raw materials. As to what bearing this

291

had on the treaty of peace, Franklin made clear in the letter to Lord Kames on January 3, 1760, the letter in which he used the expression "awe the world," what that was. "No one," Franklin said, "can more sincerely rejoice than I do, on the reduction of Canada; and this is not merely as I am a colonist, but as I am a Briton,[115] I have long been of opinion, that the *foundations of the future grandeur and stability of the British empire lie in America;* and though, like other foundations, they are low and little seen, they are, nevertheless, broad and strong enough to support the greatest political structure human wisdom ever yet erected. I am therefore by no means for restoring Canada. If we keep it, all the country from the St. Lawrence to the Mississippi will in another century be filled with British people. Britain itself will become vastly more populous, by the immense increase of its commerce: the Atlantic sea will be covered with your trading ships: and your naval power, thence continually increasing, will extend your influence round the whole globe, and awe the world."[116]

The policy of Franklin eventually prevailing in the mother country, and in the Treaty of Paris, 1763, France was stripped of Acadia, Canada, Cape Breton, and all of Louisians east of the Mississippi except for the Island of Orleans, and two small islands at the mouth of the St. Lawrence River. All in all, the treaty was a great triumph for the imperialists on both sides of the Atlantic, in England and America.

And in America the cause for celebration was particularly great in New England. This was because of the Canada decision. Canada was a bone in the throat for our New England ancestors, and for a century and a half they fought to gain the possession. Now it was safely ours, and the victory was especially dear to the hearts of the men of Massachusetts, for, as John A. Schutz said, "in their hearts New Englanders still considered the war a Protestant crusade, France an impediment to their western expansion, and Louisbourg, the St. Lawrence, and the Great Lakes the frontier of New England."[117]

The British decision to acquire Canada, pleasing as it was to the Americans in general, and to Massachusetts men in particular, was a rash one from the point of view of power politics. It failed to take into consideration the one element that had been the cornerstone of British policy for more than a hundred years.

This was the principle of the balance of power. By virtue of this principle Britain had always been able to maintain an equilibrium in Europe, and with her power she could prevent it from being upset by any single power, or even an unfriendly coalition. This was her secret weapon in all the wars and broils of Europe, and why she was always able to keep the upper hand. As long as France was in Canada England could play the same game in America, but with France gone this was impossible. The danger was particularly great in the New World because, as should have been apparent, the strength of the American colonies was growing by leaps and bounds, and growing to the point where collectively they would soon be more than a match for the mother country. That this was no idle threat was evident to many Englishmen at the time, and was commented on in the debate by opponents of the Canada policy. To brush this argument aside was to jettison the one policy that had made England a world power. The presence of France in Canada was the only guarantee England had that she could continue to maintain the same position in North America that she had always enjoyed in Europe. The Canada decision was to cost England her empire in the short run, and her world position in the long run. Machiavelli would not have acquiesced to the Canada decision.

The only way the Canada decision could have redounded to the benefit of England would have been for the nother country to have taken advantage of the wisdom of some of the American sages such as Franklin, who would have hitched American power to the engine of the British Empire so that it could, indeed, have been expanded round the globe, and awed the world, creating eht greatest political structure ever known. Such was not to be the case, however; there was not enough talent and good will on both sides of the water to support such an undertaking. To conquer the great empire was one thing, but to hold it together and rule it was quite another. The men of that period of history were up to the former, but not to the latter.

Up to this time, England's record as a governing power had been spotty. The policy of "salutary neglect" had been good as far as it went in the days before what Lawrence Henry Gipson called "the Great War of the Empire," but in the post-war period it was apparent that a policy of "tight controls" was needed to cope with the new problems that began to settle in on the mother country. These were problems of money, and that was a touchy subject in the colonies. It was also a touchy subject with the electorate in England, who failed to see why all the burdens of the Great War should be borne by the taxpayers in England, while the colonists got off scot-free, even though the war had been fought, so the English politicians said, for the purpose of protecting the American colonies. The result was the great constitutional squabble over whether taxation without representation was tyranny. The Americans were jubilant when the Stamp Act was repealed, but it really didn't settle anything. On the same day the Act was repealed, March 18, 1766, the Declaratory Act was passed, reasserting the right of king and parliament to make laws binding on the colonists "in all cases whatsoever."

The constitutional crisis bubbled up again on the occasion of the Boston Tea Party, and this led to the Intolerable Acts, which led in turn to the convocation of the First Continental Congress. On October 20, Congress adopted a resolution of *"Association,"* which sought to impose an economic boycott on the mother country unless their grievances had been satisfied by December 1, 1774. The delegates then said they found "that the present unhappy situation of our affairs is occasioned by a ruinous system of colony administration, adopted about the year 1763, evidently calculated for inslaving these colonies, and, with them, the British Empire."[118]

Memorials and Addresses were then prepared for the inhabitants of the British colonies, and for the people of England, telling the former that there was no alternative to the *"Association,"* and the latter that the "general Welfare of the British empire" was at stake. More than that. The people of England were warned "to take care that you do not fall into the pit that is preparing for us." Finally, the people of England were told that, hopefully, "the magnanimity and justice of the British Nation will furnish a parliament of such wisdom, independence and public spirit, as may well save the violated rights of the whole empire from the devices of wicked Ministers and evil Counsellors."[119]

Another important message prepared by this first Congress was one to the inhabitants of the province of Quebec. The message was both a promise and a warning. The promise was that by joining the American union the

294

Canadians would not have to depend "on the small influence of your single province" in any quarrels, but could depend on the "consolidated powerrs of North-America." On the other hand, the Canadians were warned that if they decided to go it alone, they might become our "inveterate enemies," in which case the Canadians were further warned that "you are a small people, compared to those who with open arms invite you into a fellowship."[120]

The so-called battles of Lexington and Concord took place on April 19, 1775, and on May 10 the second Continental Congress assembled at Philadelphia. On June 3, the Congress resolved to appoint four committees to draw up Petitions and Memorials to the King, to the people of Great Britain, to the people of Ireland, and to the inhabitants of Jamaica. These began to come in on July 8, and the first two were the Address to the inhabitants of Great Britain, and the Petition to the King (both on July 8).

To the Friends, Countrymen, and Brethren in England, the colonists again referred to their objective, the furtherance of the "Welfare of the Empire," and renewed their pledge to support any laws designed "for the Purpose of securing the commercial Advantages of the whole Empire" (external taxation), but pointedly asked whether the present acts were designed for this purpose? If not, the colonists raised a series of questions, "will Britons fight under the Banners of Tyranny? Will they counteract the Labours, and disgrace the Victories of their Ancestors? Will they force Chains for their Posterity? If they descend to this unworthy Task, will their Swords retain their Edge, their Arms their accustomed Vigour? Britons can never become the Instruments of Oppression, till they lose the Spirit of Freedom, by which alone they are invincible."[21]

In conclusion, the Address said, "we grieve that rash and inconsiderate Councils should precipitate with destruction of an Empire, which has been the envy and admiration of Ages, and call upon God to witness, that we would part with our Property, endanger our Lives, and sacrifice every thing but Liberty, to redeem you from ruin. A cloud hangs over your Heads and ours; 'ere this reaches you, it may probably burst upon us; let us then (before the remembrance of former Kindness is obliterated) once more repeat those appellations which are ever grateful in our ears; let us entreat Heaven to avert our Ruin, and the Destruction

295

that threatens our Friends, Brethren and Countrymen, on the other side of the Atlantic."[122]

The Petition to the King also emphasized the perils to the Empire inherent in the struggle between the mother country and the colonies. They pointed out that the solidity of the union made it possible for England to win the last war, and thereby to excite the wonder and envy of other nations, as they were forced to be a witness to "Great Britain riseing to a power the most extraordinary the world has ever known." Naturally, as loyal subjects and faithful servants, the colonists said, they desired to share with their King, as well as with the rest of the empire, "the blessings of peace, and the emoluments of victory and conquest." The colonists also said it was their sincere and fervent prayer "that your Majesty may enjoy a long and prosperour reign, and that your descendants may govern your dominions with honor to themselves and happiness to their subjects."[123]

The Address to the people of Ireland was in some ways the most interesting of the group. After making common cause with the Irish as to grievances, and observing that "the fertile regions of America would afford you a safe assylum from poverty, and, in time, from oppression alos," the colonists said that they were "pleased to find that the design of subjugating us, has persuaded administration to dispense to Ireland, some vagrant rays of ministerial sunshine." But the most important point of the Address was the pregnant observation that "the important contest, into which we have been driven, is now become interesting to every European state, and particularly affects the members of the British Empire."[124]

What do all these colonisl petitions, addresses and memorials mean? Could it be that they meant exactly what they said? If London could neither see nor understand that the Britch Empire was federal in principle that it was a union of distinct states under the same sovereign in right of the same Crown, which was an American heritage drawn from an experience of over a century and a half; if London feared the democracy of free Englishmen; if London was determined to destroy an imperial structure that had been built up over a century and a half; if London had lost its imperial vision in pursuit of a narrow point of sovereignty; then there was only one thing for the conservative elements in America to do: they must draw away from London all the outlying parts of the Empire, and make them part of an American Confederation, until the lit-tle-Englanders could see more clearly, more broadly, more imperially.

These appeals of the colonists over the heads of the King and his Ministers, directly to the other peoples of the empire, are the most convincing evi-dence one could wish of the way Americans looked at themselves as all equally parts of the empire, though with a certain primacy for Americans; and of the inten-tion to continue that way without London, if London could neither be persuaded nor coerced to the imperial point of view. America's first established policy, its one fixed idea, was empire, an empire certainly contin-ental in scope, "from Sea to Sea," including also "all the Islands lying within one hundred Miles along the Coast of both Seas."[125]

The appeal to the Irish mentioning the fact that "the important contest into which we have been driven, is now become interesting to every European state," was dated July 28, 1775. On November 29, 1775, Con-gress established a Committee of Secret Correspondence to correspond with friends of the colonies not only in Great Britain and Ireland, but in "other parts of the world" as well. In December, the Committee took a bolder step in sending Arthur Lee to make inquiries as to the disposition of foreign powers toward the strug-gle, particularly France and Spain, England's tradi-tional rivals and enemies.[126]

At the time, Lee was already in London as a colo-nial Agent, and the inquiries led to the connection with Pierre A.C. de Beaumarchais, author of The Barber of Seville, and the formation of a fictitious trading company, Hortales & Co., which illegally furnished arms to the Americans by way of Haiti and Martinique.

One week prior to the adoption of the address to the people of Ireland, Franklin broke his long silence on the subject of independence. He had arrived in America only four days before the second Continental Congress convened, and though he attended all the ses-sions had said nothing. His silence had begun to grate on the radicals to such an extent that some of them began to suspect that he was in cahoots with the enemy, that he could not throw off his lifetime dedication to building the British Empire, and that when the show-down came he would be found on the side of the British. Franklin allayed these suspicions on July 21, 1715,

297

when he broke his silence, and submitted his Articles of Confederation for the consideration of Congress.

The Articles clearly demonstrated the fact that though the author still favored the British Empire, and favored it strongly, he was now casting his vote for Independence, and for an American Empire. This came out in the membership clause of the Franklin plan, where it was provided that "any ~~other~~ and every Colony from Great Britain upon the Continent of North America and not at present engag'd in our Association ~~shall~~ may upon Application and joining the said Association be receiv'd into this Confederation, viz (Ireland) the West India Islands, Quebec, St. Johns, Nova Scotia, Bermuda, and the East and West Floridas; and shall thereupon be entitled to all the Advantages of our Union, mutual Assistance and Commerce."[127]

Even so, Franklin was not totally reconciled to the idea that the breach with the mother country was final. This was clear in the section dealing with the duration of the Articles. Franklin said that these Articles were "to continue firm till the Terms of Reconciliation proposed in the Petition of the last Congress to the King are agreed to; till the Acts since made restraining the American Commerce and Fisheries are repeal'd; till reparation is made for the Injury done to Boston by shutting up its Port; for the Burning of Charleston; and for the expence of this unjust War; and till all the British Troops are withdrawn from America. On the Arrival of these Events the Colonies (shall) return to their former Connection and Friendship with Britain; But on Failure thereof this Confederation is to be perpetual."[128]

The month prior to the submission of Franklin's Articles to the Congress, George Washington was appointed commander-in-chief of the Continental Army, and the battle of Bunker Hill was fought on June 17, 1775. This was followed by the siege of Boston, and the abortive campaign to reduce Canada into "liberty."

The plan of conquering Canada to make her the fourteenth colony in the Union was approved by Congress in early June 1775. In a letter to James Warren, John Adams probably spoke for the colonies when he said, "the Unanimous Voice of the Continent in Canada must be ours; Quebec must be taken."[129] However, no attempt was made to reduce the colony until June 27, and then it was a failure. Nevertheless, the ill-fated attempt to pluck the Canadian rose had one advantage after all. It forced the British to reinforce the Canadian garrison, and if it had not been for this, it is altogether possible that "Gentleman Johnny" Burgoyne would not have suffered his defeat at Saratoga in October 1777, which stirred France to come out openly in support of the United States. How important this was can be gathered from the fact "that ninety percent of American war materials came from France during the first year after the Declaration of Independence."[130]

Accordingly, a committee was appointed on June 11, 1776, to prepare a treaty plan to be proposed to foreign powers, particularly France and Spain. John Adams was the draftsman for the Committee, and on July 18 his report was submitted to Congress. It was debated in Congress on three days in late August, and then referred back to the Committee. The final report was submitted to Congress on September 17. A week later, Conress gave its approval to the treaty plan, and on September 26 Benjamin Franklin, Silas Deane, and Thomas Jefferson were named as commissioners to France.

The original draft of the plan of treaties was in the handwriting of John Adams, and did not even include the names of the participating parties. Thus the first article read, "there shall be a firm, inviolable, and universal peace, and a true and sincere friendship between A. and B." Some changes were made in the territorial clause of the original draft before it was approved, and the way the draft was changed is indicated by the following:

> Art. 8. In Case of any War between the most Christian King and the King of Great Britain, the most Christian King, shall never invade, nor under any pretence attempt to-invade-or-get Possession-for, to possess himself of Labradore, New Britain, Nova Scotia, Acadia, Canada, Florida, nor any of the Countries, Cities, or Towns, on the Continent, of North America, nor of the Islands of Newfoundland, Cape Breton, St. John's, Anticosta, nor of any other Island, lying near to the said Continent, in the Seas, or in any Gulph, Bay, or River, it being the

true Intent and meaning of this Treaty,
that the said united States, shall
have the sole, exclusive, undivided
and perpetual Possession of all the
Countries, Cities, and Towns, on the
said Continent, and of all Islands
near to it, which now are, or lately
were under the jurisdiction of or
subject to the King or Crown of Great
Britain, whenever the same ~~can be in-~~
~~vaded, and conquered by the said~~
~~united States, or shall in any manner~~
~~submit to or be~~ shall be united or confederated with the said united
States.[131]

The nineteen words from can to be are crossed out.
The Resolution as adopted in September 1776 proposed
this plan of a treaty to the King of France with the
words "invaded and conquered" and "submit to" changed
to "united or confederated." One may unite in any number of ways. The word unite is just as good as invade,
conquer, or subdue. It covers all those words, and
does not have the same harsh sound, particularly in regard to those possessions which "are now" subject to
the King or Crown of Great Britain, as Canada was.

This treaty plan of 1776 is good evidence of what
was in the minds of Americans at the time. It is
strong proof of the continuance of the imperial plan
of evolution, even if Americans had to strike out
alone, and without the little-Englanders who were dir-
ecting the policy of the London government. Further,
the treaty plan is evidence of the significant fact
that not even the ally, whoever that might be, not
even mighty France, was to be permitted by the slight-
est act to interfere with the American imperial evolution.

In the treaty that was finally drawn up, signed,
and ratified, the following article stands out:

The Most Christian King renounces forever the possession of the islands of
Bermudas, as well as of any part of
the continent of North America which,
before the Treaty of Paris in 1763, or
in Virtue of that Treaty, were acknowledged to belong to the Crown of Great
Britain, or to the united States here-
to fore called British colonies, or

300

which are at this time, or have lately
been under the power of the King and
Crown of Great Britain.[132]

Thus, in the treaty plan of 1776 was embodied the
first, foremost, and most fundamental of the policies
and principles of American diplomacy. That policy was,
in 1776, already almost two centuries old. Ever since
the first permanent settlements in America, Americans
had been struggling for the possession of the entire
continent. They meant to drive the French and the
Spanish into the seas. They were, as Alexander Hamilton said at the time, providing for the safety and welfare, "the face of an Empire, in many respects the
most interesting in the world."[133]

President Monroe's historic statement in 1823,
extending the American fiat to the southern continent
as well, was no more than an expression of a traditional attitude as old as the Charter of Virginia, and as
firmly entrenched in the minds of every American as
ever were the liberties of Magna Carta, or the political principles of the Mayflower Compact. President
Monroe was a Virginian. The fixed policy of empire and
the Monroe Doctrine spring from the same root. The
treaty plan of 1776 reiterated this idea, as did Monroe's Doctrine in 1823.

The steady march of American progress toward the
attainment of this goal is obvious in our history. A
glance at a map of North America and "the islands near
to it" should be proof of the imperial tradition. So
successful has it been that a Secretary of State,
Richard Olney, could challenge the world at the end of
the 19th Century with the ringing declaration:

> Today the United States is practically
> sovereign on this continent, and its
> fiat is law upon the subjects of which
> it confines its interposition. Why?
> It is not because of the pure friend-
> ship or good will felt for it. It is
> not simply by reason of its high char-
> acter as a civilized state, nor be-
> cause wisdom and justice and equity
> are the invariable characteristics of
> the dealings of the United States. It
> is because in addition to all other

301

grounds, its infinite resources combined with its isolated position render it master of the situation and practically invulnerable as against any or all other powers.[134]

William Seward's panegyric of empire is another example of how early Americans looked at themselves on the subject of empire. In an address to an Ohio audience on "The Destiny of America" the Secretary of State said that if the future you seek consists of this:

> that the borders of the federal republic so peculiarly constituted shall be extended so that it shall greet the sun when he touches the tropic, and when he sends his glancing rays toward the polar circle, and shall include even distant islands in either ocean, that our population, now counted by tens of millions, shall ultimately be reckoned by hundreds of millions; that our wealth shall be enhanced in proportion with this wide development and that mankind shall come to recognize in us a successor of the few great states which have alternately borne commanding sway in the world--if this, and only this is desired, then I am free to say that if, as you will readily promise, our public and private virtues shall be preserved, nothing seems to me more certain than the attainment of this future, so surpassingly comprehensive and magnificent.[135]

It is not enough to explain all the thinking men in America as so many opportunists or demagogues. Still less can they be explained as creators. Thomas Jefferson, for example, was a strict constructionist who did not believe that the Constitution could be stretched to cover the acquisition of Louisiana, and yet he did not hesitate to make the purchase when he had an opportunity to do so. The evolution of empire was an established and firm policy before some of the so-called founding fathers were even born. The policy had become a primary and integral part of their lives. In other words, the leaders and statesmen of the early

Republic and the colonial period were "stern men with empires in their brains."

The last thing the colonial Founding Fathers should be made out to be is an 18th Century version of the modern peaceniks. They did not come to America because they were seeking a safe haven from the bad old wars of wicked Europe. They were not opposed to empires. They did not throw themselves into the colonial wars merely because they were continuous and the parent governments were fighting in Europe. They were also not country bumpkins who did not understand what the European wars were all about. And they *were* directly involved not only in the outcome of all these wars, but in their causation. In fact, some of the great wars, if not all of them, started in America, and spread to the mother countries. Colonial life was freely given, and colonial funds were lavishly expended, in the pursuit of the American empire, first as a part of the British Empire, and later on our own. Nothing is more fundamental to an understanding of our own history than an appreciation of the fact that the polar star of our existence for the first 300 years was the policy of empire. It was also a fixed star until all the natural boundaries of our empire were reached, to the north and south as well as to the west. "Every people," Hans Delbruck said, "is the child of its history, its past, and can no more break away from it than a man can separate himself from his youth."[136]

FOOTNOTES--CHAPTER V

[1]Lord Macauley, *Critical and Historical Essays* (Boston: Houghton, Mifflin and Company, 1900), 247.

[2]Reuben Clark, *Memorandum on the Monroe Doctrine* (Washington: Government Printing Office, 1930), 9-10.

[3]Robert A. Divine, *American Foreign Policy* (New York: The World Publishing Company, 1965, 5th pr.), 21.

[4]Thomas A. Bailey, *A Diplomatic History of the American People* (New York: Appleton-Century-Crofts, 7th pr., 1964), 19-20.

[5]Samuel Flagg Bemis, *A Diplomatic History of the United States* (New York: Holt, Rinehart and Winston, 4th pr., 1955), 12.

[6]Benjamin Franklin, *The Writings of* (Collected and Edited with a Life and Introduction by Albert Henry Smyth (New York: The Macmillan Company, 1906), iv, 4.

[7]Halford J. Mackinder, *Democratic Ideas and Reality* (New York: W.W. Norton & Company, 1962), 150, a paraphrase of the famous saying.

[8]Frances Gardiner Davenport, *European Treaties bearing on the History of the United States and its Dependencies to 1648* (Washington: The Carnegie Institution of Washington, 1917), 319.

[9]Francis Parkman, *Pioneers of France in the New World* (New York: The Library of America, 1983), I, 323.

[10]Thomas Hutchinson, *The History of the Colony and Province of Massachusetts-Bay* (Cambridge: Harvard University Press, 1936), i, 28.

[11]*Ibid.*

[12]John Winthrop, *The History of New England, from 1630 to 1649* (Boston: Phelps & Farnham, 1825), II, 42.

[13]Thomas Hutchinson, *op. cit.*, I, 111.

[14]*Ibid.*

[15]*Ibid.*

[16]*Ibid.*, i, 112.

[17]*Ibid.*

[18]Francis Parkman, *The Old Regime in Canada* (New York: The Library of America, 1983), I, 1089.

[19]Thomas Hutchinsin, *op. cit.*, I, 114.

[20]James Brown Scott, *Treaty-Making Under the Authority of the United States* (Presidential Address Delivered at the Twenty-eighth Annual Meeting of the American Society of International Law, April 2, 1934), 4.

[21]Thomas Hutchinson, *op. cit.*, I, 114.

[22]*Ibid.*

[23]*Ibid.*, I, 115.

[24]John Winthrop, *op. cit.*, II, 218.

[25]Thomas Hutchinson, *op. cit.*, I, 115.

[26]*Ibid.*

[27]*Ibid.*, I, 115-16.

[28]*Ibid.*, I, 426.

[29]Max Savelle, *The Origins of American Diplomacy* (New York: The Macmillan Company, 1967), 163.

[30]Max Savelle, "Colonial Origins of American Diplomatic Principles" (*The Pacific Historical Review*, III, no. 3, Sept. 1934), 334.

[31]*Ibid.*, 339.

[32]Thomas Hutchinson, *op. cit.*, I, 153.

[33]*Ibid.*, I, 154.

[34]*Ibid.*

[35] Francis Newton Thorpe, *The Federal and State Constitutions, Colonial Charters, and other Organic Laws of the United States* (Washington: Government Printing Office, 1909), i, 79.

[36] Thomas Hutchinson, *op. cit.*, i, 155.

[37] Robert A. Divine, *op. cit.*, 21.

[38] John Marshall, *A History of the Colonies of North America* (Philadelphia: Published by Abraham Small, 1824), 147.

[39] John Fiske, *The Dutch and Quaker Colonies in America* (Boston: Houghton Mifflin Company, 1899), i, 291-92.

[40] Francis Parkman, *Count Frontenac and New France under Louis XIV.* (New York: The Library of America, 1983), II, 92.

[41] *Ibid.*, 151.

[42] *Ibid.*, 171.

[43] John Fiske, *op. cit.*, II, 196-97.

[44] Francis Parkman, *Count Frontenac and New France under Louis XIV, op. cit.*,

[45] Thomas Hutchinson, *op. cit.*, I, 337.

[46] Francis Parkman, *Count Frontenac and New France under Louis XIV, op. cit.*, II, 196.

[47] *Ibid.*, II, 197.

[48] *Ibid.*, II, 204.

[49] *Ibid.*, II, 314.

[50] Francis Newton Thorpe, *op. cit.*, VII, 3795.

[51] *Ibid.*, I, 69.

[52] *Ibid.*, V, 2762.

[53] John Marshall, *op. cit.*, 208.

[54] Anthony F. C. Wallace, "Origins of Iroquois Neutrality: The Grand Settlement of 1701," (*Pennsylvania History*, 24, 1957), 235.

[55]Francis Parkman, *Count Frontenac and New France under Louis IV, op. cit.,*

[56]Douglas Edward Leach, *The Northern Colonial Frontier 1607-1763* (New York: Holt, Rinehard and Winston, 1966), 118-19.

[57]Thomas Hutchinsin, *op. cit.,* II, 108.

[58]Francis Parkman, *A Half-Century of Conflict* New York: The Library of America, 1983), II, 420.

[59]*Ibid.,* II, 424.

[60]Samuel Vetch, "Canada Survey'd" (*Great Britian, Calendar of State Papers, Colonial, American and West Indies,* 1708-09, No. 60), 41.

[61]*Ibid.,* 42.

[62]*Ibid.*

[63]Max Savelle, *The Origins of American Diplomacy, op. cit.,* 514.

[64]Francis Parkman, *A Half-Century of Conflict, op. cit.,* II, 432-33.

[64]John Marshall, *op. cit.,* 203.

[66]*Ibid.,* 204.

[67]Francis Parkman, *A Half-Century of Conflict, op. cit.,* II, 453.

[68]*Ibid.,* 454.

[69]Peter H. Wood, *Black Majority* (New York: W.W. Norton & Company, 1975), 314.

[70]John Marshall, *op. cit.,* 251.

[71]*Ibid.,* 254.

[72]Benjamin Franklin, *op. cit.,* IV, 412-48.

[73]Margaret Davis Cate, "Fort Frederica--Battle of Bloody Marsh" (*Georgia Historical Quarterly,* vol. xxvi, June 1943), 167.

[74] *Ibid.*, 162.

[75] Thomas Hutchinson, *op. cit.*, II, 309

[76] John Marshall, *op. cit.*, 263.

[77] Francis Parkman, *A Half-Century of Conflict, op. cit.*, II, 622.

[78] John A. Schutz, "Imperialism in Massachusetts during the Governorship of William Shirley, 1741-1756" (*Huntington Library Quarterly*, 1960), v. 23, p. 319.

[79] Francis Parkman, *A Half-Century of Conflict, op. cit.*, II, 633.

[80] John A. Schutz, *op. cit.*, v. 23, p. 221.

[81] *Ibid.*, v. 23, p. 222.

[82] *Ibid.*

[83] *Ibid.*, 222-23.

[84] Francis Parkman, *A Half-Century of Conflict, op. cit.*, II, 675.

[85] *Ibid.*, II, 676

[86] Arthur H. Buffinton, "The Canada Expedition of 1746" (*American Historical Review* (1939-40), v. 45, p. 568.

[87] Thomas Hutchinson, *op. cit.*, II, 324.

[88] *Ibid.*, II, 325.

[89] John Marshall, *op. cit.*, 269.

[90] Thomas Hutchinson, *op. cit.*, II, 325.

[91] Arthur H. Buffinton, *op. cit.*, v. 45, p. 563.

[92] *Ibid.*, v. 45, p. 564.

[93] John A. Schutz, *op. cit.*, v. 23, p. 226.

[94] *Ibid.*

[95] *Ibid.*, v. 23, p. 229.

[96]*Ibid.*,

[97]Francis Parkman, *Montcalm and Wolfe, op. cit.*, II, 1041.

[98]James Thomas Flexner, *Lord of the Mohawks* ton: Little, Brown and Company, 1979), 125.

[99]Thomas Hutchinson, *op. cit.*,

[100]Francis Parkman, *Montcalm and Wolfe, op. cit.*, II, 1164.

[101]Thomas Hutchinson, *op. cit.*, IIi, 45.

[102]John Marshall, *op. cit.*, 311-12

[103]Francis Parkman, *Montcalm and Wolfe, op. cit.*, II, 1463.

[104]Thomas Hutchinson, *op. cit.*, III, 49.

[105]*Ibid.*, III, 50.

[106]*Ibid.*

[107]Francis Parkman, *Montcalm and Wolfe, op. cit.*, II, 1248.

[108]*Ibid.*, 1250.

[109]*Ibid.*, II, 1258.

[110]Thomas Hutchinson, *op. cit.*, III, 57.

[111]Francis Parkman, *Montcalm and Wolfe, op. cit.*, II, 1371.

[112]William L. Grand, "Canada versus Guadeloupe" (*American Historical Review*, 1911), v. 17, 735 & 737.

[113]*Ibid.*, 742.

[114]Benjamin Franklin, *op. cit.*, vol. iv., pp. 32-84.

[115]Carl van Doren, *Benjamin Franklin* (New York: The Viking Press, 1938), 217.

[116]Benjamin Franklin, *op. cit.*, IV, 4.

[117]John A. Schutz, *op. cit.*, v. 23, p. 236.

[118]*Journals of the Continental Congress 1774-89* (Washington: Government Printing Office, 1904), I, 76.

[119]*Ibid.*, I, 90.

[120]*Ibid.*, I, 113.

[121]*Ibid.*, II, 116.

[122]*Ibid.*, II, 170.

[123]*Ibid.*, II, 161.

[124]*Ibid.*, II, 212-13.

[125]*The Federal and State Constitutions, Colonial Charters, and other Organic Laws* (Washington: Government Printing Office, 1909), 3795.

[126]Paul A. Varg, *Foreign Policies of the Founding Fathers* (East Lansing: Michigan State University Press, 1963), 15.

[127]*Journals of the Continental Congress 1774-89, op. cit.*, II, 198.

[128]*Ibid.*, II, 198-99.

[129]Edmund C. Burnett, *The Continental Congress* (New York: The Macmillan Company, 1941), 113.

[130]Paul ℞. Varg., *op. cit.*, 22.

[131]*Journals of the Continental Congress 1774-89* (Washington: Government Printing Office, 1904). V. 576 & 579. (The original of the Plan of Treaties is in the handwriting of John Adams, and is in the Papers of the Continental Congress, No. 47, folios 129-49).

[132]*Journals of the Continental Congress 1774-89, op. cit.*, XI, 450.

[133]Alexander Hamilton, *The Federalist* (New York: E. P. Dutton & Co., 1934), 1.

[134]Reuben Clark, *Memorandum on the Monroe Doctrine* (Washington: Government Printing Office, 1930), 59.

[135]William Henry Seward, *The Works of,* ed. George E. Baker (4 vols., New York: 1853-61), Iv, 112; Ernest N. Paolino, *The Foundations of the American Empire* (Ithaca: Cornell University Press, 1973, 1 & 7.

[136]Gordon A. Craig, "Delbruck: the Miliysty Historian," in *Makers of Modern Strategy,* Edward Mead Earle (Princeton: Princeton University Press, 1971), 276.

Abercromby, James, 276-77, 283-86, 288.

Acadia, 215-18, 219, 211, 238, 246-47, 250, 252, 260-61, 268, 271, 273, 292, 299.

Adams, John, 212, 269, 298-99.

Adams, John Quincy, 122.

Adams, Sam, 83, 147.

Admission on New States, 132.

Agents, duties of, 32-36.

Agents, qualifications required, 36-37.

Agents, salaries, 37-38.

Agents, terms of office, 38.

Agency System, 29-31, 33, 35, 38, 52-54, 59.

Aix-la-Chapelle, Treaty of (1741) 187-88, 268,70.

Albany, 181, 185-86, 195, 203-04, 235-37, 239, 244-46, 249, 276, 281

Albany Congress (1754), 78, 191-93

Albany-Montreal Corridor, 203, 235, 237, 261, 266, 279, 281, 285.

Albany Plan of Union (1754), 78, 191.

Alexandria Conference, 105-06.

Algonquin, 180-81

Allen, Ethan, 95.

Altahama River, 253.

"ambassadors to the other colonies", 77.

Amherst, Jeffrey, 282, 284-87, 288-89.

Andrews, Charles M., 22.

Andros, Sir Edmund, 73-75, 236.

Anglo-Dutch War (1652-54) 71-72, 227-28, 230-31.

Annapolis, 260-61.

Annapolis Convention, 107

Argall, Sir Samuel, 216-17, 250, 268.

Arnold, Benedict, 203-04.

Articles of Confederation 6, 11, 13, 78, 86, 95-97, 102-03, 111-15, 128, 145, 298.

Atlantic Coast, 71, 133-36, 189, 233, 261, 280.

Aubry, Charles, 200-01.

"A Virginian", 76.

Azilia, Margravate of, 253.

Bailey, Thomas, 213-14, 230, 270

balance of power, 293.

Battle of the Maps, 188.

Beaumarchais, Piere A.C. de, 297.

Beaver Wars, 182-84.

Bedford, Duke of, 268.

Bedford, Gunning, 125-28.

Berkeley, Sir William, 7, 37.

Bemis, Samuel Flagg, 213-14, 270.

Biglow Papers, 14.

Bloody Marsh, Battle of, 257, 259.

Blount, William, 118.

Boscawen, Admiral Edward, 272, 275-76.

Bouquet, Henry, 197, 199-200.

Bowdin, James, 147.

Braddock, Edward, 50, 194-97, 200-01, 257, 270-75.

Braxton, Carter, 99-100, 104.

Breda, Treaty of (1667), 234.

"Briefe and Plaine Scheam" 75.

Bradstreet, John, 286.

Broom, Jacob, 125.

Bull, William, 256.

Burgoyne, Gen. John, 203-04.

Burke, Thomas, 85-87.

Burr, Aaron, 164.

Butler, John, 97-98.

Butler, Pierce, 114, 133.

Butler, Zebulon, 97.

Calhoun, John ., 103, 212.

Canada, 34, 39, 82, 139, 172, 180, 182, 187-88, 203, 213, 216-18, 233-240, 246-51, 253, 260, 263, 265-72, 275, 278-79, 281, 284-85, 289-90, 292-93, 295, 298-99.

"Canada Survey'd", 248.

Canseau, 260-61, 264.

Cape Breton Island, 215, 218, 252-53, 260-62, 264, 267, 269, 279, 284, 292, 299.

Carolina, 6, 60-61, 234, 243-44, 253-55, 258.

Carolina, Fundamental Constitutions of, 161-62

Carroll, Daniel, 125.

Cartagena, 50, 256, 270, 272.
314

Carthage, 263.

Cate, Margaret David, 257-58.

Champlain, Lake, 252, 266, 281, 288.

Champlain, Samuel de, 180, 217.

Charles I, King, 217-19, 243.

Charles II, King, 5, 33, 66, 231-32.

Charleston, 257, 260, 298.

Charters, 24-25, 28-29, 32, 34-35, 60, 65, 67, 72.

Chase, Salmon P., 102.

Chase, Samuel, 106

Chesapeake Bay, 104-06, 225.

Chisholm v. Georgia, 10.

Chittenden, Thomas, 96.

Church, Col. Benjamin, 246, 250.

Clark, J. Reuben, 211-12.

Churchill, Winston, 282.

Clausewitz, Karl von, 53.

Clemenceau, Georges, 112.

Cleveland, Grover, 3.

Clinton, George, 109-10, 148-50, 191

Coercive Acts, 80, 82.

Golden, Cadwallader, 42, 180, 184.

Committee of Correspondence, 36, 53.

Committee of Style, 138.

Concord, 83.

Confederation 5-6, 9, 14, 23, 147.

Congress, 21, 30.

Articles of Confederation, 83, 103, 104, 197, 116.

Connecticut, 5-6, 33-35, 62-64, 66, 68-73, 94, 97-98, 104, 109, 131, 137-38, 145, 150, 191, 220, 228-29, 237, 250-51, 266-67, 273.

Connecticut River, 151, 226.

Consotiation, 63.

Constitution, U.S. 12, 20, 88, 97, 103, 107, 112, 115-17, 123, 132-33, 144-52.

Cornwallis, Lord, 97.

Cromwell, Oliver, 71-72, 228, 230-31.

Crown Point, 194, 226-67, 269, 271-72, 273-77, 279, 284-85, 289.

Cubans, 258.

Cutler, Manasseh, 120.

Dale, Sir Thomas, 167.

D'Aunay, Charles de, 219-21, 223-25.

Declaration of Independence, 5, 12, 20, 24-25, 87, 89, 93, 95, 97, 100, 102-03, 117, 214.

Declaratory Act (1766), 79, 94, 294.

DeLancy, James, 191.

Deerfield, 246, 262.

Delaware, 94, 106, 113, 128, 135, 145, 525.

Delbruck, Hans, 303.

Democracy, 18-19, 21, 93.

Dickinson, John, 84-85, 125, 130, 132, 145.

Dieskau, Baron Ludwig, 270, 275.

Dinwiddie, Robert, 189.

Diplomacy, 1-3, 6, 17-23, 28, 53, 59, 61-62, 65, 31, 116, 168-69, 175, 177, 186, 191-92, 204, 211, 225.

diplomatic revolition, 277.

"divide and command" (Publius), 101.

Divine, Robert A., 212.

Dominion of New England, 73-75, 236.

Dongan, Gov. Thomas, 235.

Drake, Sir Francis, 255.

Dudley, Gov. Joseph, 246-47, 250.

Dutch, 22, 70-71, 75, 246-217, 219, 225, 226-29, 231-32, 234, 237, 245.

Easton Conference, 196-97, 199, 200.

Elizabeth, Queen, 7, 23-24.

Ellis Island, 60.

Ellsworth, Oliver, 118, 131, 143-44.

empire, 19, 20, 22.

England, 8, 19, 22-23, 28, 30, 33, 35, 44, 59, 72-74, 84, 187, 189, 191, 193, 196, 204, 213, 215, 217, 225-26, 228, 231-39, 241, 244-45, 248, 250, 252-55, 258-61, 266=70, 271, 277, 281, 282-83, 287, 390, 292-96, 300.

Fay, Bernard, 168, 170, 173, 177.

Federal Convention, 110, 112-18, 123, 131-32, 135, 143-50.

Federalist, 10, 116, 142, 150.

First Continental Congress, (1774), 80-81.

316

Fiske, John, 84, 109-10, 233.

Flexner, James Thomas, 201.

Florida, 234, 243, 253-55, 269, 298, 299.

Forbes, Gen. John, 174, 284, 286.

Fort Duquesne, 189-90, 194-95, 197-201, 271-72, 274, 277, 279, 281, 284-86.

Fort Edward, 281.

Fort Frederica, 253-54, 256-58.

Fort Frontenac, 194, 276.

Fort Necessity, 190-01, 271.

Fort Niagara, 194, 200-01, 271, 274, 275-76, 277, 279, 286-87, 289.

Fort Oswego, 195, 203, 274, 276-78, 281.

Fort San Marcos, 244.

Fort Stanwix, 203.

Fort Ticonderoga, 197, 203, 276, 281, 284-85- 288.

Fort William Henry, 195, 241, 279, 280-81.

France, 9, 22-23, 30, 51, 53, 70, 73, 75, 95-96, 112, 168-69, 178, 183-97, 200-18, 228, 231, 233-38, 241-250, 252-53, 260-72, 275-90, 293, 297, 300-01.

Franklin, Benjamin, 8, 27-29, 37-41, 44-52, 76-78, 94, 113, 118, 120-21, 125, 139, 145, 152, 165-66, 170, 180, 191, 195, 201, 249, 256, 261, 290-93, 297-98.

Franklin's Examination, 44-52, 84, 256.

Frederick the Great, 282-83.

French and Indian War, 188, 190-91, 201, 270.

Frontenac, Comte de, 235-42.

Frontier settlements, 163-68.

Fundamental Orders of Connecticut, 62, 151.

Fur trade, 60, 61, 162, 181-82, 185, 188.

Gage, Thomas, 83.

Garden, Comte de, 2, 6, 18-19, 28.

Gates, Horatio, 204.

George III, King, 53, 80.

Georgia, 37, 39, 43, 52, 60-61, 79, 93, 94, 145, 253-54, 257, 260-61.

Germain-en-Laye, Treaty of, 218, 219.

Gerry, Elbridge, 128, 133-34, 138.

Gibbons v. Ogden, 13, 102

Gipson, Lawrence Henry, 293.

Glorious Revolution, 75.

Gorham, Nathaniel, 128, 133, 135.

Grand Settlement of 1770, 185-87, 244-45.

Green Mountain Boys, 95.

Great Meadows, 190.

Grenville, Lord, 28, 41-42.

Guadeloupe, 290.

Halifax, 278-80, 284.

Hamilton, Alexander, 40, 100, 107, 124, 130, 138, 141-42, 147, 150, 301.

Hancock, John, 83, 93, 95-96, 147.

Hartford, Treaty of, 226-27.

Hartford Convention, 110.

Havana, 257.

Hawkins, Sir John, 255.

Heath, Sir Robert, 243.

Heathcote, Col. Caleb, 248.

Hendrick, King of the Mohawks, 190, 192-94.

Henry, Patrick, 42, 81, 87, 108, 148-49, 161.

Henry IV, King, 152.

Herkimer, Nicholas, 203.

Hill, Brigadier John, 25.

Holbourne, Admiral Francis, 278-79.

Holland, 235.

Howe, William, 282, 285.

Hudson, Henry, 181.

Hudson Bay, 241, 252.

Hudson River, 150, 181, 217, 225, 226, 233, 252, 281, 288.

Hurstfield, Joel, 19.

Hutchinson, Thomas, 32, 37, 43, 70, 72, 191, 219, 224, 226-27, 267, 280, 283-84, 389

Imperialism, 19, 291-92.

Indians, 3-4, 21, 23, 29, 34-37, 50-51, 60-63, 70-71, 75, 97, 159-205, 213, 228-29, 234-35, 237-39, 241, 243, 246, 248, 254, 256, 260, 272, 274-75, 280, 282, 286-87.

318

Ingersoll, Jared, 125.

Iredell, James, 101.

Ireland, 8, 296-98.

Iroquois, 174, 177-83, 185-87, 190-92, 194-96, 201-02, 235-37, 241, 244-45, 252, 274.

Isolation, 20, 213, 231, 242, 270.

"Italick Regiment", 258.

Jackson, William, 122-23.

James I, King, 215.

James II, King, 66, 74, 231.

Jamestown, 20, 25, 216-17.

Jamaica, 256, 295.

Japanese, 261.

Jay, John, 39, 150.

Jefferson, Thomas, 95, 117,119, 139, 141, 180, 212, 302.

Jenkins' Ear, War of 1871, 254-55, 260.

Jenson, Merrill, 87.

Jersey, East and West, 74

Jesuits, 168, 173, 178.

Johnson, Sir William, 191, 194, 200-01, 272, 274, 275-76, 287, 389

Johnson, William Samuel, 130, 138.

Jumonville, Coulon de, 189-90, 271

Kames, Lord, 215-292.

Kammen, Michael G., 30.

King George's War, 187, 213, 234-35, 242-45, 253.

Kirke, Gervase, 217-18.

Lake George, Battle of, 194, 275, 276.

Lancaster Conference, 170-71, 175.

Lansing, John, 123.

La Potherie, Bacqueville de, 186.

La Rochelle, 217.

Latin, 222.

LaTour, Charles de, 219, 221, 223, 225.

Law of Love, 70.

Leach, Douglas Edward, 132.

League of Nations, 67, 132.

Le Boeuf, 188-89.

Lee, Arthur, 30, 37, 39, 53, 297.

Lee, Richard Henry, 84.

319

Leisler, Jacob, 236-37.

Leverett, John, 230.

Lexington, 83.

Lexington and Concord, 295.

Livingston, Robert, 76, 98, 99, 150.

Locke, John, 161.

Logstown, Treaty of (1758), 188.

Long Island, 226, 231.

Lon, Ella, 30, 37.

Loudown, Lord, 277-84, 288.

Louis XIII, King, 217-18

Louis XIV, King, 235-36.

Louisbourg, 195, 253, 261-66, 267-70, 275, 278-81, 283-85, 292.

Louisiana, 139, 188, 233, 253, 272, 281, 292, 302.

Lowell, James Russell, 14.

Machiavelli, Niccolo, 17, 65, 69, 186, 293.

Macaulay, Lord, 211.

Mackinder, Sir, Halford, 216, 233.

Madison, James, 98, 105-06, 111-12, 116, 118, 123-25, 127, 130, 136-38, 140-42, 144, 150, 212.

Madrid, Treaty of (1670), 234.

Magna Carta, 24-25, 28, 79, 93.

Maine, 63, 66, 73, 187, 215-16, 241, 246, 271

Malthus, Thomas, 291.

Manifest Destiny, 265.

March, Col. John, 247, 250.

Marshall, John, 12-13, 71, 89, 102, 163. 232, 243, 251, 255, 281.

Marshe, Witham, 170-74, 176.

Martin Luther, 117, 131, 139, 144.

Maryland, 6, 12, 60, 87, 94, 96, 99, 104-05, 106, 117, 130-31, 139, 144-45, 164, 174, 175, 190-91, 233, 237, 241, 249, 266.

Mason, George, 106, 111, 115, 124, 143, 148, 167.

Massachusetts, 5, 23, 33, 35, 37-40, 42-43, 52, 61, 63-66, 68-74, 76, 79-80, 82-83, 94, 104, 107, 109, 120, 128, 133, 135, 138, 142, 145-47, 187, 190, 191, 219-24, 226, 228-31, 236-39, 241-42, 246-47, 250-51, 261-63, 266-70, 273-74, 277, 281, 283, 292.

Mather, Increase, 74, 167, 168.

Mayflower Compact, 4, 26, 87.

Membership problem, 66-67, 132-39.

Memorials and Addresses, 294-97.

Menneville, Marquise Du-quesnne de, 188.

Michilimack, Michigan, 235.

Minuit, Peter, 160, 226.

Mississippi, 23, 243, 266, 281.

Mohawks, 177, 179, 184, 187, 190, 192, 194, 200, 203, 237, 275.

Mohawk Valley, 274, 276.

Monckton, Robert, 194, 272.

Monroe, James, 20, 211-12, 301.

Monroe Doctrine, 211-12, 301.

Montcalm, Marquis de, 195, 277-80, 286, 289, 290.

Monteano, Ge. Don Manuel, 258-60.

Montgomery, Sir Robert, 253.

Montour, Catharine, 171-72.

Monts, Sieur de, 215.

Morris, Gouverneur, 112, 124, 138, 131-34, 136, 138-39, 149.

Mount Vernon, 256.

Mont Vernon Compact, 106.

Nathan v. Commonwealth of Virginia, 8.

New Amsterdam, 227, 232.

New Brunswick, 215.

Newcastle, Duke of, 264.

New England, 61-62, 64-66, 74, 76, 82, 104, 106-07, 147, 180, 187, 195, 201, 203, 215-16, 222, 227, 231, 233, 238, 241, 244-47, 262, 266-67, 269, 273, 280, 283-84, 290, 292.

New England Confederation, 5, 6, 14, 62-63, 65-73, 220, 222-23, 227-30, 239.

Newfoundland, 217, 241, 247-48, 252-53, 280, 299.

New France, 236, 246, 248.

New Hampshire, 38, 43, 63, 73, 79, 87, 93-96, 136, 147-50, 186, 190-91, 250, 226, 273

New Haven, 63-64, 66, 68-72, 220, 228-30.

New Jersey, 6, 37, 52, 94, 105-06, 109, 128, 130, 145, 150, 190-91, 251, 266, 275.

New Jersey Plan, 128-30, 143.

New Netherland, 63, 71-72, 215, 227, 231-33.

New Scotland, 215.

New Sweden, 215.

New York, 6, 23, 37, 42, 73-74, 76, 79, 94-97, 105-06, 109, 111, 120, 145, 148-51, 172, 181, 187, 191, 195-96, 201, 232-33, 236-37, 242, 245, 249, 251, 261, 266, 273, 279-81, 283.

Nicholson, Sir Francis, 249-52.

Nicolls, Richard, 232-33.

Normandy, 264.

North Carolina, 43, 79, 85, 94, 105, 136, 148, 151, 266.

Nova Scotia, 188, 194, 215, 217, 225, 260-63, 267, 270, 272-73, 276, 281, 298-991.

Oglethorpe, James Edward 253-55, 258-60.

Ohio, 50, 180, 188-90, 195-96, 198-99, 233, 271-72, 274, 285.

Olney, Richard, 301-02.

Oriskany, 203.

Paine, Tom, 212, 269.

Paris, Treaty of (1763), 201, 292, 300.

Parkman, Francis, 160, 174, 178-79, 188, 190, 195, 198, 218, 240-41, 252, 263, 273, 285, 289.

Paterson, William, 118, 124-25, 128, 143.

Paxton Boys, 165-66.

Penhallow v. Doanne, 10-11, 101.

Penn, William, 6, 75-76, 165.

Pennamite War, 97-98.

Pennsylvania, 6, 10, 23, 30, 39, 51-52, 76, 81, 84, 94, 98-99, 106, 110-11, 128, 135, 137, 145-49, 165, 171-74, 190-91, 196-97, 215, 246, 266, 272.

Pennsylvania v. Connecti= cut, 97-99.

Pepperrell, William, 264.

Pequot War, 62.

Philadelphia, 6, 110, 146.

Philadelphia Convention, 107-08

Phips, Sir William, 238-41, 250, 259.

Pierce, William, 118, 121-22, 124.

Pilgrims, 4, 14, 26.

Pinckney, Charles, 125, 130, 132, 145.

Pitt, William, 196, 249, 266, 268, 282-85, 287, 290.

Plains of Abraham, 389-90.

Plymouth, 5, 20, 26, 63-64, 68-73, 220, 226, 229-30, 237, 246.

Pocohontas, 159-60.

Pontis, John, 29.

Port Royal, 217-18, 238, 240-41, 246-51.

Post, Christian Frederick 198-99.

post-war planning, 85.

Potomac River, 60, 105-06.

Presque Ile, 188.

Prideux, John, 287, 289.

proportional representation, 76, 81, 112, 131, 139.

Puritans, 72.

Quebec, 201, 215-18, 239-42, 248-51, 261-62, 266, 275, 285, 287-89, 294, 298.

Queen Anne's War, 213, 243, 245-47, 253, 272.

Randolph, Edmund, 88, 106, 111, 112, 148-49.

Razilly, Claude de, 219.

Rhode Island, 5-7, 38, 63, 66, 73, 94, 109, 148, 511, 191, 250, 266, 273.

Richelieu, Cardinal de, 217-18.

Roosevelt, Franklin D., 20.

Rossiter, Clinton, 111-12.

Rum, 60, 169-71, 175.

Rutledge, John, 125, 133.

Ryswick, Treaty of (1697), 187, 241.

Salmon Falls, 237.

sanctions, 67, 139-44.

Saratoga, 85, 203-04.

satellites, 234.

Satow, Sir Ernest, 1, 18-19, 29.

Savannah River, 60, 253.

Savelle, Max, 22-23, 227.

Saybrook, Fort, 68-69, 226.

Schenectady, 237.

Schutz, John A., 269, 292.

Scotland, 7-8.

Scott, James Brown, 67, 110, 222.

secrecy, rule of, 114-18, 122, 125, 129.

sectionalism, 76.

Sedgwick, Robert, 230-31, 250.

Seven Years' War, 41, 190, 213, 219, 249, 270.

Seward, William, 302.

Shay's Rebellion (1786), 104, 107, 142.

Sherman, Roger, 124-25, 137-38.

Shirley, Gov. William, 194, 261-66, 268, 270-79, 286.

shortfall in American history, 110.

Singapore, 261.

Singletary, Amos, 146.

Six Nations, 4, 77-78, 172, 176-87, 191-92, 199, 201-03.

slave uprising, 254, 257.

Smith, Captain John, 159, 163.

Smith, Jonathan, 146.

Sons of Liberty, 43, 79.

South Carolina, 94, 105, 114, 120, 130, 133-34, 145, 234, 243-44, 249, 253, 255-47, 260, 273.

sovereignty, 64, 66, 80, 86, 89, 93, 94, 103, 114, 142, 145, 151.

Spain, 19, 22-23, 30, 51, 60, 75, 167-69, 178, 255, 257-61, 269, 297, 301.

Spanish Armada, 267.

Spanish Main, 256.

Spenser, Edmund, 7.

Springfield, 68.

Stamp Act, 41-42, 46-47, 52, 79-80, 294.

Stamp Act Congress, 43, 79-81.

St. Augustine, 215, 243-244, 254-55, 257-60, 269.

St. Lawrence River, 185, 216, 245, 248, 253. 261, 266, 281, 885, 287, 289, 292.

St. Leger, Barry, 203-04.

St. Simons Island, 257.

Stone Age, 182.

street people, 42-43, 48, 79.

Stuart Kings, 73.

Stuyvesant, Peter, 71-72, 226-27, 232.

Susa, Treaty of, 218.

Susquehana River, 97.

Swedes, 75, 225-26.

taxation without repre-sentation, 40.

Tanner, E. P. 29-30, 33, 40.

Texas v. White, 11.

treaties, 4.

Treaty-Plan 1776, 299-301.

Trenton Arbitral Board, 97-98

Trojan horse, 232.

Underhill, Ruth Marray, 179-83, 202.

unit crystallization, 75.

United Nations, 67, 132.

Utopia, 25.

Utrecht, Treaty of (1713), 174, 187, 252, 261.

Vaughan, William, 262.

Venago, 188.

Vermont, 6, 95-97, 109.

Vernon, Admiral Edward, 255-256, 259, 270.

Vetch, Samuel, 247-49.

Virginia, 6-8, 13, 23, 25, 27, 29, 33, 38, 43, 60, 73, 76, 79, 81, 87-88, 94-95, 99, 102, 104-09, 111, 116, 120, 128, 145, 147-49, 164, 167, 174, 190-91, 195-97, 216, 233-34, 243, 246, 249, 253, 258, 266, 270, 272, 301.

Virginia cabal, 111-12.

Virginia Plan, 112, 126, 128, 130.

Walker, Sir Hovenden, 251, 253, 272.

Wallace, F.C., 186, 200.

Walpole, Robert, 255.

Ware v. Hilton, 102.

Warren, Commodore Peter, 262, 264-67.

Warren, James, 298.

Washington, George, 10, 105-06, 108, 113, 118, 121-22, 145, 162, 180, 189-90, 195, 197, 256, 271.

Washington, Lawrence, 256.

Webster, Noah, 104.

"We, the people," 88.

Whitehall, Treaty of (1686), 228.

Wilkinson, James, 164.

William and Mary, 74-75.

Williamson, Hugh, 136.

Wilson, James, 137, 147, 152.

Wilson, Woodrow, 20.

Winslow, John, 272, 277.

Wolfe, James, 233, 282, 284, 285, 287, 289-90.

Wotton, Sir Henry, 17.

Wyoming Valley, 97-99.

Yamasee War, 254.

Yates, Robert, 123.

Yorktown, 8, 10, 97, 304.